Includes National Dire
Plus 2,200 Farms Where You Can Buy Fresh, Locally Grown Food

WELCOME TO THE
AGRIHOOD

Housing, Shopping, and Gardening for a
Farm-to-Table Lifestyle

ANNA DeSIMONE

HOUSING 2020 PUBLISHING
NEW YORK, NY

Housing 2020 Publishing, LLC
477 Madison Avenue #6014
New York, NY 10022
www.housing2020publishing.com

First Edition: April 2020
ISBN 978-0-578-56158-5

Anna DeSimone is author of Housing Finance 2020, *New Mortgage Programs for the New Generation of Homebuyers*, Silver Medalist Winner of the 2019 Axiom Business Book Awards in Personal Finance, Retirement Planning and Investing.

Anna frequently serves as an industry expert in news articles published by national media including: Apartment Therapy, Forbes.com, Boston Globe, Chicago Tribune, Dallas Business Journal, Log Home Living, Michigan Chronicle, Newsday, The Penny Hoarder, Source Weekly, The Simple Dollar, and The Washington Post.

Acknowledgments

Special thanks to my copy editor, Doris E. Castagno, for your invaluable copy editing, cross-checking editorial references, cross-checking endless names and places contained in the resource directory. Thanks to Joanna Breen for your librarian perspective, and Santiago McCarthy for your health and nutrition review.

Special thanks to the many enthusiastic and dedicated people who shared their photographs and provided helpful information: Lisette Templin and Beth Ann Luedeker at Texas A&M University; Leslie Aberlin, Aberlin Springs agrihood in Ohio; Paige McLaughlin and Brandy Pfalmer, Fox Hill in Colorado; John Dewald at Serosun Farms in Illinois; John Lennon at River Bluffs in North Carolina; Andy Salafia, Mike Hoye, and Jack Skelley, representing the Freehold Communities of Arden in Florida, Orchard Ridge in Texas, and Miralon in California.

Cover design: Yvonne Fetig Roehler, Jenkins Group, Inc.
Cover photo: Shutterstock Images
Author photo: NYC Portraits
Infographics created with Shutterstock images

Contents

PART 1

Chapter 1
The Local Food Sensation   11

How Far Food Travels
Know Your Farmer, Know Your Food
The Food Safety Modernization Act (FSMA)
Organic Certification
Biodiversity
Sustainable Agriculture
Genetically Modified Organisms (GMOs)
Carbon Footprint
Ecolabels

Chapter 2
Say Hello to Your Farmer   19

A New Generation of the Family Farm
Where to Buy Food from Local Farmers
The Cost of Food
Trends in Grocery Shopping
Restaurant Trends
Food Waste
The Intersection of Food and Housing
Housing Choices

Chapter 3
Urban Agriculture   27

Sustainable Development Goals (SDG)
Hydroponics, Aeroponics, Aquaponics
Vertical Farming
Greenhouses
Rooftop Farming
Urban Ag Initiatives
Urban Agrihoods – Rental Communities

Chapter 4

Agrihoods

35

Land Conservation
Features of an Agrihood
The Amenities:
 Community Centers
 Boating and Fishing
 Golf
 Horseback Riding
 Walking, Hiking, Biking
 Children and Schools
 Active Adult Communities
 Multi-generational
 Mixed-use Communities
The Farms:
 Examples of Working Farms
 Garden Spaces for Residents
The Homes:
 Sustainable Construction
 Energy Efficiency
 Energy Tax Credits and Incentives
 Home Features
 Lot Size
 Neighborhoods
 Open Space
 Home Styles

Chapter 5

Backyard Farming

69

Healthy Soil
USDA Natural Resources Conservation Service
Organic Gardening
Regenerative Agriculture
Permaculture
Hydroponics
Aquaponics
Microgreens
Bees
Local Laws and Regulations
Farm Animals

Sale of Food

Composting

Food and Water Safety

USDA Plant Hardiness Zone Map

Early Bird Planting

Vegetable Growing Season

Vegetable Planting Guide

Shade-tolerant Vegetables

Raised-bed Gardening

Container Gardening

Chapter 6

Community Supported Agriculture (CSA)　　　87

Box Share

Harvest Season

Food Box Contents

Market-style Food Box

Food Share Add-ons

Food Box Pick-up or Delivery

Pick Your Own

Member Activities and Benefits

CSA Pricing

CSA Terms

Box Sharing

Multi-farm CSAs

CSA Locator

Chapter 7

On-Farm Markets　　　95

Products Sold on the Farm

Ranchers, Fisheries, and Other Purveyors

Pick Your Own Events

Farm Activities and Amenities

Farm History

Farmers' Markets

On-farm Market Locator

Chapter 8

Food Hubs
101

The Role of Food Hubs
Food Hub Structure
Food Value Chains
Services for Producers
Services for the Community
Food Hub Locator

PART 2

State Resource Directory
105

Alabama	*106*
Alaska	*107*
Arizona	*108*
Arkansas	*109*
California	*110*
Colorado	*114*
Connecticut	*117*
Delaware	*118*
District of Columbia	*119*
Florida	*120*
Georgia	*123*
Hawaii	*126*
Idaho	*127*
Illinois	*129*
Indiana	*132*
Iowa	*134*
Kansas	*136*
Kentucky	*137*
Louisiana	*138*
Maine	*139*
Maryland	*140*
Massachusetts	*142*
Michigan	*144*
Minnesota	*147*
Mississippi	*149*
Missouri	*150*
Montana	*152*

Nebraska   153

Nevada   154

New Hampshire   155

New Jersey   157

New Mexico   159

New York   160

North Carolina   164

North Dakota   168

Ohio   169

Oklahoma   172

Oregon   173

Pennsylvania   176

Rhode Island   180

South Carolina   181

South Dakota   183

Tennessee   184

Texas   186

Utah   190

Vermont   191

Virginia   193

Washington   196

West Virginia   199

Wisconsin   200

Wyoming   203

References   205

About the Author   209

Index   211

Introduction

 Live close to the farm.

Agrihoods are healthy lifestyle communities centered around a professionally managed farm. Communities are often built on heritage farmland, where historic barns and silos dot the pastoral landscape. The daily routine for residents often begins with a walk to the farm store to buy food freshly harvested from the farm, or to enjoy a cup of coffee at one of the gathering spaces at the community center.

With amenities such as clubhouses, swimming pools, boating, fishing, golf, horseback riding, and miles of groomed walking and biking trails, it's no surprise that agrihoods across the nation are winning many "best places to live" awards. Even the K-12 schools located within agrihood developments are winning awards for academic excellence.

Agrihoods are designed for people to connect with nature, and many communities are built on conservation land, where natural wetlands, forests, and mountains provide panoramic views. Because the agrihood concept is relatively new, homes are energy-efficient and sustainably built by select home builders.

The latest trends in multifamily housing are rooftop organic farms and on-site restaurants offering healthy meals prepared from the chef's garden. Apartment buildings are starting to include community gardens into the landscape or provide individual garden spaces for tenants.

There are opportunities to buy or rent in a farm-centric community for people of all ages and financial affordability. This book will take you on a virtual tour through dozens of communities, with photos of homes, descriptions of the endless amenities, and a directory of agrihoods throughout the U.S.

Shop at your local farm.

Learn the story behind your food. Your local farmer is your neighbor, and their harvest season is *your* harvest season. Healthy food requires a healthy ecosystem. The story behind your food begins from the ground up—how food is farmed. This book spells out the rules for sustainable agriculture, such as organic certification, food safety, traceability, and GMOs. You'll learn about how far food travels, and how buying locally sourced food can reduce your household's carbon footprint.

The *Know Your Farmer, Know Your Food* initiative from the U.S. Department of Agriculture has helped thousands of local farmers across the nation bring fresh, healthy food to local markets. Many new innovations in urban agriculture are bringing farms to our cities, and commercial food growers are utilizing techniques that use less land, less water, and less energy.

This book covers all your options for buying food from your local farmer, a food hub, or through a community-supported agriculture (CSA) program. The 50-state directory in this book lists over 2,200 farms that offer a wide variety of fruits, vegetables, and other sustainably sourced food products.

Grow your own organic food.

Porches are the new backyard. Occasionally people are described as "serious gardeners" due to their extensive level of gardening activities. It doesn't matter whether your garden is an acre, or you're just growing tomatoes on your porch—if you are growing food organically then you *are* a serious gardener.

This book spells out the steps for at-home soil testing, organic gardening, composting, food safety, farm animals, beekeeping, local laws, and more. You might be inspired to grow microgreens or try the latest indoor growing systems such as aeroponics, aquaponics, and hydroponics. With lots of helpful tips, planting guides, and resources, you're ready to farm!

Anna DeSimone

CHAPTER 1

The Local Food Sensation

LOCALLY PRODUCED FOOD is the fastest-growing market sector of the United States Department of Agriculture (USDA). Sales from local farmers reached $20 billion in 2018, and across the nation there are now more than 160,000 farmers and ranchers selling to local markets. The number of farmers selling directly to consumers at local farmers' markets quadrupled over the past ten years. The nation's total organic food sales reached $50 billion in 2018, with over a third of the market attributed to fruits and vegetables.[1]

The USDA defines local food as product that is raised, produced, aggregated, stored, processed, and distributed in the locality or region in which the final product is marketed. Foods that the USDA considers local are comprised of product that is sold directly to consumers, as well as foods that are commercially sold by distributors.[2]

In accordance with the 2008 Farm Act,[3] food product can be marked as locally or regionally produced if it is purchased within the same state or not transported more than 400 miles from its origin. Definitions of "local food" differ by region due to varying climates and populations, and state agricultural organizations may establish specific boundaries, such as 100 miles. At local farmers' markets, shoppers are more likely to see product sourced from a specific farm, county, or region within the state.

How Far Food Travels

It is estimated that food in the United States travels about 1,500 miles, according to a number of studies completed by the Leopold Center for Sustainable Agriculture at Iowa State University.[4] According to ATTRA National Sustainable Agriculture Information Service, food miles refers to "the distance of travel from the location where the food is produced to the location where it will eventually be consumed." The farther food travels and the longer it takes to reach the consumer, the more its freshness declines, and its nutrients are lost. Taste and nutritional values will decline for fruits and vegetables that are engineered to preserve shelf life.[5]

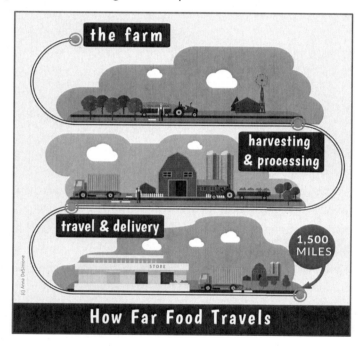

In its study, *Food, Fuel, and Freeways*, the Leopold Center utilized a Weighted Average Source Distance (WASD) formula to evaluate the sustainability of global food systems in terms of energy use. The farther food travels, the more fossil fuels are required for transport. The burning of fossil fuels leads to the emission of greenhouse gases, contributing to global warming.[6]

Know Your Farmer, Know Your Food

In 2008, then Senator Barack Obama pledged to promote local and regional food systems to help farmers and ranchers get full retail price for their food, and also enable families to remain on their farms doing the important work that they love.[7] The following year, the USDA launched the *Know Your Farmer, Know Your Food* initiative to increase economic opportunities for local farmers and stakeholders. The USDA's 17 agencies and offices collaborate on projects, share information with the public, and fulfill mandates related to local and regional food.[8]

The *Know Your Farmer, Know Your Food Compass* is a centralized hub of resources for local and regional farmers. The *Compass* maps over 4,200 federal investments that have been made by the USDA and other agencies since 2009. As of January 2017, the USDA has invested $1 billion in over 40,000 local and regional businesses.[9] The *Compass* refers to the following quote:

"Over the last four years, I've seen a shift. People who have never been on a farm are becoming interested in where their food comes from. Towns and neighborhoods that didn't have regular access to fresh fruits and vegetables are getting them. Farmers and ranchers are tapping into new markets and keeping more money in their pockets by selling locally. And all across the country, innovative local food businesses are starting up and staffing up. Local food systems work for America: when we create opportunities for farmers and ranchers, our entire nation reaps the benefit."

—President Barack Obama

Under the leadership of former U.S. Secretary of Agriculture, Thomas Vilsack, the USDA helped local farmers expand their growing season, reduce costs, and conserve natural resources through the construction of 15,000 high tunnels, commonly known as "hoop houses." The number of certified organic operations grew to 21,700—a 300% increase since 2002, and the number of farmers participating in local farmers' markets skyrocketed to 8,500. The number of local food vendors that accept Supplemental Nutritional Assistance Program (SNAP) vouchers grew from 753 in 2008 to more than 6,400 in 2016. Two-thirds of rural counties demonstrated job growth and considerable reductions in unemployment.[10]

The Food Safety Modernization Act (FSMA)

The FSMA was signed into law by President Barack Obama on January 4, 2011, giving the U.S. Food and Drug Administration (FDA) new authorities to regulate the way foods are grown, harvested, and processed. The law granted the FDA a number of new powers, including mandatory recall authority. The FDA finalized a number of foundation rules, including the establishment of accredited third-party certification that includes traceback mechanisms to allow commercial, institutional, and retail buyers to trace back produce to the originating farm. Preventive controls include steps that a food facility would take to prevent or significantly minimize the likelihood of problems occurring. The FSMA significantly enhances the FDA's ability to achieve greater oversight of the millions of food products coming into the United States from other countries each year.[11]

The FDA is responsible for regulating 80% of the U.S. food supply, while red meat, poultry, and processed egg products are regulated by the USDA. The FDA works closely with other federal, state, and local agencies in establishing regulatory guidelines.

Organic Certification

Organic is a labeling term found on products that have been produced using cultural, biological, and mechanical practices that support the cycling of on-farm resources, promote ecological balance, and conserve biodiversity. The USDA National Organic Program (NOP) enforces regulations and ensures the integrity of the USDA Organic Seal.

In order to make an organic claim or use the USDA Organic Seal, the final product must follow strict production, handling, and labeling standards, as well as go through the organic certification process. Organic certification allows a farm or processing facility to sell, label, and represent its products as organic. The organic brand provides consumers with more choices in the marketplace.[12] Labeling requirements apply to raw, fresh products and processed products that contain organic agricultural ingredients. Agricultural products that are sold, labeled, or represented as organic must be produced and processed in accordance with the NOP standards. There are exceptions for certain small farmers.

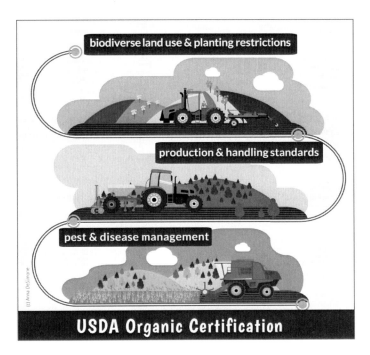

USDA Organic Certification

For multi-ingredient products in the "made with" organic category, at least 70% of the product must be certified organic ingredients. Up to three ingredients or ingredient categories can be represented as organic. Any remaining ingredients are not required to be organically produced, but must be produced without excluded methods, such as genetic engineering.

Biodiversity

Organic systems mirror nature by maintaining a balanced ecosystem on the farm and using methods that support conservation of natural resources. Farmers can protect habitats for birds and mammals, and protect waterways by controlling livestock access to sensitive areas along rivers, creeks, streams, and wetland areas. Organic producers often plant native vegetation throughout a certified organic farm. The vegetation provides food, cover, and corridors for beneficial organisms such as pollinators like bees and bats, slows wind and water down for erosion control, provides groundwater recharge, and filters pollution.[13]

Sustainable Agriculture

According to the USDA's National Institute of Food and Agriculture (NIFA), the term "sustainable agriculture" refers to an integrated system of plant and animal production practices. Sustainable agriculture seeks to provide more profitable farm income, promote environmental stewardship, and enhance the quality of life for farm families and communities.[14]

Farmers and ranchers can choose many ways to improve their sustainability, and these vary by region, state, or farm. New practices have emerged, many aimed at greater use of on-farm or local resources. Summarized below are practices that contribute to long-term farm profitability, environmental stewardship, and improved quality of life: [15]

- *Integrated Pest Management*
- *Rotational Grazing*
- *Soil Conservation*
- *Water Quality / Wetlands*
- *Cover Crops*
- *Crop / Landscape Diversity*
- *Nutrient Management*
- *Agroforestry*
- *Alternative Marketing*

Genetically Modified Organisms (GMOs)

GMOs are living organisms whose genetic material is artificially manipulated in a laboratory. A genetic engineering process is used to create combinations of plant, animal, bacteria, and virus genes that do not occur in nature or through traditional crossbreeding methods. Most GMOs have been engineered to withstand the direct application of herbicide and/or to produce an insecticide.

"Non-GMO" means a product was produced without genetic engineering and its ingredients are not derived from GMOs. "Non-GMO Product Verified" means that a product is compliant with the *Non-GMO Project Standard*, which includes stringent provisions for testing, traceability, and segregation. Third-party technical administrators evaluate products at accredited testing laboratories to assess compliance.[16]

Carbon Footprint

The greenhouse effect is a natural phenomenon that insulates the earth from the cold of space. In 2017, agriculture was responsible for 8.4% of the total U.S. greenhouse gas emissions. The Center for Sustainable Systems at the University of Michigan describes the effect of a household's carbon footprint as it relates to food: "A carbon footprint is the total greenhouse gas (GHG) emissions caused directly and indirectly by an individual, organization, event or product."[17]

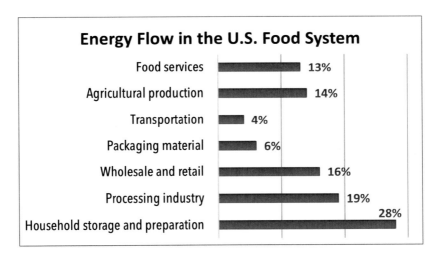

Data source: Center for Sustainable Systems, University of Michigan, 2019

Food-related energy use accounts for 16% of the national energy budget. Consolidation of farms, food processing operations, and distribution warehouses often increases the distance between food sources and consumers. Local food reduces dependence on fossil fuel energy, and vulnerability to changes in oil prices. Food accounts for 10 to 30% of a household's carbon footprint, with the higher portion in lower-income households. A vegetarian diet greatly reduces an individual's carbon footprint, since meat-based diets use more energy to produce. A single serving of beef uses 20 times more energy to produce than a single serving of vegetables. Choosing less carbon-intensive meats can make a major difference. For example, switching from beef to chicken for one year reduces an individual's carbon footprint by 882 pounds of carbon dioxide.[18]

Ecolabels

Ecolabels are used to educate consumers about locally grown and sustainably produced foods. The seal or logo indicates the product has met certain ethical and environmental standards. Some ecolabels may include such disclosures as: "no pesticides used," or "CO_2 emissions are known to contribute to global warming." Ecolabels may also identify the type of produce and geographic location where the product was sourced, such as:

- *Farm-to-store distance in food miles*
- *Number of farm-to-store shipping days*
- *Mode of transportation (airplane, ship, truck)*
- *# pounds carbon dioxide emitted per pound of product*

Examples of Ecolabels	
FAIR TRADE	Guarantees fair wages to workers and sustainable land cultivation.
DIRECT TRADE	Shows that farmers and workers involved are offered a better deal; considered more trustworthy than fair trade label.
NON-GMO	Guarantees the product's ingredients and land where cultivated were not genetically modified.
USDA ORGANIC	Certifies the product was made using organic methods: no use of pesticides and synthetic fertilizers in the land, no use of antibiotics or hormones in animals, no GMO ingredients.
AMERICAN GRASS FED	Certifies that the animals have been fed only natural milk, fresh grass or hay, have not been treated with antibiotics or hormones, and were not raised in confinement.
ANIMAL WELFARE APPROVED	Certifies that the animals were raised outdoors, using sustainable high-welfare farming methods.
RAINFOREST ALLIANCE	Guarantees the product comes from a farm that follows environmentally friendly standards and offers fair treatment to workers and their families.
CARBON REDUCTION	Implies that the producer is committed to reducing its carbon footprint during all food production processes; measured every two years.

Information source: Food Packaging Labels Corp.

CHAPTER 2

Say Hello to Your Farmer

WHETHER YOU OWN OR RENT YOUR HOME, you can enjoy the farm-to-table lifestyle. Shopping at an "on-farm" market allows you to engage with the people who do the work. They are your neighbors, and *your* harvest season is *their* harvest season. This book gives readers a basic primer on organic farming. What your local farmer can tell you about how they manage the soil, plant, feed, and harvest food is *priceless*.

At the heart of every agrihood community is a working farm and store. Many agrihoods were built on land that was once a farm, and often members of the original farming family stay on board to manage agricultural activities. Whether your farmer is managing 30 acres or producing microgreens in the rooftop garden of your apartment building, you have the opportunity to learn something every time you stop by to say hello.

A study completed in 2015 by Dr. Ion Vasi at Tippie College of Business at the University of Iowa determined that local food markets were more likely to develop in areas where residents had a strong commitment to civic participation, health, and the environment. Dr. Vasi noted:[19]

> *"The local food market is about valuing the relationship with the farmers and the people who produce the food, and believing that how they produce the food aligns with your personal values."*

A New Generation of the Family Farm

The American Farm Bureau reports in its *2018 Edition, America's Diverse Family Farms*,[20] two million farms dot America's rural landscape. About 98% of U.S. farms are operated by families, including individuals, family partnerships, or family corporations. Only 2.2% of U.S. farms are run by non-family members. The number of Hispanic and Latino farmers and African American farmers continues to increase, and women make up 36% of the total number of U.S. farm operators. At least one female decision maker works in 56% of America's farms. Just over 10% of farms are owned by retired farmers who continue to farm on a smaller scale.

According to the Pew Research Center, there were 14,000 certified organic farms in America in 2016, presenting a 56% increase from 2011, the earliest comparable year. California has the largest number of organic farms at 2,713, followed by Wisconsin at 1,276 and New York at 1,059. States with more than 500 organic farms are: Pennsylvania, Iowa, Washington, Ohio, Vermont, Minnesota, and Maine. New organic farming certifications have risen significantly in Arkansas, Alabama, South Carolina, and Missouri.[21]

Where to Buy Food from Local Farmers

This book explores all the places where you can *live* as well as where you can *shop* for fresh, locally grown food. The national directory includes a listing of agrihoods located throughout the country, urban agriculture initiatives, and over 2,200 resources of on-farm markets, food hubs, and Community-Supported Agriculture (CSA) programs.

If you are living in an agrihood community, most of your fruits and vegetables would be grown right around the corner. Food is purchased at a discount either at the farm store or through a CSA program. Many agrihoods, including those with a professionally managed farm, also set aside acreage for residents to freely grow food in a community garden. Some urban agrihoods have a site-managed farm, which can be located on a rooftop or adjacent to an apartment complex. Such farms sell produce at a discount to residents, as well as supply food to cafes located on the premises.

Where to buy fresh, locally grown food

By enlisting in a CSA program, you'll be able to visit the farm each week to pick up your "box" or "co-op share." Some CSAs offer home delivery services, or pickups at designated places. *(See more in Chapter 6, Community-Supported Agriculture.)*

On-farm markets are generally larger farms, and often have "pick your own" opportunities. In addition to fruits and vegetables, these farms may sell their own poultry, eggs, and dairy, as well as food from local artisans, fisheries, and ranchers. *(See more in Chapter 7, On-Farm Markets.)*

Food hubs serve as a consolidated marketing point for regional farmers and artisans to sell their products to consumers, restaurants, and grocers. Many food hubs distribute food to schools, churches, and shelters. America's food waste reduction program works with food hubs throughout the country to bring excess or unsold food from local businesses to charitable organizations. *(See more in Chapter 8, Food Hubs.)*

Free food is in abundance for any type of food-centric neighborhood that sets aside acreage for a community garden. A popular trend in multifamily apartment buildings is incorporating edible landscapes, community gardening spaces, or small private garden plots for residents. Vegetables are easily grown in containers placed in sunny locations such as a porch, patio, or balcony. There are some innovative indoor gardening systems designed to grow microgreens and vegetables year-round inside your home. *(See more in Chapter 5, Backyard Farming.)*

The Cost of Food

Monthly Food Expenditure

$ 449
single person

$ 726
two adults

$ 1,075
two adults +
two children

The average household in America spends $644 per month on food, according to the Bureau of Labor Statistics (BLS) report released in April 2019, *Consumer Expenditures in 2017*.[22] Data is based on 130,000 households, of which 63% own their own home. Average household size is 2.5 persons, with a pre-tax annual income average of $73,573. The above illustration reflects $449 per month for a single person, $726 for two adults, and $1,075 for two adults and two children. Data for the family of four category includes children between the ages of 6 and 17.

The farm-to-table lifestyle has many benefits that help offset any additional costs associated with the purchase of organic and sustainably grown food. First, knowing where your food comes from, and how it was handled, gives you peace of mind. Second, you are supporting local farmers in your area. Third, you are helping the environment.

Trends in Grocery Shopping

In February 2018, the National Grocers Association announced survey results from households surveyed by Harris Poll and the Nielsen Company which analyzed shopper behaviors at independent grocers.[23] In response to the query, "what matters most in the presentation of fresh foods," 76% of respondents stated that they wanted products that are *fresh*. Other notable preferences reported by consumers included: locally grown, organic, sustainability, and source traceability. 54% of respondents stated they would like grocers to clearly indicate what products are fresh and in season.

A number of studies over the past five years by global consulting company A.T. Kearney have revealed trends in consumer perception of local foods. In its study, *Firmly Rooted, the Local Food Market Expands,*[24] almost all (96%) consumers describe local food as products grown or produced within 100 miles from its source. 65% of respondents consider food that is grown or manufactured in the same state as local. 78% expressed willingness to pay more money for fresh food, and 67% would make a special trip to the market because they knew the local produce was in season.

Health and wellness continue to be drivers for shoppers, as reported by the Food Marketing Institute's (FMI) 2019 Report on *Retailer Contributions to Health and Wellness.*[25] The institute's research continues to illustrate countless positive attributes of communal eating, such as family meals.

> *"Health is now a bigger umbrella; health is about overall well-being, life balance, a sense of community—that comes along with the addition of fun, new, and nutritious food to consumers' diets."*
>
> —Food Marketing Institute

Restaurant Trends

Consumers enjoy eating food outside their home, and that trend is not slowing down. Data from the aforementioned Bureau of Labor Statistics (BLS) consumer expenditures report[26] indicates that 43% of the average annual expenditure on food is spent outside the home. What is considered "off premises" by restaurant trade groups includes: carryout, delivery, drive-through, and mobile apps used by consumers for purchasing food.

In its *Restaurant Industry 2030, Actionable Insights for the Future* report by the National Restaurant Association,[27] America is at a crossroads in how people dine. Restaurants are swiftly adapting their floor plans to meet the needs of guests, serving them wherever they want to be served. Some restaurants will morph into a hybrid model, offering counter service, full service, takeout and delivery, and meal kits. New food halls will feature retail and restaurant pairings to make it easy for people to both eat and shop for food they can take home. With a greater number of consumers working from home, people are seeking dining experiences where they can engage socially and become "regulars" in an atmosphere such as the German Biergarten or European-inspired outdoor cafes. Interior designs will offer a greater variety of seating choices and gathering spaces.

Restaurants will continue to focus on healthy options, local foods, and a product's farm-to-table journey. Some restaurant chefs are growing their own herbs and produce in mini-farms on the restaurant's premises. Restaurants are becoming more innovative about creating healthy meals for children and people with dietary restrictions. With consumers expecting an increasing level of transparency, food-safety certification and management systems will be critical. By 2030, sustainability will be integrated into every aspect of a restaurant's operations.

"If your menu has the words 'sustainably sourced,' your ingredients are considered 'clean,' and you're prepared to tell the stories behind the food you're serving, then you're already living in the restaurant of the future."

—National Restaurant Association

Food Waste

In the United States, food waste is estimated at between 30 and 40% of the food supply.[28] This estimate, based on data from the USDA's Economic Research Service, projects that 31% of food loss is at the retail and consumer levels. Wholesome food that could have helped feed families in need is sent to landfills. Land, water, labor, energy, and other inputs are used in producing, processing, transporting, preparing, storing, and disposing of discarded food.

Food loss occurs for many reasons, with some types of loss—such as spoilage—occurring at every stage of the production and supply chain. Between the farm gate and retail stages, food loss can arise from problems during transporting or processing that expose food to damage. At the retail level, equipment malfunction, over-ordering, and culling of blemished produce can result in food loss. Consumers also contribute to food loss when they buy or cook more than they need.

The Food Waste Reduction Alliance (FWRA) [29] is an industry-led initiative focused on reducing food waste by increasing food donations and sending unavoidable food waste to productive use (energy, composting) and away from landfills. The alliance is comprised of the Grocery Manufacturers Association, Food Marketing Institute, and the National Restaurant Association. Committed to improving the environment and communities, FWRA members have taken on the challenges of food waste to shrink America's environmental footprint, and simultaneously address hunger in America.

The Intersection of Food and Housing

Home builders and multi-family housing developers have recognized the growing trend of consumers being connected more closely with food. The incorporation of food elements in construction has demonstrated positive outcomes for both developers and consumers, as well as supported the environment. Real estate developers are increasingly collaborating with chefs, farmers, and artisans to bring their craft to the community. Apartment complexes are being designed with more community space for social gatherings, and include cafes, bars, and demonstration kitchens.

The Urban Land Institute (ULI) has developed comprehensive guidance and consults globally with developers, owners, property managers, designers, investors, and others involved in the real estate decision. ULI's best practice guide, *Cultivating Development: Trends and Opportunities at the Intersection of Food and Real Estate,*[30] explores the mutually beneficial relationship between food-based amenities—such as working farms, community gardens, food halls, restaurants, and grocery stores—and real estate. It highlights how the growing interest and awareness in fresh, local food is spurring innovation in development projects.

Housing Choices

The 2018 *Housing and Community Preference Survey* completed by real estate advisory firm RCLCO[31] shares insights on the types of amenities consumers are seeking in a home, and their depth of interest in a master-planned community. Survey results from 23,500 respondents revealed the majority of respondents view the following amenities to be somewhat important or a strong priority:

- *Trails*
- *Fitness centers*
- *Resort pool*
- *Pocket parks*
- *Arts and culture*
- *Sports courts*
- *Dog park*
- *Farmers' market*
- *Community garden*

Nearly every agrihood featured in the national directory in this book includes most, or all, of the amenities noted above. Chapter 4 in this book, *Agrihoods,* explains the master planned community concept and highlights certain amenities found in various agrihoods across the U.S. The scientific advances made in the area of urban agriculture significantly expand options for a farm-to-table lifestyle in the city, as explained in Chapter 3, *Urban Agriculture.*

CHAPTER 3

Urban Agriculture

SUSTAINABLE DEVELOPMENT GOALS, known as SDGs, were established by the United Nations in 2015. Adopted by 193 UN member-countries, the goals are a blueprint for long-term planning toward social, economic, and environmental well-being. Of the 17 Sustainable Development Goals, SDG Number 11 is "Sustainable Cities and Communities." Today, 55% of the world's population live in an urban area or city, and over the next 20 years, two-thirds of the global population will live in cities.[32]

Farmers and members of the food industry across the U.S. have been developing innovative farming systems to help meet the challenges of urbanization. To maximize available space for farming, city-based industrial farming operations generally consist of three types: rooftop farms, located on the top of commercial buildings, generally the food packaging center; climate-controlled greenhouses, which may be located on rooftops, and often produce food year-round; and vertical farming. The vertical structures used by commercial farmers can be a system where flat trays are stacked in layers, or systems where food is grown in towers.

Commercial food growers are increasingly utilizing new farming techniques that use less land, less water, and less energy. Some systems enable year-round production and have reduced or totally eliminated the need for pesticides. Because crops are grown in controlled environments with precise nutrients, lighting, temperatures, and risk-monitoring, there is traceability from seed to packaging.

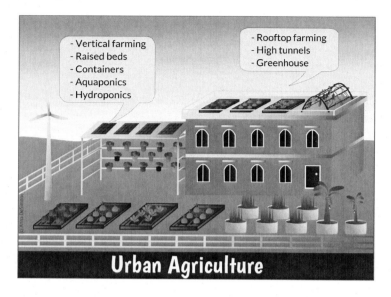

- Vertical farming
- Raised beds
- Containers
- Aquaponics
- Hydroponics

- Rooftop farming
- High tunnels
- Greenhouse

Urban Agriculture

Products grown by urban farmers include fresh vegetables, fruits, herbs, meat, and poultry. These farmers sell their products at local farmers' markets, and to grocers, schools, restaurants, and food hubs. Many urban farms donate excess produce to churches, food shelters, and charitable organizations. Outdoor urban farms also use high tunnels, known as hoop houses, raised beds, and containers.

Indoor farming methods used by commercial growers in greenhouses, buildings, or on rooftops can include any of the following methods: crops in soil, soil-free crops, or watering through a closed-loop system. Such systems would utilize one of the following growing techniques:

- *Hydroponics—plants are grown in a soil-free nutrient solution; plants use 90% less water; the predominant growing system used in vertical farms.*

- *Aeroponics—developed by the National Aeronautics and Space Administration (NASA); plants are grown in an air/mist environment with no soil and using 95% less water than field farming.*

- *Aquaponics—a closed-cycle watering system that combines plants and fish in the same ecosystem. Generally used in smaller scale food production.*

Across the nation, colleges and universities are expanding educational programs for students to learn the latest technologies and eco-farming solutions in the areas of urban agriculture, vertical farming, plant science, soil science, and animal science. Universities are developing and testing innovative farming methods and integrating their work as part of the institution's goals for sustainability. Campus farms, managed by students, are feeding students as well as local food shelters from their farms.

The *Aggie Green Fund* grant through the Texas A&M University Office of Sustainability funded the launching of the vertical aeroponic tower garden initiative at Texas A&M's *Urban Farm United* (TUFU). Lisette Templin, faculty member in the Department of Health & Kinesiology, and Broch Saxton, a student from the Department of Soil and Crop Science, led TUFU's "grow to serve" mission to introduce a sustainable method of farming that promotes hyper-local food using 90% less land and 90% less water. The fresh food harvest serves the *12th Can*, a campus food pantry.[33]

From seedlings to harvest, up to 150 varieties of vegetables are grown in the towers, fed by a closed-loop system. With growth from 24 tower gardens, TUFU supplies fresh food to 120 families twice monthly.

Texas A&M AgriLife photo by Beth Ann Luedeker, Department of Soil and Crop Science

Vertical Farming

Vertical farming ensures year-round crop production in non-tropical regions, and production is much more efficient than land-based farming. A single indoor acre of a vertical farm can produce a yield equivalent to more than 30 acres of farmland. Vertical farms eliminate the need for tractors and other farm equipment, thereby increasing job safety. Crops are shipped to outlets that are very close to the production facility, reducing the farm-to-store transportation time as well as the carbon footprint. Organic certification can be awarded to vertical farmers who meet certain criteria, such as organic inputs to the hydroponic operations.[34]

Sometimes called "high-rise farms," vertical farming systems include multi-level systems where plants are grown in stacked layers. Larger warehouse systems can reach several stories tall. A popular method used in vertical farms are 40-foot shipping containers, refurbished as self-contained vertical farms.

New Jersey-based Aerofarms has developed eco-friendly aeroponic technology for indoor vertical farming where plants are grown in stacked trays, enabling productivity 390 times greater per square foot than commercial field farming. Aerofarms' patented reusable cloth medium is used for seeding, germinating, growing, and harvesting. Plants are grown using an aeroponics system to mist the roots of the greens with nutrients, water, and oxygen.

The closed loop system uses 95% less water than field farming. LED lights are used to create a specific light recipe for each plant, giving the greens exactly the spectrum, intensity, and frequency they need for photosynthesis. Data is collected from sensors that monitor plant biology and help increase plant health, growth, and yield. For every harvest, plant scientists monitor more than 130,000 data points. To date, the company has had success in growing over 500 million plants of more than 300 varieties.[35]

Greenhouses

Hydroponic greenhouses are used to grow plants without soil in environmentally controlled greenhouses for year-round growth and production. The nation's largest greenhouses were built by Gotham Greens, currently operating 500,000 square feet of urban indoor farms in five states across the country. Gotham Greens, which built its first facility in New York City, uses a hydroponic method known as nutrient film technique. Greenhouses are situated on rooftops, where plants can benefit from natural sunlight. Crops grow in trays where plants receive a constant stream of irrigation water that is enriched with a mineral nutrient solution. Greenhouses operate in a controlled growing environment, allowing plants to thrive in light levels, temperature, humidity, and air composition at exactly the right balance.[36]

Shenandoah Growers operates the nation's largest USDA-certified organic, soil-based indoor growing system. With 12 locations across the country, the company provides produce to over 18,000 stores. Shenandoah utilizes a bioponic growing method, a type of hydroponic system that involves the use of certified organic nutrients in a hydroponic solution and a soil-based substrate. The closed-loop micro-ecosystem eliminates the need for synthetic fertilizers and reduces the use of water and land resources.[37]

Rooftop Farming

New rooftop farms are emerging everywhere across the nation, in both the residential and commercial farming sectors. Brooklyn Grange is the leading rooftop farming business in the U.S. Three farms are spread across 5½ acres located on New York City roofs, growing over 80,000 pounds of organically cultivated produce per year. To date, the company has sold over 400,000 pounds of vegetables to CSA members, restaurants, and at weekly farm stands. Through its nonprofit partner, City Growers, the company has hosted 50,000 New York City youths on the farms for educational field trips, after-school programs, and summer camps. Brooklyn Grange also provides urban farming and green roof consulting services, and designs, installs, and maintains green spaces for clients. The business also operates an apiary, keeping bees in dozens of naturally managed hives dispersed throughout NYC.[38]

Urban Ag Initiatives

Boston—Fenway Farms

Fenway Farms provides fresh, organically grown vegetables and fruit to Red Sox fans at Fenway Park's restaurants and concessions. The 5,000-square-foot rooftop farm utilizes a unique modular milk crate growing system, allowing easier, contained growing throughout the season. The 10,600-square-foot farm has a total growing space of 2,400 square feet, and grew 5,980 pounds of produce in 2018. The farm is located on the third base side of the Dell EMC Level, and can be viewed by the general public at the Gate A staircase. Designed and maintained by Green City Growers.

Detroit—Michigan Urban Farming Initiative

The Michigan Urban Farming Initiative (MUFI) is located in Detroit's North End community on nearly 3 acres and has been in operation since 2011. With the help of over 10,000 volunteers, MUFI has grown and distributed over 50,000 pounds of produce, grown using organic methods, to 2,000 local households at no cost to the recipients. Individual households subscribe to a pay-what-you-can model. MUFI also supplies to local markets, restaurants, vendors, food pantries, churches, and shelters.

Pittsburgh—Hilltop Urban Farm

Hilltop Urban Farm is located on 107 acres of land, with 23 acres dedicated to farming. The community is a multi-pronged initiative that produces locally grown crops, provides agriculture-based education, generates entrepreneurial opportunities, and strengthens communities. Hilltop Urban Farm is set to become the largest urban farm in the United States. The three core programs include youth-centered education, workforce training for new adult urban farmers, and an active, accessible farmers' market. The Farmer Incubation Program (FIP) is a 3-year workforce development program for new small-scale organic urban farm enterprises.

Urban Agrihoods—Rental Communities

Bronx, New York

Arbor House is an eco-friendly and health-promoting residential building in the South Bronx. The 120,000-square-foot building provides 124 units of affordable housing. Located on the roof is a 10,000-square-foot hydroponic farm that functions as a community-supported agriculture (CSA) arrangement where Arbor House residents can purchase shares of healthy food produced by the farm. About 40% of the produce is made available to local community schools, hospitals, and markets.

Seattle, Washington

Stack House Apartments is a mixed-use, green-living community that includes a 188-unit apartment building, a 96-unit apartment building, and a commercial building. Buildings are LEED-certified energy-efficient. The development includes a professionally managed rooftop farm, community gardens, and an on-site farm stand that offers free produce for residents.

Santa Clara, California

Win 6 Village consists of mixed-use, mixed-income, and multigenerational housing with a working organic farm. The site includes aquaponic rooftop gardens, and walkable space located in Santa Clara Valley's native oak woodland and grassland plant community. The Win 6 plan includes housing for 359 residents—165 low-income seniors, 16 moderate-income apartments, 144 market-rate apartments, and 34 market-rate townhouses. (Under development)

Note: See Part 2, Resource Directory, Agrihood listings for additional information for each urban ag initiative featured.

CHAPTER 4

Agrihoods

IT'S A BEAUTIFUL DAY IN THE AGRIHOOD. Stepping into an agrihood community, you just might find yourself singing the beloved *Mister Rogers* tune. You'll see children of all ages scampering in and out of pocket parks, owning the road as they confidently ride their bikes through pedestrian-friendly streets. You'll see teenagers carrying foraged scraps of lumber into the woods to build their own forts. The daily routine of pre-school children is petting rabbits and goats, gathering eggs from the chicken coop, and waving hello to Jack, the farm's resident donkey. This is the agrihood lifestyle at *Aberlin Springs* in Morrow, Ohio, a historic farm community that residents describe as a "neighborhood of free-range chickens and free-range kids."

The term agrihood, which combines the words *agriculture* and *neighborhood,* was coined by the nation's earliest developers of these farm-centric communities. An agrihood is a residential community centered around a working farm. Generally designed as "master planned communities," agrihoods include amenities similar to golf course developments, such as club houses and swimming pools.

The heart of an agrihood, however, is its working farm. "We've traded golf greens for salad greens," says Leslie Aberlin, who built an agrihood on the 141 acres of woods and tillable farmland where her Swiss parents put down roots to begin their American dream.

Land Conservation

Agrihoods are designed with a purpose—*to connect people with the land*—not just for agricultural activities, but to also protect and support conservation of farmlands, forests, watersheds, and wildlife habitat. Many agrihoods are built on heritage farmland or conservation land.

In his book, *Creating Value with Nature, Open Space, and Agriculture*, author Edward T. McMahon states: "Conservation development is a practice of land use planning and community design that strives to maintain a respectful relationship with nature. Through a broad range of techniques and strategies, conservation development is intended to achieve specific development objectives parallel to the protection of the landscape's essential natural and environmental values."[39]

Mr. McMahon, who serves as Sustainable Development Chair at the famed Urban Land Institute, helps provide support and educational guidance to planners and developers in the area of agrihood development. He further states in his book that "a *conservation subdivision* is a residential development that achieves the maximum number of permitted dwelling units through the use of smaller lots, setting aside the majority of the remaining land as permanently protected open space, natural areas, or working land."[40]

An agrihood community can be comprised of up to 70% open space, including land dedicated to agriculture activities and animal pastures. Residents not only benefit from access to fresh food, they enjoy the close connection to the farm and participating in agricultural activities. Neighbors connect with nature, and each other as they walk, hike, or bike alongside pastures, orchards and woodlands. Many agrihoods are built on heritage farmland, and, where possible, developers hire original farm family members to help plan and manage agricultural operations. Instead of displacing a farmland for housing development, agrihood developers help a community farm thrive by providing capital and infrastructure, and by supporting the local economy.

"As Citizen Farmers, residents learn how to give the land more than what they take from it, facilitating action that fosters healthier, more sustainable food systems." [41]

—Daron "Farmer D" Joffe, Farmer D Consulting

36

Features of an Agrihood Community

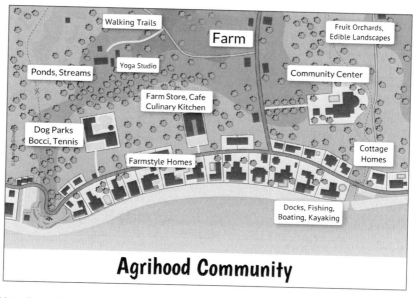

Agrihood Community

Listed are features generally found in agrihoods:

- Professionally managed farm
- Community gardens
- Farm store
- Restaurant, café, culinary kitchen
- Community center
- Clubhouse, fitness center, pool
- Children's play area, splash pool
- K-12 Schools, farming and environmental education
- Fruit and nut orchards
- Edible landscapes
- Trails for walking, hiking, biking, horseback riding
- Pocket parks, dog parks
- Sports courts, ballparks, yoga studios, meditation gardens
- Boating, fishing, kayaking, archery
- Single-family residences
- Condominiums, townhomes
- Rental apartments
- Age-restricted residences
- Income-restricted residences
- Multi-generational housing

Agrihood developers collaborate with municipal planners, conservationists, architects, and builders to help design a sustainable community that preserves farmland and supports responsible agriculture. Agrihoods are often referred to as "development supported agriculture." Developers also recognize the types of homes people want, their respect for sustainable construction, and their commitment to energy conservation. This chapter spotlights a number of agrihoods around the country in three categories: the amenities, the farms, and the homes.

The Amenities

Community Centers

Agrihoods can be considered "lifestyle communities," since they offer a diverse range of amenities. *Arden*, a healthy-living community in Palm Beach County, Florida, was named winner of the *2020 Gold Award* for "Best Amenity" by the National Association of Home Builders. *Arden* was recognized for its extraordinary community amenities, including the resort-style Lakehouse, and The Barn, where residents gather for seasonal themed events and workshops.

Gathering spaces are an important part of the agrihood lifestyle, and most agrihoods include a clubhouse or community center that serves as the agrihood's centerpiece. The center is a place to connect with neighbors and host events, club meetings, educational workshops, and activities for children and teens. Alternatively called a recreation center or clubhouse, centers typically include a café, gathering spaces, meeting rooms, and a culinary or demonstration kitchen. Some agrihoods have one or more restaurants.

Most agrihoods have at least one swimming pool, and in warmer climate areas, there may be several types of pools, including salt-water, toddler, and splash pools. Health and wellness features might include a fitness center, yoga studio, or meditation garden. Some facilities have guest suites for overnight visitors. Community centers are generally designed with architectural features compatible with the local area. They may be situated in the middle of a nostalgic town square, where streetscapes are reminiscent of landmark American villages, or they might be midwestern-style with sleek, modern features.

Aberlin Springs in Morrow, Ohio, welcomes visitors with a striking Swiss chalet, a repurposed timber-framed building that formerly housed members of the original farm family. The chalet includes guest suites for overnight visitors, a health and wellness spa, and multiple gathering spaces.

Willowsford, located in Loudoun County, Virginia, spans over 4,000 acres and is comprised of four distinctive, interconnected villages. There are two community recreation centers, each with teaching and demonstration kitchens, a state-of-the art fitness center, and resort-style pools.

Hidden Springs in Boise, Idaho, offers a centrally located community clubhouse with gathering spaces, a pool, a fitness center, and a kitchen. Residents have access to a second pool, and a quaint red barn and surrounding lawn for private events.

Through a partnership with *Messina Hof Wine Cellars, Inc., Harvest Green*, an agrihood in Richmond, Texas, is adding a winery to its agrihood and a 130-seat restaurant and event-hosting venue. *Harvest Green* has been awarded a top selling community, and was voted *2018 Master Planned Community of the Year* by the Greater Houston Builders Association. The heart of *Harvest Green* is The Farmhouse, featuring an expansive clubhouse, resort-style pool, fitness center, lakeside amphitheater, event hall, and lawn.

A large-scale, master-planned community that focuses on wellness, *Serenbe* in Chattahoochee Hills, Georgia, encompasses four hamlets, each having complementary commercial centers focused on the elements of a well-lived life: arts for inspiration, agriculture for nourishment, health for well-being, and education for awareness. Year-round cultural events include outdoor theater productions from Serenbe Playhouse, culinary workshops, festivals, music events, films, lectures, boutique shopping, art galleries, a spa, and trail riding, plus a robust Artist in Residence program featuring dinners and talks.

Photo courtesy: Miralon, Palm Springs, CA

Miralon, in Palm Springs, California, offers residents its central amenity, The Club, which can be described as a "luxurious 5-star international resort." The above photo is a rendering by Robert Hidey Architects. The Club includes pools, a spa, outdoor recreation space, a state-of-the-art health club, a coffee bar, and a full-service bar and lounge. Inside and out, the design and furnishings reflect a chic desert esthetic including poolside cabanas, expansive mountain views, and an outdoor demonstration kitchen.

The Cannery at the Packing District in Orlando, Florida, a new mixed-use community, includes apartment complexes, townhomes, retail shops, and office space. Amenities include indoor and outdoor health and wellness facilities, pools, restaurants, a food hall, a micro-brewery, and the *4 Roots Farm and Agricultural Center*.

Fox Hill in Franktown, Colorado, is anchored by a 1912 Charleston-style farmhouse, pictured above, along with the barn and silos from the original homestead. Fox Hill Farm includes an English-style greenhouse furnished with an aquaponic system to support a year-round growing season. Fox Hill creates a sustainable living environment that preserves history, conserves the land, and offers homebuyers eco-friendly energy options such as geo-thermal heating and cooling, and 1G fiberoptic technology.

Historic barns that were restored to community centers or gathering spaces can be found at *Elliott Farm* in Loveland, Ohio; *Creekside Farm at The Cliffs at Mountain Park*, South Carolina; the *Farmstead at Corley Ranch*, Gardnerville, Nevada; and *Prairie Crossing* in Grayslake, Illinois. The community center *at Tryon Farms* in Michigan City, Indiana, is an iconic dairy barn.

At *Orchard Gardens* in Missoula, Montana, you can rent a modern apartment right in the middle of a historic farm that is deeply rooted in agricultural traditions. *The Grow* in Orlando, Florida, is a new master planned community featuring vintage architectural features reminiscent of the homes and farmhouses of the 1940s. An authentic wood barn will include gathering spaces and a farm-to-table restaurant.

Photo courtesy: River Bluffs, Castle Hayne, N.C.

Boating and Fishing

Pictured above is the *Riverwalk,* the longest, privately funded overwater walk in the country, measuring 2,700 feet in length. The Riverwalk is an amenity at *River Bluffs*, located in Castle Hayne, North Carolina. This unique waterfront community sits on 313 acres with a working farm as well as a 10-acre community farm for residents. Situated along the scenic Cape Fear River, water is a large part of the community's lifestyle. The marina complex has an average water depth of 35 feet and includes 188 boat slips, state-of-the-art floating docks, and two gazebos on the Riverwalk.

Olivette, a 346-acre agrihood community located along the French Broad River in Asheville, North Carolina, provides residents with seven acres of riverfront beach. Residents can enjoy tubing, smallmouth bass fishing, kayaking, and canoeing. Winner of the *2019 Best in America Living Award for Best Green Community* by the National Association of Home Builders, *Olivette's* residents can enjoy parks, creeks, and views of the Blue Ridge Mountains.

Winner of numerous awards, *Prairie Crossing* in Grayslake, Illinois, offers residents the opportunity to swim, canoe, sail, and ice skate on its 20-acre *Lake Leopold*, named after the conservationist, Aldo Leopold.

At *Arden* in Palm Beach County, Florida, residents can enjoy walking or biking through 20 miles of trails that wind through the community and around Arden lake, or enjoy kayaking, bass fishing, and birdwatching on the 275 acres of lakes and 500 acres of greenspace at Arden.

Residents of *Pine Dove Farm* in Tallahassee, Florida, have exclusive access to two lakes designed for paddle-boarding, fishing, canoeing, and kayaking. *Bundoran Farm* in North Garden, Virginia, has two private lakes for fishing and kayaking. *Kukui'ula*, located in Kauai, Hawaii, includes a 20-acre lake for canoeing, fishing, and watersports. Boating and fishing opportunities are available in the many ponds through *Willowsford* in Loudoun County, Virginia; at *Serosun Farms* in Hampshire, Illinois; *Aberlin Springs*, Morrow, Ohio; *Tryon Farm*, Michigan City, Indiana; and *Chickahominy Falls*, Glen Allen, Virginia.

Pringle Creek in Salem, Oregon, is a 32-acre development located in the heart of the *Willamette Valley*. Running through the length of the community is *Pringle Creek*, which has been restored and certified as "Salmon Safe," with the watershed clean enough for native salmon to spawn and thrive.

Palmetto Bluff in Bluffton, South Carolina, is a 20,000-acre community offering residents low-country sporting activities on 32 miles of waterfront, including fishing, kayaking, canoeing, and paddle-boarding. The *May River* is stocked with largemouth bass and bream, and saltwater fishing for tarpon, cobia, redfish, and sea trout is available in spring and summer. *Palmetto Bluff* is also a vacation resort, and offers tours, cruises, and boat rentals.

Golf

The Cliffs at Mountain Park, Marietta, South Carolina, has seven nationally acclaimed golf courses, including a *Gary Player* signature course, where residents can play, take lessons, and compete in tournaments. *The Cliffs* is home to the University of North Carolina at Asheville Women's Golf Team, and hosts the annual LPGA-USGA Girls Golf Academy.

Creekside Farm, at *The Cliffs at Walnut Cove*, in Arden, North Carolina, includes a signature Jack Nicklaus golf course, with views of the Blue Ridge Mountains surrounding Walnut Cove. *Balsam Mountain Preserve* in Sylva, North Carolina, offers ownership or fractional ownership in its cabins, set on 3,000 acres of preservation land. In addition to a full range of outdoor amenities, Balsam Mountain Preserve includes an Arnold Palmer golf course and practice park at an elevation of 3,700 feet surrounded by mountain views and wildlife. Golfing is available at *Kukui'ula* in Kauai, Hawaii, and *Palmetto Bluff* in Bluffton, South Carolina.

Photo courtesy: Serosun Farms, Hampshire, IL

Horseback Riding

Serosun Farms, located in Hampshire, Illinois has built a state-of-the-art equestrian facility, shown in the above photo, which was designed to be a boarding and training facility for both competitive and recreational riders. Serosun offers world-class trainers a holistic approach to horse care, emphasizing the physical, nutritional, and social aspects of horse care. Residents of the 400-acre agrihood can enjoy 8 miles of trails along picturesque countryside.

Prairie Crossing in Grayslake, Illinois, has 10 miles of riding trails, and residents can enjoy a heated lounge and tack room inside the 13-stall stable. *Serenbe* in Chattahoochee Hills, Georgia, offers miles of riding trails, and residents can purchase lot sizes large enough to include a horse stable.

Dry Creek Ranch in Boise, Idaho, has horse stables and an equestrian facility where residents can enjoy dressage, western pleasure riding, lessons, and competitions. Groomed trails are located throughout the neighborhood. Dry Creek Ranch's larger home lots provide an option for residents to construct modest horse stables.

The Cliffs at Mountain Park, Marietta, South Carolina, includes an equestrian center *at Keowee Vineyards*, offering stables, riding rings, and training. Residents have access to more than 200 miles of riding trails throughout the Jocassee Gorges Wilderness Area. The Cliffs is located close to the renowned Tryon International Equestrian Center.

Palmetto Bluff in Bluffton, South Carolina, has an equestrian facility that includes a covered arena, outdoor lawn, and dressage area. Horseback riding is available at *Balsam Mountain Preserve* in Sylva, North Carolina, *Bundoran Farm* in North Garden, Virginia, and *Pendry Natirar Residences* in Peapack, New Jersey. Two new agrihoods with plans to include equestrian facilities are *The Grow* in Orlando, Florida, and *Agape* in Mukwonago, Wisconsin. Residents of Agape will be able to board a horse or other animal.

Walking, Biking, Hiking

Agrihoods are built for healthy lifestyles, and you'll see outdoor trails for walking, biking, and hiking in just about every community. Urban agrihoods, including rental apartments, have connections to trails. Many agrihood trails are bordered by edible landscapes, fruit and nut orchards where residents are free to enjoy a healthy snack.

Photo courtesy: Miralon, Palm Springs, CA

Miralon, a new agrihood by Freehold Communities in Palm Springs, California, has planted 7,000 olive trees within its 300 acres. The 7 miles of walking trails are recreated from the cart paths of a former golf course. Trails are surrounded by species of Spanish, Italian, and California olives, as well as citrus groves, dog parks, and gardens. Pictured above are the mature olive trees.

45

Balsam Mountain Preserve agrihood in Sylva, North Carolina, has 35 miles of groomed trails that were created on former logging roads that ran through the Nantahala National Forest. *Fox Hill*, located in Franktown, Colorado, is home to Castlewood Canyon, filled with hiking trails, rolling hills, majestic ponderosa pines, and spectacular views of the Colorado Rockies. *Prairie Crossing* in Grayslake, Illinois, has 10 miles of trails for walking, biking, or skiing, with trails that connect to the 5,800-acre Liberty Prairie Reserve.

Fanita Ranch in Santee, California, is a new agrihood with more than 2,000 acres of open space. Residents will have 35 miles of trails for hiking, biking, and walking through pocket parks and preserves. Trails include connections to Goodan Ranch, Sycamore Canyon, Stowe Trail, and Mission Trails Regional Park.

North River Farms, a new agrihood in Oceanside, California, includes 16 acres of parks and recreation, trails for hiking, biking, and walking, and a public mountain bike trail.

Pine Dove Farm in Tallahassee, Florida, has nearly 115 acres of conservation land with over 3 miles of marked walking trails among native forestry and habitat. *Etowah*, a new agrihood in Cumming, Iowa, includes 100 acres of forest park with accessible points throughout the community for hiking or biking.

Middlebrook in Cumming, Iowa, has trails that lead to the Great Western Bike Trail. *Baseline*, a new agrihood in Broomfield, Colorado, has 145 acres of open space and dedicated farmland, with numerous parks among its villages with connections to regional trails. *Bundoran Farm* in North Garden, Virginia, offers 15 miles of hiking and bridle trails.

Orchard Ridge, a Vital Community™ located just north of Austin in Liberty Hill, Texas, won the 2019 National Association of Home Builders (NAHB) Gold Award for Landscape Design which, along with its community gardens, emphasizes "healthy living." The land gradually slopes into an expansive basin of seasonal creeks and ponds integrated with an expansive system of walking trails, playgrounds, and neighborhood parks in a true Texas Hill Country setting.

Mesilla Vineyard Estates, in Las Cruces, New Mexico is near the Rio Grande and bordered by vineyards.

Residents have incredible views of the Organ Mountain Range, and access to a number of parks and trails in the nearby Organ Mountains Desert Peaks National Monument.

Organ Mountain photo source: Shutterstock Images

Mesilla Vineyard Estates is just a few minutes away from historic Old Mesilla, known for its rich Old West history that has included the legendary Sheriff Pat Garrett, outlaw Billy the Kidd, and local hero, Colonel Albert Fountain.

Willowsford in Loudoun County, Virginia, has varied terrain trail systems for all ages and skill level throughout its four-village community. *Hidden Springs* in Boise, Idaho, has miles of hiking and biking trails through the community, foothills, and valleys.

A number of agrihoods have bike trails that lead to a city center, public transportation, or other trail system. Those include: *The Cannery* in Davis, California; *Arden* in Palm Beach County, Florida; and *Farmers Park* in Springfield, Missouri. *Orchard Gardens* in Missoula, Montana, connects residents to the central Missoula Valley. *Elliott Farm* in Loveland, Ohio, is 1 mile from the Little Miami Scenic Trail. Miles of walking and hiking trails can be found at *Whisper Valley* in Austin, Texas, and *The Cliffs at Mountain Park* in Marietta, South Carolina.

The Village at Stone Barn in Peterborough, New Hampshire, the nation's first "regenerative agrihood," sits on a 32-acre hillside near the popular rock-climbing spot, Mount Monadnock. Walking trails are surrounded by fruit orchards and berry patches. Winter activities are also available at a number of agrihoods. In Illinois, residents can enjoy ice skating at *Prairie Crossing* in Grayslake; and snow-shoeing or cross-country skiing through 40 acres of woodlands at *Serosun Farms* in Hampshire. Groomed cross-country ski trails are available at *Cobb Hill Cohousing* in Hartland, Vermont.

Children and Schools

Agrihoods are family-friendly, and you'll find plenty of playgrounds, swimming pools, treehouses, and kids' bike paths. Activities often include learning programs about farming and the environment. A number of agrihoods are featured in this section due to their unique amenities for children. Also listed are agrihoods with on-site schools, and a few that have announced plans to build a school.

Prairie Crossing in Grayslake, Illinois, has 14 parks with swings, sandboxes, and climbing structures located throughout the community, along with baseball, basketball, and soccer fields. The Prairie Crossing Charter School (PCCS) enrolls 432 students in K-8. The school was awarded the *2019 Niche Award* as top charter school in the state and has received more than 25 awards for academic excellence since 2004, including two awards in 2018 as being in the top 4% of elementary schools in the nation.

Balsam Mountain Preserve in Sylva, North Carolina, offers many activities, including a Kids' Camp with trout fishing, horseback riding, hiking, and camping under the stars. Educational programs are led by naturalists at Balsam's Nature Center. Balsam Mountain Trust provides education, research, conservation leadership, and administers the Birds of Prey program.

The Cliffs at Mountain Park, Marietta, South Carolina, has activities for children as well as a summer camp for kids of all ages. Adventures include hiking, biking, camping, swimming, rafting, and zip-lining. *Hidden Springs* in Boise, Idaho, offers several bike trails for children of various ages and riding abilities, a swim club, a kids' camp, and before/after school activities. The community includes Hidden Springs Elementary School and the Smart Start Preschool.

Willowsford, in Loudoun County, Virginia, has two recreation centers, three treehouses, walk-in family-sized tents in camping areas, a kids' mountain-bike trail, a 10-line archery range, snow-sledding hills, disc golf, numerous pools and splash parks, a swim team, fishing and boating, and fields for volleyball and soccer. Within the development are a grade school and a middle school.

Located in Argyle, Denton County, Texas, *Harvest* has two on-site elementary schools, with plans to build the Argyle Middle School. Children residing at Harvest can attend schools in either the Argyle or Northwest school districts. A third option is the Liberty Christian School, located five miles from *Harvest*, offering academics for students in pre-K through 12th grade. The Harvest Farm provides a farming education program called *Harvest Littles*.

Agrihoods that have on-site K-8 schools include: *Fanita Ranch* in Santee, California; the *Village of Esencia*, part of *Rancho Mission Viejo* in California; and *Hidden Springs* in Boise, Idaho. *Dry Creek Ranch* in Boise, Idaho, has donated land for an elementary school in the West Ada school district.

Agrihoods currently under development that include schools in their master plan are *Carlton Landing* in Lake Eufaula, Oklahoma; *The Grow* in Orlando, Florida; *Baseline* in Broomfield, Colorado; and *Whisper Valley* in Austin, Texas. *Olivette* in Asheville, North Carolina, is building a K-8 school and *Little Free Libraries*. Children can enroll in farming education classes at *Rancho Mission Viejo* in California.

Active Adult Communities (Over 55)

There are agrihoods that are exclusively active adult communities. Those include *Del Mesa* in Carmel, California, with 289 condominiums, a clubhouse, restaurant, dog park, walking/hiking trails, fitness center, and pool. Located one mile east of *Carmel by the Sea*, the community has a 24-hour security gate. The community has about 20 clubs and committees. A key amenity includes the *Art House,* a place where painters and crafters can gather to work and store art supplies. Classes and events are held at the *Art House*, including trips to museums.

Chickahominy Falls in Glen Allen, Virginia, is an over-55 community near Richmond of 400 homes. Homes are clustered into small neighborhoods connected by walking trails. Amenities include a clubhouse, outdoor pool and patio, walking trails, birdwatching, and fishing. The professionally managed farm includes areas for beekeeping.

The *Village of Gavilan*, part of *Rancho Mission Viejo* in California, is a resort-style over-55 community offering single-story or easy two-story living, and more than 50 clubs.

Farmstead at Corley Ranch in Gardnerville, Nevada, is an over-55 community of 250 homes set on the historic *Corley Ranch* in Douglas County. The *Farmstead* clusters eco-friendly artisan studios, commercial space, and cottage and ranch homes. Residents can grow their own food utilizing *Farmstead's* greenhouse and orchard, with the assistance of an expert cultivator.

Multi-generational

Architects and home builders are now designing floorplans with "multi-generational features" for homebuyers who wish to share their home with extended family members. Multi-generational homes are usually designed with a suite on the first floor that includes a living room, bedroom, bathroom, small kitchen, and porch.

Fox Hill in Franktown, Colorado, offers a traditional farmhouse model with multi-generational features. *Edwards Addition* in Monmouth, Oregon, lists a 3,000-square-foot multi-generational home. Most agrihoods that showcase various builders would certainly welcome the opportunity to discuss any expanded options for building a multi-gen home.

Aria in Denver, Colorado, includes multi-generational co-housing condominiums and affordable rental apartments. *Middlebrook* in Cumming, Iowa, is a large agrihood with 1,000 dwellings, including an area for senior living. *Springbrook Farm* in Alcoa, Tennessee, is a new agrihood that will include residents for senior living.

Agritopia in Gilbert, Arizona, has assisted-living and independent-living centers in partnership with *Investment Property Associates* and *Retirement Community Specialists*. *The Urban Farm at Aldersgate* in Charlotte, North Carolina, is built on a 231-acre retirement care community founded as the *Methodist Home* in 1943.

Mixed-use Communities

"Mixed-use" communities blend together residential, retail, and commercial characteristics. Residential structures may include single-family homes, multi-family homes, condominiums, townhomes, and apartment buildings. Apartment buildings can be garden-level, mid-rise, or high-rise. For the most part, homes, condos, and townhomes are owned and apartments are rented.

"Mixed-income" is an additional element found in planned communities, where all or a certain portion of residential units are set aside for low-income households. Mixed-use and mixed-income communities are rapidly gaining in popularity across the country. The examples shown below are a few communities that include agricultural amenities.

Win6 Village, a new project in the city of Santa Clara, is a mixed-use community that will include mixed-income and multi-generational households. The development includes an organic farm agrihood, community gardens, an urban farm plaza, fresh food emporium, and marketplaces. *The Dows Farm Agri-community,* a mixed-use community built on conservation land in Ames, Iowa, will include commercial space, single-family homes, multi-family homes, and apartments. Under development in Alcoa, Tennessee, is *Springbrook Farm*, a mixed-use community that will include single- and multi-family homes, townhomes, a hotel, and senior living residences.

The Farms

Every agrihood includes some type of agricultural feature, and many communities include more than one farming amenity. The majority of agrihoods have "working farms," where experienced farmers are employed by the developer to manage agricultural activities. Also referred to as "professionally managed farms," the extent of services provided by the farm team varies depending upon the size of the community and farm.

A number of agrihoods were built on heritage farms, and members of the original farm family or other stakeholders are hired to help manage agricultural activities. Some agrihoods contract with outside farming entities to operate the farm and sell food at the farm store and/or through a community supported agriculture (CSA) program.

"Community farms" can also refer to professionally managed farms, however, structures can vary. For example, in smaller agrihoods, a community farm might be managed by one or two agriculturalists who welcome volunteer help from residents. A community farm may also represent a farm structured as a "cooperative," where residents work on the farm in exchange for a free share of the harvest.

Alternatively, community farms can be an area where all farming activities are completed by residents. Individual gardening plots for residents, generally called "community gardens," are discussed further in the next section called "gardening spaces for residents."

Land preservation is fundamental to the mission of any agrihood built on farmland. For that reason, some agrihoods form trusts so that the farmland, forests, wetlands, and wildlife habitat are held as conservation land in perpetuity. The farm entity generally operates as a nonprofit. Agrihood developers try to preserve the characteristics of heritage farmland wherever possible and will restore barns, silos, windmills, farmstead homes, and other structures. Buildings are often repurposed to serve as community centers, gathering spaces, or to host events and educational workshops.

In master-planned communities, the placement of the farm is important, since developers want residents to have convenient access to the farm store and also enjoy the pastoral views of grazing farm animals. At the same time, developers are also careful to place homes away from the distractions of heavy farm equipment noises, as well as noise and odors from livestock.

According to the Urban Land Institute's guide, "Agrihoods: Cultivating Best Practices," small farms consisting of less than five acres employ at least two full-time agriculturalists who engage closely with community residents and participate in activities, education, and events. Medium-sized farms that are less than 20 acres require more staff, while larger farms that are greater than 20 acres are more likely to have more machinery with greater operational efficiencies.[42]

Food distribution methods can include farm stores, seasonal farm stands, "pick your own" options, hosting farmers' markets, and offering season-long subscriptions to a CSA program. CSAs may also be available to non-residents. Most agrihoods operate on a "seasonal flat fee" for residents to purchase set quantities of fruits and vegetables, based on family size. Others may work under a system where no money is exchanged, and food is included in the homeowner's association fee. A few agrihoods operate on a year-round basis, and some also produce meat, poultry, eggs, and honey from their beehives.

Miralon in Palm Springs, California, in partnership with Temecula Olive Company, will press on-site olives harvested from its grove of 7,000 trees, and the community will sell *Miralon*-branded olive oil.

Examples of Working Farms

Founded 20 years ago, *Agritopia* in Gilbert, Arizona, is situated on 160 acres and includes an 11-acre working farm. The farm includes a citrus grove and produces certified organic fruits and vegetables and heirloom vegetables. Residents can purchase produce from the farm as well as grow their own in raised-bed community gardens.

A Planned Agricultural Community (PAC), *Pine Dove Farm* in Tallahassee, Florida, utilizes organically grown practices in its farm products, fruit trees, and pecan orchards. Pine Dove residents can subscribe to a CSA program, take part in the gardening process, and participate in gardening workshops.

Rancho Mission Viejo, near San Juan Capistrano, California, includes 6,500 acres of permanently preserved natural space including protected creeks, canyons, wetlands, woodlands, and native grasslands. The farm includes avocado, walnut, and bay trees along with organic fruits and vegetables. Residents can volunteer for planting and harvesting or attend culinary or gardening workshops.

Photo courtesy: Arden, Palm Beach County, FL

Arden, in Palm Beach County, Florida, has a 5-acre working farm that produces fruits, vegetables, herbs, and flowers, pictured above. Residents can volunteer to work with the full-time farmers as they manage their crops, and also share in the harvest. More than 50 varieties of produce and flowers are shared among residents through a Farm Share program. The program is managed organically, with special care taken to recycle nutrients, increase biodiversity and preserve air, water, and soil quality. The farm is a living classroom where residents can connect with where food comes from and be a part of the production through regular volunteer days.

Serenbe, located in Chattahoochee Hills near Atlanta, Georgia, is a 1,000-acre community surrounded by greens, wetlands, watershed areas, and hills. The 25-acre certified organic farm provides over 300 varieties of fruits, vegetables, herbs, and flowers.

Olivette Riverside Community and Farm, located in Asheville, North Carolina, was built on a historic farm that grows salad greens, specialty produce, flowers, fruit, and honey for local farmers' markets and restaurants, as well as CSA memberships to the Olivette and Asheville communities.

Creekside Farm at The Cliffs at Walnut Cove located near Asheville in Arden, North Carolina, has a 5-acre farm called Broken Oak Organics, which produces over 300 varieties of heirloom vegetables, herbs, and flowers. *River Bluffs* in Castle Hayne, near Wilmington, North Carolina, includes a 10-acre community farm, CSA, and farmers' market.

In Bluffton, South Carolina, the working farm at *Palmetto Bluff* offers fresh produce to residents, and serves the community's nine restaurants, food-based events, educational events, community farm stand, and partnerships with local food banks.

Fresh food is delivered to residents by the "Town Farmer" at *Carlton Landing* in Lake Eufaula, Oklahoma. The farm also provides food for the farm-to-table menus at local restaurants.

In Nevada, *The Farmstead at Corley Ranch,* an over-55 community in Gardnerville, includes a working farm, greenhouse, and orchard, where fresh fruits and vegetables are sold at the Farmstead's Farmers' Market. Residents can also grow their own produce in the community garden.

Millican Reserve in College Station, Texas, offers its residents a year-round CSA program for fresh produce and eggs, a farmers' market on the green, and other activities hosted by the farm team.

*S*Park* in Denver, Colorado, is an "urban agrihood," formerly known as Sustainability Park. The mixed-use development offers condominiums and townhomes. The farm consists of a 15,000-square-foot urban farm and greenhouse, professionally managed by Altius Farms. Residents purchase fruits and vegetables from the farm or grow their own in a solar-powered community garden of raised beds.

Fox Hill in Franktown, Colorado, operates a sustainable farm that includes apple and pear orchards, a berry-picking patch, row gardens, flowers, farm-fresh eggs, and honey. Fox Hill Farm operates at a biological level, a step above organic farming, with proactive soil amendments and testing.

Serosun Farms in Hampshire, Illinois, is a conservation community with a 160-acre working farm that supplies fresh produce, flowers, farm-raised meat, and a variety of specialty items. Serosun also grows heirloom varieties and specialty vegetables in its 5-acre demonstration garden.

Founded in 1987, *Prairie Crossing* in Grayslake, Illinois, is a conservation community on 675 acres and includes a 100-acre organic farm and CSA. Residents are invited to harvest fruit on Prairie Crossing's edible landscape and orchards.

Aberlin Springs in Morrow, Ohio, is a conservation community with a working farm, CSA, wellness center, and features a demonstration kitchen in its community center. The farm and greenhouse produce a wide variety of greens and microgreens.

Dry Creek Ranch in Boise, Idaho, is set on 1,400 acres and includes both a community farm and a professionally managed farm that utilizes natural growing methods for seeding, growing, and harvesting. Residents can enjoy weekly produce delivered to their door. Located 10 miles north of Boise is *Hidden Springs* created around a 135-year-old agricultural heritage site of 1,844 acres. The 40-acre working farm produces organic vegetables and offers a CSA program.

Middlebrook, located near Des Moines in Cumming, Iowa, has dedicated more than 100 acres of land to agricultural endeavors. The agrihood includes a town farm, neighborhood gardens, a community farm, edible landscapes and animal pastures. *Garden View* is a 62.5-acre community in Lincoln, Nebraska, offering abundant natural landscapes. The site includes a farm, an orchard, and community gardens.

Willowsford, located in Loudoun County, Virginia, raises several breeds of livestock on its 300 acres of farmland, and cultivates more than 150 varieties of vegetables, herbs, fruit, and flowers. Willowsford residents purchase food from the farm stand and CSA program.

Mesilla Vineyards Estates in Las Cruces, New Mexico, features a 14-acre working farm managed by a professional horticulturist. The farm provides a relaxing environment for walks and includes a community gazebo for private use.

Chickahominy Falls is an active adult community located in Glen Allen, Virginia, near Richmond. The community includes a professionally managed farm, farmhouse, farmers' market area, and areas for beekeeping.

Broomgrass, located in Gerrardstown, West Virginia, is a 320-acre community consisting of 16 residences and farmland that is protected in perpetuity. Each year, community members have a winter meeting to coordinate the agricultural intentions for the coming year. Residents can optionally work on the farm.

The Village at Stone Barn in Peterborough, New Hampshire, includes a "beyond organic" working farm, surrounded by orchards, berry patches, vegetable and flower gardens, and small livestock.

Cobb Hill Cohousing in Hartland, Vermont, is built on 270 acres of forest, pasture, and agriculture soils, with 26 varieties of vegetables grown on the farm. Members own their own homes plus a share in the commonly owned land. Cobb Hill is home to Cedar Mountain Farm and CSA, a maple syrup enterprise and group of beekeepers.

South Village in Burlington, Vermont, has a 12-acre organic farm, chickens, bees, and community gardens. The Farm at South Village participates with the Intervale Food Hub, providing fresh farm food on a year-round basis.

Hawaii has two agrihoods with working farms. *Hōkūnui* in Maui, once a diverse native forest, has set aside over 230 acres for permanent agricultural and cultural operations, with 10% of the land dedicated to housing. Walking trails lead residents from their backyard through the green pastures alongside cattle, sheep, and chickens, to the community area and farm store, offering fresh produce, meat, and ready-to-eat meals.

Kukui'ula in Kauai is an upscale agrihood that includes the Upcountry Farm, a 10-acre natural wonderland where residents can pick their own organic produce, help with harvesting, just relax, or partake in gardening lessons from the farm team.

A new agrihood under development in Broomfield, Colorado, is *Baseline*, an 11,000-acre site of 6,000 homes in a mixed-use community. Unique to Baseline's master plan is its Butterfly Pavilion, bringing a pollinator-friendly ecosystem throughout the agriculture areas. *Baseline* will be home to the Center for Invertebrate Research and Conservation.

Garden Spaces for Residents

A large number of agrihoods provide community gardens for residents to grow their own produce in addition to operating a professionally managed farm. A few agrihoods exclusively offer a community garden and/or private gardening spaces for residents. General maintenance and irrigation of community gardens are provided by the developer or homeowner's association. Some agrihoods employ agriculturalists or horticulturalists to provide assistance to residents in setting up their gardens or to conduct educational workshops. Many agrihoods have a "young farmers" program.

Harvest, located in Argyle, Texas, provides homeowners with ample opportunities to grow their own produce, pitch in to harvest community crops, share surplus food with the North Texas Food Bank, or deepen their agricultural knowledge through on-site gardening classes.

Harvest Green, an agrihood located near Houston in Richmond, Texas, gives homebuyers the option to have their builder include a "ready-to-grow" backyard garden. Harvest Green works in partnership with Enchanted Nurseries & Landscapes of Richmond to install the gardens and help new homeowners set up soil and seed.

Tryon Farm in Michigan City, Indiana, is a community of country weekend homes on historic Lake Michigan, where 120 acres of preserved meadows, dunes, and oakwood forests are home to roaming cows and chickens. A historic dairy barn serves as the community hall, offering educational workshops on beekeeping, habitat restoration, fish stocking, and environmental education. Community gardens are available for residents.

There are a number of agrihoods where residents can purchase large-size lots in order to plant their own vegetable gardens. *Cooke's Hope*, located in Easton, Maryland, offers both inland and waterfront lot sizes ranging from 2 to 57 acres.

Pictured above is the Founders Garden at *Orchard Ridge*, located in Liberty Hill, Texas, just north of Austin. A master-planned, porch-friendly Vital Community,™ residents enjoy fresh food from the working farm with no exchange of money. Residents can also grow produce in their own private space within the Founders Garden. Tools and equipment can be borrowed from the nearby farm shed, and help is always around the corner from the community's staff agriculturalists. In addition to its community gardens, Orchard Ridge brings families together in its Activity Center, designed for indoor and outdoor activities. It includes a Clubhouse with community room, a courtyard for events, an outdoor pavilion with fireplace and BBQ grills, plus an upscale, family-friendly pool with splash pad. The Fitness Center includes innovative cardio equipment, strength training sets, and weights.

The Homes

Agrihood developers generally partner with local builders to construct residential homes. Builders are selected for their reputation in the industry, work quality, and because their principles and standards align with agrihood developers. Because the agrihood concept is fairly new, the majority of homes have been built over the past ten years. For that reason, you'll find that the homes in agrihood developments are sustainably built with many eco-friendly features.

Sustainable Construction

Referred to as "green homes," or "eco-friendly" homes, a sustainably built home requires builders to be environmentally responsible in the design and construction of properties. This applies to all types of residential dwellings, including multi-family apartments, condominiums, and townhouses. Sustainable homes are built with durable materials for long-term use, lower replacement costs, and are made from renewable sources that did not harm or burden the environment. An "eco-smart" home typically involves the use of technology and applications to monitor and control energy use.

You might see homes in agrihoods that are LEED-certified, which is a designation from the Leadership in Energy and Environmental Design. LEED is a worldwide green building certification program developed by the U.S. Green Building Council. The National Association of Home Builders (NAHB) administers a certification process under its National Green Building Standard (NGBS) program. NGBS standards aim to minimize the home's impact on the environment, and apply to site design, energy-efficiency, water conservation, resource conservation, indoor environmental quality, and homeowner education. [42]

Green building standards for master-planned communities are often rated according to the Building Research Establishment's Environmental Assessment Method (BREEAM). To comply with BREEAM criteria, community standards are applied in the early design stages of a development to help create sustainable communities that are good for the environment. [43]

Energy Efficiency

Sustainable homes will include some type of energy conservation feature. The term "energy-efficiency" relates to the environmental impact of a specific material, home appliance, or energy source. A number of agrihood home models are classified as "net-zero" homes. This means that, on an annual basis, the total amount of energy used is equal to the amount of renewable energy created by the home. Some model homes might be described as "net-zero capable," which means the homebuyer has the option to upgrade to energy-efficient features that would render a net-zero rating. Outlined below are a number of energy-efficient features that are commonly found in agrihood developments.

 The Energy Star Certified Home Program was introduced by the U.S. Department of Energy in 1996. There are about two million homes in America that currently have the Energy Star whole-house certification label. [44]

 The Zero Energy Ready Home (ZERH) is a certification issued by the U.S. Department of Energy for high-performance homes whose total annual energy use is offset by renewable energy. [45]

 Solar photovoltaic panels absorb sunlight and convert the light energy to electricity. The system generates no pollution and no greenhouse gas emissions. [46]

 Geothermal energy is considered to be the most eco-friendly solution, since an entire home can be heated and cooled without the use of fossil fuels. [47]

The list of *Energy Star*-rated home products is very extensive, and energy ratings, audits, and certifications will take each *Energy Star* feature into account for an overall whole-house rating.

Energy Star products include: thermostats, air-source heat pumps, boilers, furnaces, ductless heating and cooling, geothermal heat pumps, central air conditioners, room air conditioners, ventilation fans, refrigerators, freezers, dishwashers, washing machines, dryers, dehumidifiers, air purifiers, windows, doors, roof products, storm windows, insulation, ceiling fans, light fixtures, light bulbs, and smart home energy management systems.[48]

Over the past decade, there have been many technological advances in solar energy, and costs have been reduced. Photovoltaic (PV) panels are placed in an area that maximizes the amount of sunlight, and can be mounted on the ground, wall, or roof. Mounts can include a solar tracker to follow the sun across the sky. Solar hot water systems involve the installation of solar panels that contain water-based fluid. The fluid absorbs the sun's heat and carries the fluid down to the hot water tank.[49]

Geothermal technology comes from layers far beneath the earth. Thermal properties within the core are collected by a ground-level heat pump to heat and cool the home. According to the U.S. Department of Energy, geothermal technology reduces energy consumption by up to 65%.[50] Geothermal systems are not available in every U.S. state, and agrihood builders generally offer geothermal energy if it is available in the area. Updated maps can be viewed on the Department of Energy's website at www.energy.gov.

Energy Tax Credits and Incentives

The Bipartisan Budget Act of 2018 reinstated a bill that allows homeowners to apply for a rebate for the purchase of a photovoltaic (PV) system or a geothermal heat pump and/or cooling system. For the year 2020, the federal income tax credit is 26% based on the cost of the equipment and installation. A tax credit is a "bottom-line" reduction on the Federal 1040 return and can be carried forward if the dollar amount of the credit exceeds the tax amount.[51]

The Database of State Incentives for Renewables and Efficiency (DSIRE) is a public database for consumers to locate incentives within their state. After choosing your state from the flash map on the site's homepage, the screen will display a full list of available programs, categorized as "financial incentives," or "regulatory policies."

Examples of programs include: rebates, property tax incentives, loan programs, *Green Power* purchasing, solar renewable energy credit, and sales tax incentives. You'll see hundreds of programs, and there are filters to narrow your search to view "renewable energy," or enter a keyword such as "solar." The DSIRE program is managed and funded by the North Carolina Clean Energy Technology Center Fund, a part of the N.C. State Engineering Foundation.[52] The site can be accessed at www.dsireusa.org.

Home Features

Exterior home styles and interior features offered by agrihood builders are generally consistent with the new home construction industry. The National Association of Home Builders (NAHB) data show that consumers continue to ask for smaller homes, not only in overall square footage but also in the number of features, such as bedrooms and bathrooms. The four-year downward trend has led to the smallest average home size since 2011 at 2,520 square feet. The report lists energy-efficient features, particularly *Energy Star* windows and appliances, as a priority, as well as geothermal heat pumps, and solar electricity and hot water heating. Preferences included other eco-friendly features such as programmable thermostats and efficient lighting.[53]

Lot Size

For the most part, agrihood lot sizes are consistent with new construction housing in America. Unlike the standard residential "subdivision," agrihoods offer homebuyers an expanded range of options for pricing, home size, and lot size. A number of agrihoods offer lot sizes of one or more acres, and there are several communities throughout the U.S. that offer lots with very large acreage.

According to the National Association of Home Builders (NAHB), the median lot size of a new single-family detached home sold in 2017 was 8,560 square feet, or just under one-fifth of an acre. State-level figures are unique to the area. In New England states, for example, there may be minimum lot size restrictions, where more than half of lots exceed four-tenths of an acre. In the NAHB's Pacific division where land is scarce, half the lot sizes are under .15 of an acre.[54]

Neighborhoods

Many agrihoods build homes in "clusters," which are referred to as "hamlets," or "villages" within the community. These homes are placed relatively close together, and both home and lot sizes are smaller. Villages often have their own "pocket park," children's play area, dog park, and sometimes a separate community center and pool.

Agrihoods have been creative in planning "streetscapes" that are pedestrian-friendly, with wide paved walkways, bordered by shady trees or landscapes. There may be several hamlets which criss-cross in and out of village greens and town centers, and that are within a short distance to the farm and recreational amenities.

Larger homes and farmstead-style homes are generally located on winding roads with wider-spaced lots, along the perimeter of waterways, or areas offering premium views. Views can consist of canyons, mountains, or pastures adjacent to farmland. For years, homebuyers paid a premium for views of golf fairways—in agrihoods, they pay a premium for views of horses. A key amenity found in nearly all agrihoods is the thoughtfully placed access points throughout the development that lead to walking or biking trails.

Open Space

Building homes on smaller lots allows agrihood developers to leave a larger portion of the land to open space for agricultural purposes, conservation, wetlands preservation, or wildlife habitat. Open space is valuable to environmental sustainability. It keeps streams, creeks, ponds, and rivers available for everyone to access. Open space provides habitat for bees, butterflies, birds, bats, wildflowers, songbirds, flora, and fauna.

Expanses of undeveloped land allow rain to percolate into the ground, replenish the groundwater, and cleanse stormwater runoff prior to entry to an estuary, tributary, or river. Forests, trees, and other vegetation help the environment by absorbing carbon dioxide gases and releasing oxygen.

Home Styles

The home shown above is the Kendal Model from Pendragon Homes available at Aberlin Springs in Morrow, Ohio.

Cottage-style homes reflect the vintage character of an area. Typically, square footage is smaller, and architectural features can include vertical board-and-batten, shingle, stucco walls, gable roofs, balconies, and porches. Front porches are very common in agrihoods, which are often described as "porch-friendly" communities.

Garages are frequently placed in the back of the home, allowing for larger, "rocking chair" porches or "wraparound" porches. Cottage-style homes can be woodsy and described as "cabins" or bungalows." They are charming and might be described as "vintage" or "Victorian."

Single-floor living is popular for many homebuyers, particularly "empty nesters," who are happily settling into a retirement lifestyle at an agrihood. Throughout the nation, you'll find single-level models available, including modified floor plans, known as "easy-step multi-level" designs.

Photo Courtesy: Arden, Palm Beach County, FL

Shown above is the Carlton Model from Kenco Homes, available at Arden in Palm Beach County, Florida.

Many agrihood developers give residents the opportunity to purchase a custom-built home or modify one of the architectural plans to suit their individual needs. The "multi-generational" home feature is increasingly popular, and most agrihoods have a choice of multi-gen floor plans available. Larger homes in agrihoods can be 4,000 to 5,000 square feet, and are typically referred to as "estate homes" or "carriage house" models. The "craftsman" style home is very popular and is seen in a range of home sizes. Pictured below is a custom home from Pendragon Homes, for Aberlin Springs.

Photo courtesy: Ablerlin Springs, Morrow, OH

Photo courtesy: Freehold Communities for Miralon, Palm Springs, CA

As master-planned communities agrihood developers seek to reflect the historic landmark communities of the area, and plant native trees and shrubs along streetscapes. "Mid-century," "prairie," and "mid-western" designs are popular. Some designs have expansive floor-to-ceiling glass windows, allowing homeowners to have panoramic views of mountains or canyons. Pictured above is a rendering of the Flair Model offered by Woodbridge Pacific Group for Miralon in Palm Springs, California. The interior of the two-story Flair home is shown below.

Photo courtesy: Freehold Communities for Miralon, Palm Springs, CA

CHAPTER 5

Backyard Farming

BACKYARD FARMING IS A TIME-HONORED TRADITION. Growing our own vegetables can be very rewarding and brings back fond memories for many. Backyard farming seems relatively straightforward, since we are fulfilling the same tasks that were used for generations. Times have changed, however, and the most significant change pertains to our natural environment. In order to produce healthy food, plants require a healthy eco-system. How we plant, feed, manage, and harvest fruits and vegetables depends upon a number of biological factors. This chapter discusses environmentally conscious farming methods such as permaculture and regenerative agriculture. Such concepts build upon organic farming principles that can result in healthier food and a healthier environment.

Healthy Soil

A successful garden starts from the ground up—the soil. Soil quality is the capacity of soil to function within its natural or managed ecosystem to sustain plant productivity. Before deciding whether to grow food in your backyard, it is important to research your property history. Previous use of the land and surrounding areas can affect the quality of soil health. An assessment of soil health is based on a number of measurable indicators that test the physical, chemical, and biological properties of soil.

Soil testing is available from the *Soil Plant Nutrient Testing Laboratory* at the Center for Agriculture, Food and the Environment at the University of Massachusetts at Amherst.[55] The routine test for home gardening can provide the following information: nutrient levels, soil acidity (soil pH), and levels of toxicity from lead or heavy metals, and identify areas with excess nutrients that can pollute local waterways. The routine home gardening test costs $20 and is recommended by the USDA's *Urban Agriculture Toolkit.* Instructions on how to order and send soil to the lab are available at: www.ag.umass.edu/services/soil-plant-nutrient-testing-laboratory

USDA Natural Resources Conservation Service

The USDA's Natural Resources Conservation Service (NRCS) has a web-based portal that provides information for farmers and consumers. The upper-left side menu includes several tabs for users to search for information on a range of topics and programs. Pictured below is the home page of the USDA-NRCS site. www.nrcs.usda.gov

Image source: USDA National Resources Conservation Service

If you have concerns about your soil, you can consult with a certified Soil Scientist. Choose "Contact Us" from the row of tabs on the top of the home page, select "directories," and then select "State Soil Scientists." You'll see the name, title, telephone number, and email address of your state representative, along with the address of the USDA-NRCS state office.[56]

Image source: USDA National Resources Conservation Service

In the upper right corner of the USDA-NRCS home page, you can select "State Websites" to browse for information applicable to your state. The example shown above is for the state of Colorado. You can narrow your search criteria by selecting the tab "Browse by Audience," located under the general search bar. Choose "Homeowners" from the drop-down list to view state initiatives and conservation-conscious articles. From any page throughout the USDA-NRCS portal, you can access the "National Centers," which lists a number of divisions. Choose "National Soil Survey Center," followed by "Soil Surveys by State." After selecting your state, you will see a full list of archived soil surveys for each county.[57]

Organic Gardening

According to Rodale's *Basic Organic Gardening* by Deborah L. Martin, home gardeners can purchase organic seeds or buy plants from a grower who follows organic practices. To follow organic practices for a home garden, people are advised to make good choices when using necessary fertilizers and pesticides, and selectively apply the least toxic products. Plants will need a moderate amount of nutrition that is beneficial to soil microbiology. The *Organic Materials Review Institute (OMRI)* is a nonprofit organization that focuses on agricultural inputs such as non-synthetic fertilizers, soil amendments, and naturally derived pest-control products. Gardeners should look for products with a seal that reads "OMRI" or "OMRI Listed" to identify products that have been evaluated and deemed acceptable for use in organic production.[58]

The difference between organic and conventional farming is that conventional farming relies on chemicals to provide plant nutrition, and fight pests and weeds. Conventional agriculture increases greenhouse gas emissions, soil erosion, water pollution, and can be a threat to humans and animals. Organic farming relies on biodiversity, composting, and systems that do not involve the use of synthetic pesticides, herbicides, and fertilizers. Genetically Modified Organisms (GMOs) are not allowed. Organic farming has a smaller carbon footprint, conserves and builds soil health, and replenishes natural eco-systems for cleaner water and air. *(See Chapter 1 for more information about USDA organic certification.)*

Regenerative Agriculture

"Beyond Organic" and "Beyond Sustainable" are associated with the concept of regenerative agriculture. Regenerative agriculture is considered a philosophy based on a holistic systems approach to agriculture that encourages continual on-farm innovation for environmental, social, economic, and spiritual well-being. The term regenerative agriculture was coined by Robert Rodale, son of the American organic pioneer, J.I. Rodale. According to the Rodale Institute, regenerative agriculture improves the resources it uses, rather than destroying or depleting them.

The most important priority in regenerative organic agriculture is soil health, which is intrinsically linked to the total health of our food system. Regenerative agriculture prioritizes soil health while simultaneously encompassing high standards for animal welfare and worker fairness. In 2018, the Rodale Institute introduced a holistic, high-bar standard for agriculture certification.

Regenerative Organic Certification, or ROC, is overseen by the *Regenerative Organic Alliance*, a non-profit made up of experts in farming, ranching, soil health, animal welfare, and farmer and worker fairness. Using the USDA certified organic standard as a baseline requirement, Regenerative Organic Certification adds important criteria and builds off these and other standards in the areas of soil health and land management, animal welfare, and farmer and worker fairness.[59]

Permaculture

According to the *Permaculture Research Institute*, permaculture integrates land, resources, people, and the environment through mutually beneficial synergies—imitating the no waste, closed loop systems seen in diverse natural systems. It is a multidisciplinary system that includes agriculture, water harvesting and hydrology, energy, natural building, forestry, waste management, animal systems, aquaculture, appropriate technology, economics, and community development. Permaculture principles are applied to regenerative agriculture, as explained earlier.

The word permaculture combines the words permanent and agriculture, and the term has also been described as "permanent culture," due to the social and sustainable aspects of the farming philosophy. The term was coined in 1978 by Bill Mollison, a senior lecturer in Environmental Psychology at the University of Tasmania, and graduate student David Holmgren, who in 2002 together published the book *Permaculture: Principles and Pathways Beyond Sustainability in 2002*. Permaculture uses organic gardening and farming practices, but its principles extend beyond these practices to integrate environmental impact. [60]

Hydroponics

Briefly discussed earlier in *Chapter 3, Urban Agriculture*, hydroponics is gaining presence in vertical farming. Hydroponics enables the growth of food without soil and natural light. Instead of soil, plants grow on a layer of porous material kept moist by a closed-loop water-based nutrient solution. Most farmers use low-energy LED lighting systems. There are a number of hydroponic growing systems available for at-home use by consumers.

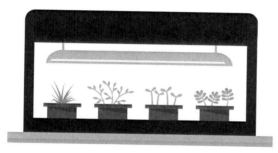

"Smart gardens" are table-top growing systems using NASA-inspired soil that hold a long-lasting water supply.

Hydroponic growing systems are made in a variety of types and sizes, and many innovative table-top products are being introduced for at-home use. There are growing systems with LED lighting for indoor use, and other types that can be placed in a covered area such as an outdoor porch. Commercial makers of hydroponic systems are also offering consumers "pre-planted" seed packs, and the pods are simply placed into the growing tank. Hydroponic systems usually require consumers to subscribe to a monthly delivery system to receive the porous soil materials and growing solution.

There are "aeroponic" products designed for at-home use that closely resemble hydroponic systems, but without the closed-loop watering system. These products are designed for indoor growing of herbs and generally utilize pre-planted seed pods. The energy-efficient LED lighting boosts growth, and consumers only need to add water.

Aquaponics

Aquaponics combines two processes—hydroponics and aquaculture—into one integrated system. Some of the indoor products for consumer use are based on an aquaponic system where the growing tank also includes fish. The fish waste provides organic food for the growing plants, and the plants naturally filter the water in which the fish live. If you are shopping for an indoor hydroponic growing system, you will see a number of products that have a fish tank on the bottom, and the upper portion of the product holds the plant garden.

Ornamental fish, such as koi and goldfish, are popular in smaller aquaponic systems. While you're at the office, your fish are feeding your plants.

Image source: Shutterstock

Microgreens

Microgreens, which are the seedlings of herbs and vegetables, are ideally suited for growing in hydroponic solutions. Microgreens are different from sprouts, which are harvested just after the seeds begin to grow. Microgreens grow from sprouts, but they have leaves. Depending on the type of plant, microgreens can be harvested 1 to 3 weeks after planting.

Microgreens can be grown in only a few inches of soil. After planting the seeds, the soil must be kept moist in order for seeds to germinate. Gently misting the soil with water from a spray bottle helps keep seeds in place. Most plants will be ready to eat within 2 to 3 weeks. Some plants can be rotated by placing new plants in the same pot after harvesting, and other types will continue to grow after leaves are cut above the soil line. Listed below are popular herbs and vegetables that can be grown as microgreens:

Amaranth	Cilantro	Mustard
Arugula	Cress	Parsley
Basil	Dill	Pea
Beet	Kale	Radish
Broccoli	Leaf Lettuce	Rocket (Arugula)
Cabbage	Leek	Spinach
Celery	Mesclun	Swiss Chard

The two commodities produced by bees are honey and wax.

Beeswax can be used to make soap, wood polish, candles, and other by-products.

Bees

According to *Bee Built*, an Oregon-based maker of hives and beekeeping supplies, bees perform approximately 80% of all pollination worldwide. Unfortunately, the United States has experienced significant loss in bee colonies in recent years, caused by the use of pesticides, from pests and diseases, and from climate change. One-third of our food supply relies on bees for pollination. The foraging season of bees varies greatly across climates, and is longer in the south. The only species in America is called *Apis Mellifera*, known as the European honeybee. A bee colony will pollinate within a 5-mile radius of its hive.[61]

Beehives can function anywhere, on balconies, rooftops, and urban yards. However, the placement of beehives is important, since there may be issues from neighbors. Many components of beekeeping are regulated by local, state, and federal authorities. Beekeepers who plan to extract, bottle, and sell honey are subject to specific rules. Some jurisdictions have zoning requirements for beekeeping, and hives may not be permitted by your homeowner's association. Local rules may require beekeepers to obtain a license, register bees, and have annual apiary inspections.

The *Apiary Inspectors of America (AIA)* is a non-profit organization established to promote better beekeeping conditions in North America and provide accurate and helpful information for the management of honey bees.[62] The website address of the AIA is: www.apiaryinspectors.org/

From the home page, select "Inspection Services," then "U.S. Inspection Services," and you will see an alphabetical directory that lists every state, with contact information for an apiary inspector. Located within the state information screen is a direct link to the state's laws and regulations. The direct link to the state directory is: www.apiaryinspectors.org/us-inspection-services/

Local Laws and Regulations

Backyard farming may be subject to zoning laws and regulations, even if food is exclusively grown for household consumption. If you are living in a community governed by a homeowner's association, the by-laws should state whether or not there are any covenants or restrictions that prohibit certain gardening activities. Generally, there are no restrictions for produce that is grown in pots or other containers.

Local regulations can also include "set-back" restrictions regarding the placement of gardening structures or greenhouses. A set-back is the minimum number of feet from a neighboring property line that a structure can be located. Many areas throughout the U.S. have adopted a "right to farm" law, giving homeowners the legal right to grow food on their property. However, most jurisdictions also have "nuisance laws" which give neighbors the right to file a complaint if there are noises or odors resulting from farm animals or agricultural activities.

If you are considering growing cannabis, it is imperative that you research all federal and state laws. The *Marijuana Break* website provides a brief summary of rules in each state in the U.S. The site is a good initial step to inquire about permissible use for growing cannabis for medical and/or recreational purposes. The summary specifies registration card requirements, the maximum number of plants per adult household member, householder age, and other rules.[63] The site can be accessed at: www.marijuanabreak.com/state-by-state-guide-to-growing-marijuana

Farm Animals

Each state and/or other jurisdiction such as county, city, or town will likely have laws pertaining to farm animals. Such laws will specifically pertain to the type of animal (e.g. chickens, goats), and rules may vary based on the size of the animal. For non-commercial farmers, rules will stipulate the maximum number of animals, such as six chickens or one goat. You may be required to obtain a license to have animals on your property and maintain veterinary records. Non-commercial farmers are prohibited from slaughtering animals or selling dairy products. Laws generally include rules for animal fencing and set-backs for buildings such as chicken coops.

Sale of Food

The entrepreneurial category of backyard farmers includes "hobby farms" and "cottage farms." These types of farms are usually operated by people who want to earn extra money, or they have an income from other sources. The USDA defines "small farmers," as an enterprise earning less than $25,000 per year. However, hobby farms and cottage farms are more unique, and often involve other activities—namely "food processing." All the rules change when food is baked, cooked, or canned because processing may also include other food products or by-products. People who operate hobby or cottage farms often sell their produce at their own farm stand in front of their home, on food trucks, or at a farmers' market.

When any type of food is sold, and whether or not it is processed, the operator is subject to federal laws for food safety, processing, marketing, labeling, and distribution. In addition, operators are subject to local zoning ordinances for their farming enterprise.

According to *Urban Ag Law*, food safety regulators do not consider fruits and vegetables to be processed if they have merely been washed and refrigerated, or if they have only had their leaves, stems, and husks removed. However, the moment a fruit or vegetable has been sliced, cooked, frozen, or mixed with other ingredients, it has been "processed" under the law.[64]

Composting

Compost provides plants with optimal nutrition from a process where organic materials are combined and encouraged to decompose. Nitrogen-rich materials such as vegetable peels, fruit rinds, and grass clippings are placed into a compost bin. Also added to the bin are carbon-rich materials, such as fallen leaves, straw, dead flowers, shredded newspaper, and cardboard. Soil is layered in between the different types of materials, and the contents of the bin are turned with a garden fork every few weeks. The compost bin must be kept moist, and slowly the contents will decompose and be ready for use as compost. Meat scraps or dairy products must not be added to the compost, and there are strict rules regarding the use of materials such as cow manure or waste from other barnyard animals. If you are considering composting, refer to the "Backyard Conservation Tip Sheet" published by the USDA National Resources Conservation Service.[65]

Food and Water Safety

The U.S. Food and Drug Administration (FDA) oversees standards for produce safety. Rules apply to commercial farmers with average annual income from sale of food greater than $25,000 annually. FDA rules do not apply to personal or on-farm consumption. Nonetheless, produce safety affects every fruit and vegetable grower. Regardless of the size, location, or commodity grown, food is subject to safety risks.

Agricultural water that is used for irrigation as well as post-harvesting activities must be safe enough for its intended use. Water from public sources is routinely tested. Well or groundwater sources can be tested for safety. Once you have determined that your farming plans comply with your local laws, your planting soil is healthy, and you'll be feeding your plants with healthy water—you're ready to farm!

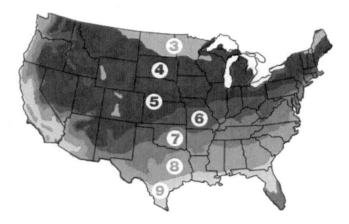

USDA Plant Hardiness Zone Map

All gardening is based on a planting season that is structured according to geographic "zones." The plant hardiness zone map is the standard by which all gardeners and growers can determine which plants are most likely to thrive at a location. The map is based on the average annual minimum winter temperature, divided into 10-degree Fahrenheit zones. When you purchase seeds or plants from a nursery, instructions will refer to the planting and harvest time according to the geographic zone.[66] By entering your zip code, you can obtain your exact zone from the USDA website: www.planthardiness.ars.usda.gov

Early Bird Planting

You can jump-start your vegetables by growing seeds indoors. The "frost date" is the first day in spring that any plant can be placed into the ground. Gardeners should refer to the prior year's frost date when planning their next season. You can extend your growing season by starting seeds indoors, or in a "cold frame" or greenhouse. Seeds can germinate indoors, be relocated to a greenhouse as outdoor temperatures begin to warm, and then be planted in the ground after the frost date. Seed packets contain specific instructions for moisture, temperature, and lighting. Many heirloom variety plants are only available as seeds, and organic-certified seeds are available from agricultural suppliers.

Vegetable Growing Season

	← Seed Indoors →		← Plant Outside →			← Harvest →			
	March	April	May	June	July	Aug	Sept	Oct	Nov
Basil									
Beans									
Broccoli									
Carrots *									
Cilantro									
Cucumber									
Dill									
Eggplant									
Kale *									
Lettuce									
Parsley									
Peppers									
Sage									
Spinach *									
Summer Squash									
Thyme *									
Tomato									
Zucchini									

Vegetable Growing Season

The chart illustrated above represents the growing season for gardening in the U.S. plant hardiness zone 6, which stretches across 35 states from east to west. The shaded bars reflect the months (or half months) that activities can be completed. The lightest shade is when seeds can be started indoors or in other protected areas. The darkest shade is planting in the ground after the frost date. The medium gray shade represents harvesting time. Not all vegetables are suitable for indoor seeding, and those are marked with an asterisk. The source of information in the chart was adapted from the *Old Farmer's Almanac.*[67] You can obtain planting and harvesting information specific to your exact location at the following site: www.almanac.com

Vegetable Planting Guide

"Plant spacing" is the number of inches required between each plant. Each plant has its own unique requirements for spacing and depth, and therefore laying out your plan can be challenging. As a first step, draw a diagram of your garden that is divided into small squares. Drawing 1-inch squares works well on paper, since it allows you enough room to pencil in the name of the plant. Each square will correspond to an actual square foot in your garden.

If your garden is 8 feet by 4 feet, you will have exactly 32 squares. Visualize four rows of planting where you could have 8 different vegetables in each row. This exercise will help simplify your plant selections and estimate how much space you will need for your garden. Keep in mind that you could have 2 or 3 different garden beds throughout your backyard. In fact, garden chores are less strenuous when you are navigating around smaller beds.

The square foot concept was pioneered by the late Mel Bartholomew, who published a number of editions of his book, *Square Foot Gardening.*[68] The "plant spacing guide" shown on the next page was inspired by the square foot concept, and based on data published by the *Old Farmer's Almanac* for U.S. hardiness zone 6.[69]

Plant Spacing Guide

Number of Plants per 12" Width	Vegetables	
1	Asparagus Broccoli Brussels sprouts Cabbage Cauliflower Corn Cucumber	Eggplant Kale Squash, summer Squash, winter Sweet potato Tomato, large Zucchini
2	Beans, bush Beans, pole Bell peppers Celery Chili peppers Chinese kale Cilantro	Cucumber, trellis Fennel Lettuce, head Okra Sweet potato Tomato, small Tomatillos
4	Arugula Basil Broccoli rabe Leaf Lettuce Parsley	Parsnip Potato Radicchio Rocket (Arugula) Rutabaga
6	Bok choy Kohlrabi Mache greens Radicchio	Shallots Spinach Spinach, baby Swiss chard
8	Beets Black-eyed peas Dill Leeks	Onions Radish Soybeans Turnips
12 to 16	Carrots Cress Garlic	Lentils Peas Scallions

After you have made your selections, your next step is to arrange your plants in the most optimum location. Some plants need more space. You might want to place them in a corner, or you can reserve two squares for one large plant. If your garden is next to a wall or fence, placing the "climbers" in the back row makes it easier for you to reach the plants, and the shorter vegetables will have more sun.

There are plants that make good companions and plants that do not make good companions. Certain plants benefit others because they deter pests or diseases, while other plant combinations do the opposite, and can attract harm. The *Old Farmer's Almanac* website provides free information, including a "Companion Planting Chart for Vegetables."[70] The most popular vegetable plants are listed along with their corresponding "friends and foes." The Companion Planting Chart is available at:

https://www.almanac.com/content/companion-planting-chart-vegetables

Shade-tolerant Vegetables

Most vegetables require at least 6 hours of sunlight a day. However, there are a number of vegetables that only require 3 or 4 hours of sunshine each day. Those include root vegetables such as beets, carrots, potatoes, radishes, and turnips. In addition, a number of green vegetables will thrive with only 3 to 4 hours of sun each day such as arugula, chard, cabbage, cilantro, kale, lettuce, parsley, scallions, and spinach. It might take longer for your plants to mature when there is less sun, and sometimes plants will be a bit smaller.

Raised-bed Gardening

There are many types of "raised-bed" gardens. The "bottomless" structure is placed directly on the ground. The beds are typically rectangular and constructed of wood. Popular size beds are 4 feet by 8 feet, which provide 32 square feet of gardening space. Many backyard farmers have several beds, separated by "walking paths." The side walls of the bottomless garden bed are typically 8 to 12 inches high.

The borders help protect the plants from intrusion and provide a firm base for gardeners to attach protective covering when needed. The ground underneath must be tilled and free of all grass. However, there is less soil preparation if the area is filled with organic potting soil and fertilizer products that are purchased from a certified organic supplier. Depending upon the depth of newly added soil, it may cover the entire rooting system of your plants.

Some gardeners place a mesh lining on the bottom of the planting bed to deter insects. Plants with completely enclosed bottoms can be placed on any flat surface such as wooden decks or concrete patios. Planters should be placed on bricks or a layer of stones for ventilation and drainage.

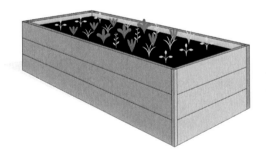

Waist-high beds are known as "elevated" planting structures and are less-strenuous for weeding and other tasks.

"Terraced" planting is when you arrange several planters of different heights to form a bi-level or tiered garden. An attractive, yet practical backyard garden could include a 3-foot high planter, as illustrated above, with a 2-foot high planter in front or on the sides. There are many do-it-yourself (DIY) structures that can be made to complement your home flower garden and overall landscape.

85

Porches are the new backyard

All you need is a sunny location, and you can grow organic produce just about anywhere—on your balcony, deck, or patio.

Containers are easy to move around. You can follow the sun or make room on your patio for your very own farm-to-table al fresco dining.

Container Gardening

For just a few minutes of your time every day, you can grow a complete "salad garden" for an entire season. All you need are a few large planters and six hours of daily sunshine. There are many vegetables that do very well when planted alone, such as beans, cucumbers, eggplant, lettuce, spinach, and tomatoes. It's easy to add a trellis to support beans or tomatoes in a planter, and vegetables will also grow in hanging pots.

Planters should be at least 18" to 24" in diameter, and 12" to 18" tall, depending on the type of vegetable. You can repurpose items made from wood or metal to use as a planter—as long as the material is non-toxic and safe for growing food. You may need to drill holes on the bottom of the container for drainage and place it on a layer of stones to keep water from settling at the base. Wooden milk crates are popular for gardening and are ideal for creating terraced gardens. Just stack planted crates above one or two rows of empty crates. Slatted wood crates need to be lined with mesh liners to keep the soil contained.

Galvanized steel "horse troughs" are popular for home gardening. These large oval containers can be spray-painted and are lightweight, inexpensive, and portable. Old-fashioned metal trash cans are also being used for growing vegetables. As long as there's drainage, sufficient space for roots to expand, and the material is safe—you have a place to grow food.

CHAPTER 6

Community-Supported Agriculture

WHAT'S IN SEASON? Instead of hearing the words "what's for dinner?" from your family, you may be surprised at how quickly your household has adapted to the "harvest season." After all, this is how our ancestors ate— and celebrated. Thanksgiving first began when the pilgrims celebrated their wheat harvest; and around the world, harvest festivals remain the heart of many cultural traditions.

By joining a Community-Supported Agriculture (CSA) program, you are making a pledge to the farm in return for a "share" of the harvest. Each week, you will receive a "share box" of the freshest food from the farm's most bountiful crops. As a CSA member, you and your family will have a connection to the farm and benefit from a season-long supply of nutritious food from the "farmer you know." In fact, your family might begin asking the question, "did these vegetables come from the supermarket or *our* farm?"

CSAs give farmers a sustainable model for anticipating crop needs and funding the cost of agricultural operations. Each subscriber commits to a certain share size and distribution schedule. Generally, "shareholders" or "members" invest in the farm by paying a flat fee at the beginning of the season. Shareholders also share in the risk, since the farm's production can be affected by weather or other unforeseen events.

There are many different CSA structures and a wide range of options. For example, instead of paying the entire seasonal fee up front, some CSAs collect fees throughout the season. Examples of various CSA programs are explained separately in the sections below.

Box Share

"Box share" is a term used by most CSAs and refers to the quantity of food that will be provided to your household in accordance with your CSA agreement. Every CSA will specify how much food can be expected, usually expressed as a number of items. For example, when describing a "full share," you will likely see the description "12 to 15 items." For any size share, the actual number of items can fluctuate throughout the season due to variations in produce size or weight.

A "half share" is typically the same quantity of food as a full share, only the box is distributed on a bi-weekly basis. Whatever schedule is chosen, the food is always freshly harvested. Box shares can also be categorized as "large," or "small," and some CSAs also provide other size options, such as "single" or "medium." The CSA agreement will be specific regarding the quantity of food, and may also include estimates regarding the number of household members the food will feed. For any size box selected, members will choose a "weekly" or "bi-weekly" distribution schedule. Your "box" might be packed in a closed-top recyclable cardboard carton, or in an open-top crate that is later returned to the CSA.

Harvest Season

Your CSA will provide a "harvest schedule" to let you know what food you can expect, and when. Typically, schedules or calendars are posted on the CSA website, and most CSAs will e-mail newsletters to members announcing the forthcoming harvest. The CSA season is generally 5 months in northern parts of the country, and 6 to 8 months in warmer climates. Southern and southwest CSAs generally operate year-round. Your harvest schedule might resemble the example shown on the following page, which reflects a growing season for zone 6.

CSA Harvest Season

VEGETABLES

Arugula	April, May	September to December
Beans	July to October	
Beets	May to November	
Broccoli	June to October	
Cabbage	May, June	September, October
Carrots	June to November	
Cauliflower	September to November	
Cilantro	April to December	
Corn, sweet	July to October	
Cucumber	May, June	August, September
Eggplant	May to October	
Kale	April to December	
Lettuce	May to December	
Peas	June, July	
Peppers	June to August	
Potatoes	July to November	
Radishes	April, May	September, October
Rhubarb	May, June	
Spinach	May to December	
Summer Squash	May to September	
Sweet Potatoes	July to November	
Swiss Chard	May to December	
Tatsoi	October to December	
Tomatoes	July to September	
Turnips	April to June	September to December
Winter Squash	September to December	
Zucchini	July to October	

FRUIT

Apples	August to October
Blackberries	July to September
Blueberries	June to August
Cherries	June, July
Peaches	July to September
Pears	July, August
Raspberries	July to October
Strawberries	May, June

Food Box Contents

Each week, the farm will pack the share boxes with the freshest fruits and vegetables from the field. What's unique about the CSA concept is that you're more likely to try a fruit or vegetable that is new to you or members of your family. Perhaps you've passed by rutabagas or turnips in the supermarket aisle; however, after seeing their glorious color in your food box, you may find yourself searching for recipes.

CSA farms make every attempt to deliver a variety of foods to members. Early in the season, there'll be strawberries and lots of leafy greens. In summer, your box will include beans, carrots, and tomatoes, followed by root vegetables in the fall. You may have the opportunity to revise your food preferences. For example, some CSAs may provide a listing of vegetables where members can select their choices from the list, and perhaps have a chance to indicate smaller or larger quantities of a specific fruit or vegetable.

Market-style Food Box

Some CSAs offer a program where members have the opportunity to fill their own share box under a program generally referred to as "market-style" food selection. At the farm, you would manually select your fruits or vegetables from a display table. There might be a few restrictions, such as limiting the number of items of a particular food, so that there is enough supply for other members. If this option is available, your box may be measured by weight or quantity of items.

Food Share Add-ons

In addition to enjoying your fresh, organically grown fruits and vegetables, many CSAs also offer other foods such as meats, fish, poultry, eggs, dairy, breads, honey, jams, and preserves. To receive an on-going supply of these foods in tandem with your food box, you can sign up for "add-ons" and, for an additional fee, these items will automatically be included in your food box. Your CSA may partner with local ranchers, fisheries, etc. and will provide applicable information as to how the food is sourced.

Food Box Pick-up or Delivery

When you sign your agreement with the farm, you'll be presented with a number of options for receiving your food box. Typically, boxes are always available for pick up at the farm, and your agreement will list what days and times the boxes are ready. If the farm offers additional pickup locations in your area, the agreement will list the address, days, and times that you can obtain your food.

Many CSAs offer delivery services. The CSA agreement will list options available for delivery to your home or other specified location. Also indicated in your agreement are the terms under which the CSA will handle any changes to the schedule, such as holidays or inclement weather. The agreement will also stipulate what notifications you must provide to the farm in the event you are away on vacation or unable to pick up your food box. Uncollected food is generally donated to a food shelter, and your CSA will list the names of any food shelters, churches, or nonprofit organizations that will receive donations of food from the farm.

Pick Your Own

Your CSA farm may offer "pick your own" events, and as a CSA member, you'll get newsletter announcements in advance. These events might be limited to certain fruits, such as strawberries, peaches, or apples. Some CSAs offer *pick your own* options on certain types of vegetable crops such as peas, beans, tomatoes, hot peppers, and herbs. The CSA will provide instructions and how the food will be counted toward your share.

Member Activities and Benefits

As a shareholder or member of the farm's CSA, you'll be receiving regular communication via email, and be able to view events and information on the CSA website. Events typically offered by CSAs include:

- *Meet your farmer day*
- *Educational workshops*
- *Discounts on food purchased at the farm store*
- *Events for children such as hayrides, petting zoo*
- *Free coupons for product specials*

CSA Pricing

Every CSA establishes its own pricing based on the number of weeks or months in the harvest season. Some CSAs charge on a per-box basis, and some offer discounts to seniors or lower-income households. Some CSAs offer a variety of options in order to accommodate single-person households and dietary restrictions. In the "pay-as-you-go" model, you might be able to purchase a different size share box with each visit to the farm. Some CSAs charge a small annual membership fee, generally, to establish your household as a shareholder.

Due to the wide range of options and the length of a CSA season, you will see a very broad range in pricing. All CSAs post fees on their websites, and you'll see prices anywhere from $300 to $700 for the entire season. As a rule of thumb, you can estimate $100 per month for a full-share box. There are a few CSAs who offer a "pay-what-you-can-afford" program for customers who meet eligibility requirements.

CSA Terms

Your CSA agreement will spell out the terms and conditions regarding fees, acceptable forms of payment, cancellation policy, and so forth. Although the "shareholder" model is popular, and generally requires the entire fee paid in advance, this option might be less expensive than the pay-weekly option. For CSAs that accept weekly (or bi-weekly) payments, members may have to provide the CSA with a debit or credit card number which is charged as food is distributed. As in any group membership, cancellation terms are unique to the CSA.

Box Sharing

"Splitting" your share with a friend is generally acceptable. Your CSA might require that one of you serve as the designated contact person, sign the agreement, and be responsible for payment. Also, there may be a requirement that the primary contact person is responsible for notifications regarding pick-ups, schedule changes, or other membership issues. In such cases, ask the CSA to add your co-sharing person to the email list to stay current on news and events at the farm.

Multi-farm CSAs

Some CSAs are comprised of more than one farm. For example, a few small farms within the same local area will band together to form one CSA program. The identity of each farm, as well as an indication of what fruits or vegetables are provided, will be disclosed on the CSA website and marketing materials. There may be other purveyors selling food products within the collaborative, such as poultry farmers or ranchers.

CSA Locator

The national directory in this book includes more than 900 CSAs, representing the majority of the 850+ CSAs that are self-registered with the USDA, plus farms located through Local Harvest. CSAs were selected based on size of operation and scope of products and services. To search for additional CSAs in your area, the two sites below have a search option to locate farms by zip code. The sites are listed below:

USDA
https://search.ams.usda.gov/csa/mobile/mobile.html

Local Harvest *(select CSA in menu)*
https://www.localharvest.org/

CHAPTER 7

On-Farm Markets

STOP AND SMELL THE ROSES. The first thing you notice when you visit the store at a farm are the displays of beautiful, fragrant flowers. From early spring to late fall, you'll see rows of baskets overflowing with colorful flowers of the season. It's a warm welcome that immediately connects you with nature. You may also be personally greeted by a member of the farm team, who perhaps is handing out free maple sugar donuts, with their irresistible aroma. These are the little things that stir up enthusiasm from your family when it's shopping day at the farm.

The "on-farm" market is different from a farmers' market, and both types are covered in this chapter. Seasonal "farm stands" are very popular and frequently seen on the side of the road as you pass by a farm. However, an on-farm market is a fully staffed enterprise that operates similarly to a grocery or produce store. In addition to selling fruits and vegetables grown on the farm, on-farm markets often sell food from other local purveyors.

Certified organic farms, and farmers who practice sustainable growing methods, often do business with ranchers, fisheries, and artisans who also subscribe to the highest standards of sustainable production. Therefore, you'll see many other products that are labeled as organic or locally sourced. In fact, you may meet some of these purveyors personally when you are visiting the farm, since they may be hosting their own display table and available to answer your questions. On-farm markets often give away samples and host cooking demonstrations, where you have a chance to inquire about the food ingredients or obtain a recipe.

Products Sold on the Farm

Stores that operate year-round often sell Christmas trees, home decorations, and holiday baked goods. Larger stores in colder climates may close after Thanksgiving, and re-open in early spring. If the farm has a bakery, products are usually baked on the store premises. Plants and flowers are often displayed throughout the store, and you might see a greenhouse adjacent to the store with a full assortment of annuals, perennials, shrubs, and plants. The chart below lists many types of foods that are often sold at farm stores.

On-Farm Market	
Products	
Baked goods	Jam
Beef	Juices
Bread	Maple products
Canned goods	Meat, other
Coffee	Microgreens
Crafts	Mushrooms
Dairy	Nuts
Dry beans	Pet food
Eggs	Plants
Flour	Poultry
Flowers	Prepared meals
Frozen foods	Preserves
Fruit	Pumpkins
Gift baskets	Soap
Grains	Tea
Herbs	Vegan products
Heirloom vegetables	Vegetables
Honey	Wine
Activities & Amenities	
Educational workshops	
Food demonstrations & samples	
Food and gift delivery	
Family and youth events	
Hayrides	
Petting zoo	
Pick-Your-Own events	
Picnic areas	
Recipes, cookbooks	
Tours	
Venue for private events	

Ranchers, Fisheries, and Other Purveyors

Many farms sell eggs, dairy, honey, or other food products that are produced by other purveyors. Typically, the other producers are selling organic, locally sourced food. You may see displays of grass-fed beef raised by local ranchers, or organic, free-range chickens raised by local poultry farmers. Also, any local fisheries that partner with organic farms are usually selling sustainably harvested seafood.

The farm may also sell frozen or prepared meals that have been produced in collaboration with other local purveyors. For example, the ingredients in a chicken pot pie may include farm-grown vegetables and chicken from the same poultry farm that is selling chicken at the farm store. At special events, you might have a chance to meet the local artisans who sell bread, baked goods, honey, jam, and preserves at the farm store. A large number of farms with stores also offer CSA programs.

Pick Your Own Events

The opportunity to fill your basket with fresh strawberries or apples can be very appealing, and fun for the whole family. However, not all fruits or vegetables are conducive to being hand-picked in the field by consumers. When you visit the farm, or subscribe to the farm's newsletter, you will see announcements for special "pick your own" events, also called "U-pick." Pumpkins are popular and some farms permit customers to pick their own green beans and certain varieties of tomatoes. Generally, you are more likely to see the following fruit for pick your own opportunities:

- *Apples*
- *Blackberries*
- *Blueberries*
- *Cherries*
- *Peaches*
- *Pears*
- *Raspberries*
- *Strawberries*

Farm Activities and Amenities

Farmers are family-friendly people and are great at organizing activities for children of all ages. Children love to visit farm animals, and they love having the chance to meet the animal's caretakers. Some farms provide full-time access to the areas where chickens, goats, pigs, or other animals reside. The farm may welcome visitors to walk along pastures to see grazing cows or sheep. For safety, there will be "no petting" signs where applicable.

Throughout the year, farms like to celebrate the harvest, and many events are scheduled around certain foods. For example, hayrides are typically used to transport kids to the area for gathering pumpkins, or apple-picking. Farms may offer birthday and private event packages that include hayrides, a petting zoo, and a healthy picnic lunch at the barn. Educational programs often include "future farmer" presentations and outside planting or exercises. Some educational programs are geared toward high school age attendees who may be interested in working as an apprentice on the farm.

Barns are popular venues for weddings and private events, and are often made available to the public. Typically, the farm will have a list of food and beverage vendors who collaborate with the farm to offer organic and healthy food options. Many farms offer tours to local schools and groups.

Farm History

Hundreds of farms have hundred-year histories. There are farms across America that have been operated by the same family for many generations. When there is a 250 year-old story to tell, you can rest assured that the farm's reputation for honesty and integrity is a strong priority. When visiting a farm store, you might see a display of cookbooks, packets of free recipes, and news articles about the farm's history. It's nice to know that a good recipe was tried and tested, but when it's made from ingredients that were grown on the farm, it's even more special. By shopping at a farm, you are supporting a local farmer. As the farm's history unfolds, your support becomes even more meaningful.

Farmers' Markets

Over the past 25 years, the number of farmers' markets around the country has more than quadrupled. In 1994, when the USDA began collecting data from the agency's self-registration site, there was a nationwide total of 1,755 markets. As of 2019, there were approximately 8,700 registered.

Farmers' markets are generally seen during the height of the growing season. For example, a city or town may sponsor a farmers' market each weekend for a period of ten weeks, even in geographic locations where the season is longer. The schedule gives merchants the most exposure for selling their goods in peak season. At farmers' markets, you might see farms that also have on-farm markets, and also see sponsors of CSA programs. A number of agrihoods invite local farmers to sell their food products at a weekly farmers market in one of the agrihood parks.

Although farmers' markets are in all shapes and sizes, representing different types of businesses, all the merchants have one thing in common—food safety rules and regulations. When you shop at a farmers' market, you are able to purchase only the types of foods that are permissible. For example, fresh meats or poultry may be excluded. However, the market may permit frozen meat or poultry, as long as the merchant has a freezer that maintains the required temperature.

Licenses, permits, registrations, etc., are requested as part as the application process by the market organizer. Food safety rules are strict and include food storage, handling, protective covers on displays, and so forth.

When local means local

The market may have restrictions with respect to the farmer's labeling of food products. If the market advertises "Fresh, locally grown food," the market's definition of "local" might be 50 miles, or 100 miles. The origin of food may require accurate labeling to identify where the produce was grown or sourced. Artisans who sell baked goods or jams may be required to adhere to labeling requirements regarding the primary ingredients of the food product. The organizer may require that dairy products, including cheese, butter, and yogurt be sourced from a dairy farm within a designated region. Other geographic restrictions can apply to fisheries, ranchers, and specialty agricultural products.

On-farm Market Locator

The USDA has over 1,500 farms in their self-registered database that operate on-farm markets. The national directory in this book includes a little over 1,000 listings, which have been selected based on size of operation and product range. Farms with seasonal stands or limited to a few produce selections are not included. The entire database can be viewed on the USDA site indicated below.

USDA
https://www.ams.usda.gov/local-food-directories/onfarm

Local Harvest *(extensive database of farms with various search options)*
https://www.localharvest.org/organic-farms/

Farmers' Market Locator

USDA
https://www.ams.usda.gov/local-food-directories/farmersmarkets

Local Harvest
https://www.localharvest.org/organic-farms/

CHAPTER 8

Food Hubs

MISSION-BASED ORGANIZATIONS are a fitting description of food hubs. Led by people with a commitment toward helping their community, local farmers, and helping the environment, food hubs are more entrepreneurial in structure. Simply put, food hubs are created to make a social impact that benefits everyone. As explained in Chapter 1, the USDA launched the "Know Your Farmer, Know your Food Initiative" in 2009. This mission strengthened the connection between farmers and consumers, and the USDA has expanded its commitment to help broaden the marketplace for farmers and ranchers through the establishment of a food hub initiative.

The USDA defines a food hub as "a business or organization that actively manages the aggregation, distribution, and marketing of source-identified food products primarily from local and regional producers to strengthen their ability to satisfy wholesale, retail, and institutional demand." Many food hubs make a concerted effort to expand their market to underserved areas where there is a lack of healthy, fresh food. Environmentally, food hubs are helping to build a farmer's or producer's capacity to develop sustainably grown products, thereby reducing energy use and waste in the distribution process.[71]

Food hubs are valued business partners to farmers and producers and provide technical assistance in product branding and to ensure they receive a fair price for their products.

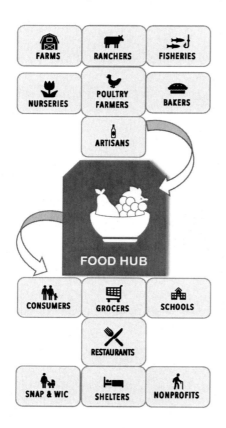

Food hubs serve as a centralized marketplace to sell locally sourced food products from a region's small farmers and food producers.

Food hubs are mission-based companies that support local farmers, provide healthy food to the community, and help the environment.

Retail customers of food hubs are consumers, grocers, and restaurants. Food hubs accept low-income vouchers and supply food to schools, nonprofits, and shelters.

The Role of Food Hubs

Many food hubs have evolved from an educational or social mission to bring consumers and producers together in the marketplace. Food hubs offer a combination of production, distribution, and marketing services that allow producers to gain entry into new and additional markets that would be impossible to access on their own. Food hubs meet the need of retail and institutional food buyers who want to "buy local," and also have a single point of purchase for consistent and reliable supplies of source-identified products.[72]

In addition to selling products, food hubs may also seek to educate consumers on the importance of retaining food dollars in the local economy. In many cases, food hubs share information on where or how food was produced, providing a greater connection between producers and consumers.

Food Hub Structure

Food hubs consist of commercial entities and nonprofits. The goals of a non-profit may be tied more to a social mission than to business profitability. Therefore, the nonprofit may emphasize products that are more expensive to source, such as organic and fair-trade products.

Some food hubs are formed through cooperatives, representing collaborations within a group of farmers, a group of retailers, or a consumer group. The cooperative structure is controlled by its members, where membership fees provide working capital for the food hub. A co-op is managed by a board that ensures the organization meets its members' needs and serves the local community.[73]

Food Value Chains

A new business strategy to the agricultural sector, "food value chains" represent an innovative business model in which agricultural producers and related supply chain entities form collaborative and transparent partnerships with a commitment to shared values and social mission goals. Unlike corporate marketing approaches which focus on the superior attributes of a product or service, value chains address social improvement. Food value chains incorporate social or environmental mission values that are focused on such issues as:

- Supporting the local economy
- Farmland preservation and visibility
- Humane treatment and animal welfare
- Expanded community access to fresh food
- Environmental stewardship

The business model responds to a growing number of today's consumers who want to know the story behind their food, and they want to support businesses with a social consciousness. Food hubs are an important subset of food value chains. By offering farmers and ranchers a combination of aggregation, distribution, and marketing services at an affordable price, food hubs make it possible for many producers to gain entry into larger-volume markets that boost their income and provide them with opportunities for scaling up production.[74]

Services for Producers

Regional food hubs actively seek to provide new market outlets for small and mid-sized local and regional producers. They also work with producers to develop product differentiation strategies. Food hubs also provide operational services to farmers, ranchers, and producers for packaging, storing, and distributing their food products. In addition, food hubs provide education and training in business management, agricultural practices, food safety, and other areas.

Services for the Community

Food hubs are firmly rooted in their community, and often carry out a number of community services. These include food banks, increasing consumer awareness on the benefits of buying local food, organizational farm tours, offering farm apprenticeships, and establishing delivery mechanisms to increase healthy food access to underserved areas. Food hubs provide transportation for consumers, recycling, and composting programs.

Food hubs carry out activities such as SNAP redemption, health screenings, nutrition counseling, and cooking demonstrations. SNAP stands for the Supplemental Nutrition Assistance Program, formerly known as food stamps, administered by the USDA. The USDA Special Supplemental Nutritional Program for Women, Infants and Children (WIC) provides federal grants to states to cover the cost of supplemental foods, nutritional education, and health care for low-income women and children under age five.[75]

Food Hub Locator

Food hubs are relatively new and there is growing interest. Across the nation, there are approximately 250 food hubs. The national directory included in this book lists nearly all food hubs. The list can be viewed in its entirety at the address below.

USDA
https://www.ams.usda.gov/local-food-directories/foodhubs

National Directory

Agrihoods

Community Supported Agriculture (CSA) Programs

On-Farm Markets

Food Hubs

Also included are several Urban Ag Initiatives

This directory includes descriptions of agrihoods located throughout the U.S. Summaries are adapted from content published on the agrihood's website. Certain information was provided by the developer or other published media. Except where noted, the agrihood is a community for homeowners. CSAs, On-Farm Markets, and Food Hubs are listed by city or town, and represent farms that offer a full range of sustainably sourced products and services.

ALABAMA

COMMUNITY SUPPORTED AGRICULTURE (CSA) PROGRAMS

Birmingham	Manna Market Organic Food Co-op	www.mannamarket.net
Coker	Snow's Bend Farm	www.snowsbendfarm.com
Dothan	Kith & Kin CSA	www.kithandkincsa.com
Goodwater	Rora Valley Farms	www.roravalleyfarms.com
Gurley	Duncan Farms	www.huntsvillefarm.com
Huntsville	Sweet City Micros	www.sweetcitymicros.com
Killen	Hines Family Farm	www.hinesfamilyfarm.com
Mentone	Mountain Sun Farm	www.MountainSunFarm.com
Mobile	Shipshape Urban Farms	www.shipshapeurbanfarms.com
Nauvoo	Slow Money Farm	www.slowmoneyfarm.com/
Prattville	Wild Yeast Kitchen	www.wildyeastkitchen.com
Rainbow City	Gardens On Air	www.GardensOnAir.com
Shorter	Joy Haven Farm	www.joyhavenfarm.weebly/com
Weogufka	Back Home Farm	www.backhomefarm.com

ON-FARM MARKETS

Eufaula	Backyard Orchards	www.Backyardorchards.com
Fairhope	LA Berry Farms, Inc.	www.weeksbayplantation.com
Flat Rock	Sheer Lark Farm	www.sheerlarkfarm.com
Gallant	Dayspring Dairy	www.dayspringdairy.com
Jemison	Mountain View Orchards	www.mountainvieworchards.com
Millbrook	Barber Berry Farm	www.barberberryfarm.com
Oneonta	Old Field Farm General Store	www.suzysfarm.com
Robertsdale	Gardner's Berry Farm	www.gardnersberryfarm.com
Robertsdale	Meme's Poultry and Quail	www.memespoultry.com

FOOD HUBS

Huntsville	Farm Food Collaborative	www.foodbanknorthal.org

ALASKA

COMMUNITY SUPPORTED AGRICULTURE (CSA) PROGRAMS

Anchorage	Arctic Harvest Deliveries	www.arcticharvestak.com
Delta Junction	Northern Roots Farm	www.northernrootsfarm.com
Ester	Calypso Farm	www.calypsofarm.org
Ester	Cripple Creek Organics	www.cripplecreekorganics.com
Fairbanks	Rosie Creek Farm	www.rosiecreekfarm.com
Fairbanks	Spinach Creek Farm	www.alaskacommunityag.org/content/spinach-creek-farm
North Pole	Alaskan Farm	www.AlaskanFarm.com
Palmer	Arctic Organics	www.arcticorganics.com
Palmer	Sun Circle Farm	www.suncirclefarm.com
Palmer	Spring Creek Farm	www.springcreekfarmak.org
Sitka	Alaskans Own Seafood	www.thealaskatrust.org/alaskans-own.php
Sitka	Sitka Salmon Shares	www.sitkasalmonshares.com

ON-FARM MARKETS

Phoenix City	Serenity Farm	www.thinkserenity.com

FOOD HUBS

Homer	Alaska Food Hub	www.alaskafoodhub.org
Juneau	Salt & Soil Marketplace	www.saltandsoilmarketplace.com
Wasilla	Bogard Food Hub	www.bogardfoodhub.com

107

ARIZONA

AGRIHOODS

Agritopia
Gilbert
www.agritopia.com

Founded in 2000, Agritopia is an established agrihood consisting of 450 homes on 160 acres. The 11-acre working farm includes a citrus grove, lambs, chickens, and heirloom vegetables. Certified organic fruits and vegetables are available to residents through a CSA as well as raised-bed community gardens. Residents enjoy a barrier-free lifestyle, with low fences, porches, parks, and shady sidewalks that connect homes to schools, gardens, restaurants, and shops. The Generations Senior Living Community is Agritopia's 117-unit assisted- and independent-living center, in partnership with Investment Property Associates and Retirement Community Specialists.

COMMUNITY SUPPORTED AGRICULTURE (CSA) PROGRAMS

Amado	Agua Linda Farm	www.agualindafarm.net
Cave Creek	JH Grassfed Beef	www.jhgrassfed.com
Chino Valley	Y C Grown Yavapai County	www.ycgrown.com
Hereford	Echoing Hope Ranch	www.echoinghoperanc.org
Mesa	True Garden	www.truegarden.com
Paulden	Whipstone Farm	www.whipstone.com
Scottsdale	North Scottsdale Organics	www.northscottsdaleorganics.com
Sedona	Verde Valley CSA	www.verdevalleycsa.com
Tubac	Avalon Organic Gardens	www.avalongardens.org
Tucson	Elderberry Edibles	www.elderberryedibles.com

ON-FARM MARKETS

Gilbert	Organic Chicken Feed and Grain	www.phoenixorganicfeed.com
Phoenix	Orchard Community Learning	www.orchardlearningcenter.org
Phoenix	Citi Farms	www.CitiFarms.com
Tucson	Elderberry Edibles CSA	www.elderberryedibles.com
Tucson	Our Garden	www.ourgardencatalina.com
Wilcox	Briggs & Eggers Orchards	www.briggs-eggers.com

FOOD HUBS

Tempe	Chow Locally	www.chowlocally.com
Tucson	Iskashitaa Refugee Network	www.harvesttucson.org

ARKANSAS

AGRIHOODS

Red Barn
Bentonville
www.redbarnbentonville.com
              Rental Community

Red Barn is an environmentally friendly community, close to downtown Bentonville, surrounded by trails, farmland, and forested areas in the heart of the Ozarks. Residents can volunteer at The Farm, and enjoy neighborly activities at The Barn, a gathering place that functions as the village square. Living spaces include energy-efficient apartments and town homes. Affordable housing discounts available.

Eco Modern Flats
Fayetteville
www.ecomodernflats.com
              Rental Community

96-unit apartment building with community gardens. Modern design, light-filled apartments with solar hot water, rainwater harvesting, and energy-efficient heating and cooling. Gathering spaces include saltwater pool, outdoor fireplace, rooftop terrace, and community activities. All-inclusive rent includes basic cable and all utilities. Full size washer and dryer. Short walk to University of Arkansas campus and Razorback greenway 36-mile trail.

COMMUNITY SUPPORTED AGRICULTURE (CSA) PROGRAMS

Cotter	Age Old Agriculture	www.ageoldagriculture.com
Eureka Springs	Sycamore Bend Farm	www.sycamorebendfarm.com
Fayetteville	Hazel Valley Farms	www.hazelvalleyfarms.net
Little Rock	Arkansas Local Food Network	www.littlerock.locallygrown.net
Little Rock	Foodshed Farms CSA	www.foodshedfarms.com
London	Bright Moon Ranch CSA	www.brightmoonranch.com
Pea Ridge	Shamba Creek Farm	www.shambacreekfarm.com
Perryville	Farm Girl Meats	www.farmgirlfood.com
Perryville	KMG Farms	www.kmgfarms.com
Perryville	Heifer Ranch CSA	www.heifer.org

ON-FARM MARKETS

Bentonville	Anglin Beef	www.anglinbeef.com
Bruno	Schot's Slopes Farm	www.schotsslopesfarm.com
Cave Springs	Ewe Bet Farm	www.ewebetfarm.com
Fayetteville	Mason Creek Farm	www.masoncreekfarm.com
Harrison	Fenton's Farm Market	www.fentonsberryfarm.com
Mt Pleasant	Earth and Foods	www.earthartandfoods.com
Pea Ridge	McGarrah Farms	www.mcgarrahfarms.com
Pettigrew	Baughmans Farm Goat Breeders	www.baughmansfarm.com

FOOD HUBS

Little Rock	Little Rock Local Food Club	www.littlerock.locallygrown.net

CALIFORNIA

AGRIHOODS

The Cannery
Davis
www.livecannerydavis.com

Own or Rent

Residences include flats, town homes, homes, large bungalows, and cottages, including homes up to 6 bedrooms. Bartlett Commons includes affordable rental apartments with access to all amenities of The Cannery. Urban farm offering organic produce. Bicycle distance to town. The Ranch House includes lap pool, spa, outdoor fireplace. The Farm House serves as gathering place and community welcome center. Amenities include 4.7 acres of neighborhood parks, bike paths, dog parks, sports courts, picnic spaces, and amphitheater. The Cannery Marketplace hosts retail stores, mixed-use residences, and office space.

Del Mesa
Carmel
www.delmesacarmel.org

Over-55 Community

Del Mesa Carmel is a community with 289 condominiums available for purchase to persons over the age of 55. Amenities include a restaurant, walking/hiking trails, dog park, fitness center, pool, putting green, bowling green, art association, and clubhouse. Located one mile east of Carmel-by-the-Sea with views of Point Lobos, Carmel River Valley, and Santa Lucia mountains. Residents plant and harvest produce in gardens located throughout the community. 24-hour security gate.

Fanita Ranch
Santee
www.fanitaranch.com

Under development. Fanita Ranch is a 2,684-acre development that will be 76% open space and habitat preservation. The community will include a solar farm for renewable energy, 348 acres for homes, a mixed-use village center, K-8 school, 35 miles of walking/hiking trails, and pocket parks. The professionally managed organic farm will use permaculture techniques that mimic natural ecosystems, minimizing the use of energy and water, and maximizing recycling.

Miralon
Palm Springs
www.discovermiralon.com

The 309-acre community includes 1,150 mid-century modern-inspired homes to harmonize with the architectural heritage of Palm Springs. All homes include solar panels as well as architectural features designed for indoor/outdoor living. Central to Miralon's status as a pioneering agrihood is its transformation of a previously constructed 18-hole golf course into working olive groves, community gardens, view corridors, and walking trails. Much of the former golf course is planted with 7,000 olive trees, along with the community gardens, trails, dog parks, and a high-efficiency community center, also designed in the mid-century style.

North River Farms

Oceanside
www.livenorthriverfarms.com

Under development. The Farm at North River Farms includes over 80 acres of agricultural land, including 30 acres of farmland, 10 acres of parks, 5 miles of trails. Farmers' market, CSA shares, hotel, arts center, education center, and multiple artisan shops. Single-family, detached homes with unique American village design and diverse architectural styles. Streetscapes derived from landmark neighborhoods throughout California.

Rancho Mission Viejo

Rancho Mission Viejo
www.ranchomissionviejo.com

The Rancho Mission Viejo community is a 23,000-acre ranch nestled between Cleveland National Forest and the historic town of San Juan Capistrano. The Ranch covers 6,500 acres of permanently preserved natural space at the Reserve at Ranch Mission Viejo, including protected creeks, canyons, wetlands, woodlands, and native grasslands. The farm includes avocado, walnut, and bay trees along with organic fruits and vegetables. Residents can volunteer for planting and harvesting, attend culinary or gardening workshops, or enroll children in farming education classes. There are multiple villages, and each one is unique.

The Village of Esencia is a neighborhood for all ages, with a wide selection of floor plans, K-8 school, several unique pools, and 47 community clubs.

The Village of Gavilan is a neighborhood for residents over the age of 55, with several single-story or easy two-story living, resort-style amenities, and over 50 clubs.

Sendero Farm is part of Rancho Mission Viejo and is comprised of 940 homes and 285 apartments on a working ranch next to a community farm.

Sendero Gateway is a rental community offering a wide range of sizes and floor plans, with resort-style amenities, pool, fitness center, spa, clubhouse, media room, pet park, business center, and children's play area. Hillside and ocean views.

Walden Monterey

Monterey
www.waldenmonterey.com

Under development. Walden Monterey is a luxury agrihood development of 200 home sites on 600 acres, situated on Monterey Peninsula. The community is focused on sustainability and communal farming, providing an average of 20 acres of land per parcel. Amenities include a sunrise yoga platform, a treehouse, and a Zen meditation garden.

Win6 Village   Own or Rent

Santa Clara
www.win6village.org

Under development. Six acres of mixed-use, mixed-income, and multigenerational housing with working organic farm. Site includes aquaponic rooftop gardens, and walkable space located in Santa Clara Valley's native oak woodland and grassland plant community. Plan includes housing for 359 residents, including 165 low-income seniors, 16 moderate-income apartments, 144 market-rate apartments, and 34 market-rate townhouses.

Community Supported Agriculture (CSA) Programs

Arcata	Deep Seeded Community Farm	www.arcatacsa.com
Atwater	Rancho Piccolo Organic Farm	www.ranchopiccolo.com
Beverly Hills	Farm Box LA	www.farmboxla.com
Camarillo	McGrath Family Farm CSA	www.mcgrathfamilyfarm.com
Escondido	Garden of Eden Organics	www.goeorganics.com
Escondido	J R Organics CSA	www.jrorganicsfarm.com
Fair Oaks	Raphael Garden	www.rudolfsteinercollege.edu/csa
Fairfield	Shooting Star CSA	www.shootingstarcsa.com
Goleta	Fairview Gardens Farm	www.fairviewgardens.org
Half Moon Bay	Ananda Valley Farm	www.anandavalleyfarm.com
Ivanhoe	Family Farm Fresh	www.familyfarmfresh.com
Moorpark	Underwood Family Farms	www.underwoodfamilyfarms.com
Pescadero	Blue House Farm	www.bluehouseorganicfarm.com
Pescadero	Fifth Crow Farm	www.fifthcrowfarm.com
Petaluma	Tara Firma Farms	www.tarafirmafarms.com
Pilot Hill	Buttercup Family Farm	www.buttercupfamilyfarm.com
Redding	Providence Garden of Hope	www.www.gardenofhopecsa.org
Redwood City	Himmelgarten	www.himmelgarten.org
San Diego	Seabreeze Organic Farm	www.seabreezed.com
San Francisco	Farm Box SF	www.farmboxsf.com
San Francisco	Marin Sun Farms	www.marinsunfarms.com
San Jose	Veggielution Community Farm	www.veggielution.org
Santa Barbara	Hello Harvest	www.helloharvest.com
Sebastopol	Green Valley CSA	www.greenvalleycsa.com
Sebastopol	Singing Frogs Farm	www.singingfrogsfarm.com
Soquel	Fogline Farm	www.foglinefarm.com
Templeton	Nature's Touch Nursery	www.ntnah.com
Valley Ford	Conlan Ranches Truegrass	www.truegrassfarms.com
Waterford	Lucky #19 Ranch	www.lucky19ranch.com
Watsonville	High Ground Organics	www.highgroundorganics.com
Winters	Terra Firma Farms	www.terrafirmafarm.com
Woodland	Say Hay Farms	www.sayhayfarms.com

On-Farm Markets

Alpine	Tzaddik Farm	www.tzaddikfarm.com
Biggs	Max's Miracle Ranch	www.maxsmiracles.org
Camino	Sun Mountain Farm	www.sunmountainfarm.com
Cherry Valley	123 Farm at Highland Springs	www.123farm.com
Clarksburg	Loving Nature Farm, Inc.	www.LovingNatureFarm.com
Corning	Maywood Farms	www.maywoodfarms.com
Creston	Olivas de Oro Olive Company	www.olivasdeoro.com
Escondido	Farm Stand West	www.thefarmstandwest.com
Fallbrook	Kendall Farms	www.kendall-farms.com
Fiddletown	Damas Vineyards	www.damasvineyards.com
Garden Valley	Berry Heaven	www.BerryHeavenUSA.com
Gaviota	Classic Organic Farm	www.classicorganic.org

Guinda	Star Rose Ranch	www.starroseranch.com
Hilmar	Anderson Almonds	www.andersonalmonds.com
Knightsen	First Generation Farmers	www.firstgenerationfarmers.org
Murrieta	Bel Cielo Villa	www.belcielovilla.com
Newcastle	Burgeson Family Farm	www.burgesonfamilyfarm.com
Newman	Open Space Meats	www.openspacemeats.com
Oak Glen	Willowbrook Apple Farm	www.willowbrookapple.tripod.com
Oregon House	High Sierra Beef, Inc.	www.highsierrabeef.com
Oroville	Morse Mandarin Farm	www.morsemandarinfarms.com
Pauma Valley	Pauma Tribal Farms	www.solidarityfarmsd.com
Pebble Beach	Monterey Gold Honey	www.montereygoldhoney.com
Penryn	Sinclair Family Farm	www.sinclairfamilyfarm.net
Placerville	Smokey Ridge Farmstand	www.smokeyridgeranch.com
Plymouth	Amador Flower Farm	www.AmadorFlowerFarm.com
Pollock Pines	Harris Family Farm	www.harristreefarm.com
Rio Oso	Derby Walnuts	www.derbywalnuts.com
Roseville	Top Hill Farm	www.tophillfarm.com
Saint Helena	Long Meadow Ranch	www.longmeadowranch.com
San Andreas	Nakagawa Ranches	www.nakagawaranches.com
San Jose	Red Barn Farm & Poultry	www.redbarnfarmpoultry.webs.com
San Luis Obispo	Growing Grounds Farm	www.growinggroundsfarm.org
Tehachapi	Knaus Apple Ranch	www.knausappleranch.com
Templeton	Templeton Valley Farms	www.templetonvalleyfarms.com
Turlock	R.A.M. Farms Pumpkin Patch	www.ramfarms.com
Ukiah	Finley's Mountain Ranch	www.finleysmountainranch.com
Valley Ford	Freestone Ranch	www.freestoneranch.com
Ventucopa	Santa Barbara Pistachio Co.	www.sbpistachios.com
Winton	Top Line Milk	www.toplinemilk.com
Woodland	Yolo Land & Cattle	www.yololandandcattle.com
Yorkville	Petit Teton Farm	www.petitteton.com

FOOD HUBS

Alpine Meadows	Tahoe Food Hub	www.tahoefoodhub.org
Chico	North Valley Food Hub	www.northvalleyfoodhub.com
Esparto	Capay Valley Farm Shop	www.capayvalleyfarmshop.com
Fresno	Food Commons Fresno	www.ooooby.org/fresno
Grass Valley	Farm 2 Family Brunswick	www.farmfreshonline.com
Los Angeles	Village Market Place	www.csuinc.org
Madera	Braga Organic Farms	www.buyorganicnuts.com
Oakland	Mandela Market Place	www.mandelamarketplace.org
Ojai	Ojai Pixie Growers Assoc.	www.ojaipixies.com
Olivehurst	Next Generation Foods	www.nextgenfoods.com
Placerville	Organic Power Foods	www.organicpowerfoods.com
Riverside	Goodwin's Organic Foods	www.goodwinsorganics.com
Salinas	Alba Organics	www.aggrigator.com
Salinas	Top 10 Produce	www.top10produce.com
Sebastopol	Sonoma Organics	www.sonomaorganics.com

COLORADO

AGRIHOODS

Aria
Denver
www.ariadenver.com

Aria Denver is a community built on the Sisters of St. Francis property, located near Regis University and eight minutes from downtown Denver. Aria is an economically and environmentally responsible development model comprised of modern, sustainable housing characteristics. The 17.5 acre site houses 400 housing units, including condominiums, town homes, affordable rental apartments, intergenerational cohousing condominiums, and 20,000 square feet of commercial space. The community features a production garden, community plots, permaculture pocket gardens, and greenhouse. Aria Denver has been thoughtfully planned to encourage active living, with walking paths and exercise facilities planned on site. Future plans include a Habitat for Humanity community.

Adams Crossing Agriburbia
Brighton
www.agriburbia.com

Under development. Mixed-use 780-acre community with commercial, retail, residential, and agricultural neighborhoods, potentially housing 2,500 multifamily units and 750 single-family homes. Design is compatible with Denver's light rail system and will include connections to Bus Rapid Transit. Adams Crossing will include a unique system of agricultural community integration, with farm plots operated independently, providing stable career paths for aspiring farmers, and offering engagement with community residents.

Baseline   Own or Rent
Broomfield
www.baselinecolorado.com

Under development. Baseline is a planned next generation sustainable urban center that includes mixed-use residential, retail, commercial, and educational centers on an 11,000-acre site. Baseline includes 6,000 homes offering a wide range of home styles for purchase, including town homes, paired homes, and single-family properties. 50-acre West Village includes two parks with links to regional trails to all things Baseline and Broomfield. Town Center includes Adams 12 STEM School, with 1,800 students K-12; Center for Invertebrate Research and Conservation; and butterfly pavilion. Plans include 145 acres of open space and dedicated farm land. Agriculture is integrated with productive landscaping, and a series of 3-5 acre plots cultivated for community gardening in a pollinator-friendly ecosystem. Part of the West Village at Baseline, Park 40 includes about energy-efficient 300 apartments and 18 3-bedroom residences. Residents will have access to over 3 acres of habitat-friendly open space with trails, central clubhouse, outdoor pool and spa, and dog park.

Buckinghorse

Fort Collins
www.buckinghorseneighborhood.com

The 160-acre agrihood features a trail system, community gardens, and a farm-to-fork restaurant serving produce grown on-site. Built around two historic farmsteads, Johnson Farm and Jessup Farm, home of the Jessup Farm Artisan Village. The site offers a 5K integrated trail system, edible landscape, a clubhouse, Olympic-sized swimming pool, and health-inspired retailers. The CSA program is administered by local non-profit, Sproutin' Up. This community provides excellent wildlife habitat for deer, birds, insects, rabbits, and small mammals that feed and live in this natural environment.

Fox Hill

Franktown
www.liveinfoxhill.com

Fox Hill is located in Douglas County, with views of Pikes Peak and the Colorado Front Range. An eco-friendly community anchored by a 1912 Charleston-style farmhouse, barn, and silos. The sustainable farm includes apple and pear orchards, a berry-picking patch, row gardens, flowers, farm-fresh eggs, honey, and yields fresh produce boxes to Fox Hill residents. The farm features an English-style greenhouse with an aquaponic system that supports a year-round growing system. Custom homes offer innovative designs, acreage home sites, and state-of-the-art 1G fiber-optic technology. Homes in Fox Hill will also have the option to add geothermal heating and cooling systems.

Mariposa   Rental Community

Denver
www.mariposadenver.com

Mariposa is a bike-friendly neighborhood of energy-efficient town homes and flats, minutes from downtown and the Santa Fe arts district. There are 87 units, ranging in size from 1 bedroom to 5 bedrooms; each unit is LEED-certified. Buildings include the Aerie, the Zephyr, and Arches. Located one block from the light rail station, amenities include outdoor living spaces, gardens, and playgrounds.

S*Park

Denver
www.liveatspark.com

*S*Park is an urban agrihood, formerly known as Sustainability Park, which served as an incubator for sustainable living and community development. The mixed-use development offers studios, 1, 2, 3, and 4-bedroom condos and town homes. Construction utilizes solar-powered energy systems, a vertical greenhouse, and urban soil farm managed by Altius Farms. Residents subscribe to an exclusive program for fruits and vegetables from gardens managed by professional agricultural experts. The S*Park offers composting, underground parking with electric charging stations, and ample greenspace. S*Park also includes a solar community garden from Microgrid Energy.*

COMMUNITY SUPPORTED AGRICULTURE (CSA) PROGRAMS

Arvada	Pioneer Farmsteaders	www.pioneerfarmsteaders.com
Ault	D & H Farms	www.dhfarms2000.com
Aurora	DeLaney Community Farm	www.dug.org
Boulder	63rd St. Farm	www.63rdstfarm.com
Boulder	Cultiva! Youth Project	www.growinggardens.org
Boulder	Cure Organic Farm	www.cureorganicfarm.com
Carr	Donoma Farms	www.www.donomafarms.com
Denver	Denver Urban Gardens	www.dug.org
Denver	Kristin's Farm Stand	www.KristinsFarmStand.com
Durango	Adobe House Farm	www.adobehousefarm.com
Hotchkiss	Ela Family Farms CSA	www.elafamilyfarms.com
Larkspur	Busy Bee Farm	www.busybeefarm.us
Mancos	Mountain Roots Produce	www.Mountainrootsproduce.com
Mancos	Southwest Farm	www.southwestfarmfresh.com
Montrose	Circle A Garden	www.circleagarden.com
Saguache	Green Earth Farm	www.greenearthfarm.com
Wellington	Grant Farms CSA	www.grantfarms.com

ON-FARM MARKETS

Aurora	Fresh Start Family Farms	www.freshstartfamilyfarms.com
Berthoud	Heritage Lavender	www.heritagelavender.com
Black Forest	High Altitude Rhubarb Organic	www.highaltituderhubarb.com
Canon City	Colon Orchards	www.colonorchards.com
Delta	Dragonfly Farm	www.dragonflychurros.com
Denver	Feed Denver Sunnyside Farm	www.FeedDenver.com
Denver	Roasted Chile	www.Roastedchili.com
Dolores	Harvest Moon Produce	www.harvestmoonproduce.farm
Fort Collins	On the Vine at Richmond	www.onthevineatrichmondfarms.com
Fort Collins	Laughing Buck Farm	www.laughingbuckfarm.com
Henderson	Palombo Farms Market	www.PalomboMarket.com
Lakewood	Everitt Farms	www.everittfarms.com
Larkspur	Crooked Clove Farm & Ranch	www.crookedclove.com
Montrose	Del Yaks	www.yakmeat.us
Montrose	Life Cycles Pasture	www.lifecyclespasture.com
Monument	Searle Ranch	www.searleranch.com
Palisade	Morton's Organic Orchards	www.mortonsorchards.com
Paonia	Desert Weyr	www.desertweyr.com
Pueblo	A Wren's Nest Farm	www.awrensnest.comnest
Walsenburg	Hugs Farm	www.HugsFarm.weebly.com

FOOD HUBS

Denver	High Plains Food Coop.	www.highplainsfood.org
Denver	US Potato Board	www.potatogoodness.com
Fort Collins	LoCo Food Distribution	www.locofooddistribution.com
Hotchkiss	Farm Runners	www.FarmRunners.com

CONNECTICUT

COMMUNITY SUPPORTED AGRICULTURE (CSA) PROGRAMS

Bethany	Ro-Jo Farms	www.ro-jofarms.com
Deep River	Deep River Farms	www.depriverfarms.com
Durham	Star Light Gardens	www.starlightgardensct.com
Guilford	Lakeside Farm Stand	www.lakesidefarmstand.com
Ledyard	Full Heart Farm	www.fullheartfarm.com
Litchfield	Laurel Ridge Farm	www.lrgfb.com
Mansfield Center	Cobblestone Farm	www.cobblestonefarmcsa.com
Middletown	Yellow House Farm	www.yellowhousefarmct.com
North Canaan	Howling Flats Farm	www.howlingflatsfarm.com
Old Lyme	Deep River Farms	www.depriverfarms.com
Ridgefield	Simpaug Farms	www.simpaugfarms.com
Shelton	Laurel Glen Farm	www.laurelglenfarm.com
Simsbury	George Hall Farm	www.georgehallfarm.com
Stafford Springs	Connecticut Farm to Table	www.ctfarmtable.com
Woodbridge	Massaro Farm CSA	www.massarofarm.org
Woodstock	Woodstock Sustainable Farms	www.wssfarms.com

ON-FARM MARKETS

Bethel	Holbrook Farm Market	www.holbrookfarm.net
Bozrah	Old Fitch Farm Vineyard	www.fitchclaremonthouse.com
Colchester	Common Ground CSA	www.commongroundcsa.com
East Haddam	Staehly Farms	www.staehlys.com
Eastford	Buell's Orchard	www.buellsorchard.com
Griswold	Standing Stone Farm	www.standingstonefarm.com
Guilford	Bishops Orchards	www.bishopsorchards.com
Harwinton	Cheney Family Farm	www.cheneyfamilyfarm.com
Litchfield	Laurel Ridge Grass Fed Beef	www.lrgfb.com
Middlefield	Lyman Orchards	www.lymanorchards.com
North Branford	Rose Orchards	www.roseorchardsfarm.com
North Granby	Lost Acres Orchard	www.lostacres.com
North Windham	Raspberry Knoll Farm	www.raspberryknoll.com
Roxbury	Mike's Beehives	www.mikesbeehives.com
Salisbury	Whippoorwill Farm	www.WhippoorwillFarmCT.com
Sandy Hook	Sepe Farm	www.sepefarm.com
Somers	Pell Farm	www.pell-farms.com
S. Glastonbury	Walnut Ledge Farm	www.walnutledgefarm.com
Wallingford	Blue Hills Orchard	www.bluehillsorchard.com
Washington Depot	Averill Farm	www.averillfarm.com
Winchester Center	White Stone Acres	www.whitestoneacres.com
Woodstock	Devon Point Farm	www.devonpointfarm.com

FOOD HUBS

East Haddam	CT Farm Fresh Express	www.ctfarmfreshstore.com
Woodstock	Woodstock Sustainable Farms	www.wssfarms.com

117

DELAWARE

COMMUNITY SUPPORTED AGRICULTURE (CSA) PROGRAMS

Bridgeville	Evans Farms	www.EvansFarmsProduce.com
Camden-Wyoming	Fifer Delmarva Box CSA	www.fiferorchards.com
Dover	Dover Dragonwool Shetland Sheep	www.dragonwool.weebly.com
Felton	Dittmar Family Farms	www.dittmarfamilyfarms.simplesite.com
Harrington	Heart and Soul	www.heartandsoulalpacas.com
Milton	Jubilee Back Forty	www.jubileebackforty.com
Newark	Kranz Hill Farm	www.kranzhillfarm.org
New Castle	Penn Farm	www.colonialschooldistrict.org/pennfarm/
New Castle	Against the Grain Farm	www.atg.farm
Townsend	Powers Farm	www.thepowersfarm.com
Wilmington	Highland Orchards	www.highlandorchardsfarmmarket.com
Wyoming	Fifer Orchards	www.fiferorchards.com

ON-FARM MARKETS

Newark	Cook Family Farm	www.coolrockstock.com
Seaford	Maebrook Produce	www.maebrookproduce.com
Wilmington	Highland Orchards	www.highlandorchardsfarmmarket.com
Wilmington	Southbridge Youth Farm	www.swpn.org

Community Supported Agriculture (CSA) Programs

Washington	Common Good City Farm	www.commongoodcityfarm.org
Washington	Loudoun Beef	www.LoudounBeef.com
Washington	Little Farm Stand	www.littlefarmstand.com
Washington	Up Top Acres	www.uptopacres.com
Washington	Good Sense Farm & Apiary	www.goodsensefarm.com
Washington	4P Foods	www.4pfoods.com

On-Farm Markets

Washington	Common Good City Farm	www.commongoodcityfarm.org
Washington	Little Wild Things City Farm	www.littlewildthingsfarm.com

Food Hubs

Washington	Arcadia's Mobile Market	www.arcadiafood.org
Washington	DC Central Kitchen	www.dccentralkitchen.org

FLORIDA

AGRIHOODS

Angeline
Land O' Lakes

Proposed development. Lennar Homes is building a new development on 7,000 acres of land that was formerly a ranch operated by the Bexley family. Plans include a 63-acre agrihood community which will include an organic farm, community garden, restaurant, playground, cattle barn and pasture, and other amenities. The overall development will include more than 10,000 homes, a corporate business park, and a cancer center and research institute. 843 acres of the land was sold to Pasco County to preserve ecological corridors. The Angeline site is located south of SR 52, bordered by the Suncoast Parkway and the CSX Railroad line. The agrihood's entrance will be at the intersection of Quail Ridge Drive.

Arden
Palm Beach County
www.ardenfl.com

Arden is a healthy-living community centered around a five-acre farm and event barn. Residents can volunteer to work with Arden's full-time farmers to plant and harvest fruits, vegetables, herbs, and flowers. Homebuyers can choose from a range of home styles such as the Artisan Collection or the Homestead Collection from Ryan Homes, or a home built by Lennar or Kenco. Nearly every home site backs up to a park, greenway, or nature trail. Residents can enjoy walking and biking through 20 miles of trails that wind through the community and around Arden Lake; or enjoy kayaking, bass fishing, and birdwatching on the 275 acres of lakes and 500 acres of greenspace at Arden. The community has a 24-hour staffed gatehouse, and a community clubhouse with pools.

Pine Dove Farm
Tallahassee
www.pinedovefarm.com

Pine Dove Farm consists of 200 acres, with nearly 115 acres of conservation land, and provides residents with organically grown produce, fruit trees, and pecan orchards. Homes are eco-friendly, farmhouse-style, with spacious lots. Pine Dove features a clubhouse with a pool, gym, summer porch, and gathering room. Residents can enjoy fishing, walking, and hiking on over three miles of walking trails. The main community garden provides a setting for residents to take part in the gardening process, and residents can subscribe to the farm's CSA program. Pine Dove residents have exclusive access to two beautiful lakes designed for canoeing, kayaking, or paddle-boarding.

The Cannery at the Packing District
Orlando
www.packingdistrictorlando.com

Under construction. 307-unit apartment complex and town homes. The Cannery at the Packing District is the residential part of the 202-acre mixed-use project near College Park. The Packing District includes residential areas, retail shops, and office space. Amenities include a swimming pool, restaurant, food hall, microbrewery, and event space. The overall plan includes indoor and outdoor health and wellness facilities, and the 4 Roots Farm and Agriculture Center.

The Grow
Orlando
www.lifeatthegrow.com

Under development. The Grow is a residential farm and garden community that welcomes its residents and visitors with a fluttering signature windmill leading to a nostalgic town center and gateway to neighborhoods that wind around a 20-acre community park of pastoral spaces, fishing ponds, lakes, wetlands, and edible walking trails. Homebuyers may choose from a diverse range of homes with lot sizes ranging up to one acre, designed with vintage architecture of homes and farmhouses of the 1940's. The community is 55% open space and includes a 9-acre revenue-generating working farm managed by a team of agriculturalists. Residents may grow their own produce on 21 acres of community gardens. At the heart of The Grow is an authentic wood barn for gathering, and farm-to-table restaurant. Weekly farmers' markets are held at the town center. Other amenities include an equestrian facility, neighborhood parks, and an elementary school.

COMMUNITY SUPPORTED AGRICULTURE (CSA) PROGRAMS

Alachua	Swallowtail Farm CSA	www.swallowtailcsa.com
Bell	The Family Garden Organic	www.thefamilygardencsa.com
Boca Raton	My Organic Food Club	www.myorganicfoodclub.com
Boynton Beach	Farming Systems Research	www.veggies4u.com
Homestead	Teena's Pride CSA	www.teenaspride.com
Indiantown	Kai-kai Farm	www.kaikaifarm.com
Jacksonville	Down to Earth Farm	www.downtoearthjax.com
Malabar	Florida Fields to Forks	www.floridafieldstoforks.com
Miami	Farm Fresh Miami	www.farmfreshmiami.com
Miami	Little River Cooperative	www.littlerivercooperative.com
Miami	Turtle Box Market	www.turtleboxmarket.com
Ocala	Florida Fresh Meat Company	www.floridafreshmeat.com
Orlando	Edgewood Children's Ranch	www.edgewoodranch.com
Placida	Boca Grande Farmers Market	www.bocagrandefarmersmarket.com
Redland	Redland Bee Heaven	www.beeheavenfarm.com
St. Augustine	KYV Farm	www.kyvfarm.com
Summerfield	Florida Fresh Family of Farms	www.floridafreshmeat.com
Tampa	Sweetwater Organic Farm	www.sweetwater-organic.org

ON-FARM MARKETS

Baker	Shockley Springs Blueberry	www.shockleysprings.com
Belleview	Abshier Blueberry Farm	www.abshierblueberryfarm.com
Bokeelia	Pine Island Botanicals	www.pineislandbotanicals.com
Campbellton	LE Farms	www.chestnutsrus.com
Christmas	Heart of Christmas Farms	www.hocfarms.com
Clermont	Marks U-pick Blueberries	www.marksblueberries.com
Clermont	Southern Hill Farms	www.southernhillfarms.com
Clermont	The Showcase of Citrus	www.showcaseofcitrus.com
Crescent City	Allison Family Farm	www.allisonfamilyfarm.com
Davie	Flamingo Road Nursery	www.flamingoroadnursery.com
Davie	Bender's Tropical Grove	www.bendersgrove.com
Deland	Stetson Farmers Market	www.stetson.orgsync.com
DeLeon Springs	Vo-LaSalle Farms	www.giftfruitfromflorida.com

121

Estero	The Farm	www.thefarm-estero .com
Gainesville	Great Tasting Pigs	www.greattastingpigs.com
Gainesville	Loftus Family Farm	www.loftusfamilyfarm.com
Grant-Valkaria	Liberty Farms of Florida	www.libertyfarms.info/home
Haines City	Ridge Island Groves, Inc.	www.ridgeislandgroves.com
Hawthorne	South Moon Farms	www.upickblueberriesgainesville.com
High Springs	High Springs Orchard Bakery	www.highspringsorchard.com
Indiantown	CoLab Farms	www.colabfarms.com
Labelle	Pattys Patch Blueberry U-pick	www.pattyspatch.com
Lake Placid	Persimmony Snickets	www.persimmonysnickets.com
Lake Wales	Sustainable Seasons Farm	www.sustainableseasons.com
Laurel Hill	The Flyin D Ranch	www.TheFlyinDRanch.com
Lithia	Herbs Erbs & Teas	www.fortlonesome.org
Live Oak	Mitillini Vineyards	www.mitillinivineyards.com
Live Oak	Rooney's Front Porch Farm	www.rooneyfarm.com
Live Oak	Sampson Family Farm	www.sampsonfamilyfarm.com
Monticello	Green Meadows Farm	www.localharvest.org/greenmeadowsfarm
Moore Haven	Gray's and Danny's Meat	www.GDMeatPlant.com
Myakka Head	Bellablue Berry Farm	www.bellablueberryfarm.com
Naples	Colusa Farms	www.colusafarms.com
O'Brien	The Back Acres Farm	www.thebackacresfarm.com
Ocoee	Tom West Blueberries	www.tomwestblueberries.com
Orlando	Brook Hollow Hydroponics	www.thebrookhollowfarm.com
Oxford	Brown's Country Market	www.brownandbrownfarms.com
Palm City	Shadowood Farm, Inc.	www.shadowoodfarm.com
Plant City	Abundant Gardens	www.abundantgardens.net
Plant City	Hardy Farms	www.hardypalmtrees.com
Ponce De Leon	Cypress Cattle and Produce	www.cypresscattle.com
Ruskin	Hydro Harvest Farms	www.hydroharvestfarms.com
Saint Augustine	Maggies Herb Farm	www.maggiesherbfarm.com
Sarasota	Honeyside Farms	www.honeysidefarms.com
Summerfield	Heirloom Country Farms	www.heirloomcountryfarms.com
Tallahassee	Goat First Network	www.goatfirstnetwork.com
Tallahassee	Windy Hill Vineyard	www.windyhillvineyard.com
Trenton	Laughing Chicken Farm	www.laughingchickenfarm.com
Valrico	Wingspread Farm	www.wingspread.farm
Vero Beach	Osceola Organic Farm	www.osceolaorganicfarm.com
Yalaha	Aquaponic Lynx	www.aquaponiclynx.com

FOOD HUBS

Bradenton	Suncoast Food Alliance	www.suncoastfoodalliance.com
Oakland Park	German Bread Haus	www.germanbreadhaus.com
Placida	Farmers Market Alliance	www.bocagrandefarmersmarket.com
Summerfield	Florida Fresh Meat Co	www.floridafreshmeat.com

Bluedress Farm

Grayson
www.facebook.com/bluedressfarm/

Proposed development. Winnett County commissioners approved a request for a farm-centric neighborhood, with plans for as many as 45 homes with a central community-shared farm, a boathouse, a market for local produce, and a coffee shop. Bluedress Farm will include 50 acres of scenic rural landscape highlighted by a 9-acre naturally stocked freshwater lake, a spoil of magnificent oak trees, rolling fields, and natural wildlife.

Eco Cottages at East Point

Atlanta
www.epecocottages.com

Under development. Located in historic Downtown East Point, the Eco Cottages community is planned on a 7.69-acre parcel and will have over 40 eco-cottages on permanent foundations. Eco Cottages is a new type of community of sustainable structures, new urbanism, and micro-agrihood. By design, cottages are significantly smaller than the average home, with customizable, efficiently designed interiors, and creative use of porches. A varied landscape includes edible landscaping, vertical gardens, potted herbs, and a community garden.

Etowah

Cumming
www.theetowah.com

Under development. Community of hamlets surrounded by forest, mountains, ravines, and Etowah River. 15-acre village center and public square. Amenities include activities center with pool, tennis, play areas, forest park, and health and wellness programs. 100 acres of Forest Park walking/hiking trails accessible at multiple trail connections throughout the community. Mountain biking trails. Working farm, orchard, hops garden, educational opportunities for aspiring farmers, and CSA program. Home styles include cottages, village homes, and canopy towers with forest views. Prime waterfront areas will include shared work spaces, brewery, and restaurants.

Gateway Heights

Macon
www.www.facebook.com/pages/Gateway-Heights-An-Urban-Agrihood/

Proposed development. Gateway Heights will be an urban agrihood with community farms occupying spaces once blighted with decay and abandoned properties. Totaling 13.17 acres within walking distance of downtown Macon, Southside was formerly home to gardens and mini-farms. Southside's greatest gift is in its terrain, consisting of well-tended land by residents of previous generations, and fertile soil ready to be developed into active farming and gardening space. The plan will repurpose 12 blighted parcels to 5 acres of fresh farmland—serving as the region's first agrihood. The neighborhood will consist of a multileveled mixed-use structure overlooking the farm house, a farm-to-fork open air restaurant, community kitchen, fitness center, and low income/affordable apartments and other retail spaces all within walking distance of Downtown Macon.

Serenbe

Chattahoochee Hills (Atlanta)

www.serenbe.com

Serenbe is a 1,000-acre community with four residential hamlets surrounded by greens, wetlands, watershed areas, and hills. The 25-acre certified organic farm and CSA provides over 300 varieties of vegetables, herbs, flowers, and fruits to residents, three on-site restaurants, local area businesses, and a Saturday farmers' market. Year-round cultural events include an outdoor theater from Serenbe Playhouse, culinary workshops and festivals, music events, films and lectures, boutique shopping, art galleries, a spa, and trail riding. The first house at Serenbe was built in 2004, and the community is now home to over 650 residents. Residents can purchase a new home, a resale, or have a home built by their own custom builder. Short and long-term leases on rentals range from one bedroom lofts and townhouses to much larger homes.

COMMUNITY SUPPORTED AGRICULTURE (CSA) PROGRAMS

Bluffton	White Oak Pastures	www.whiteoakpastures.com
Brunswick	Sapelo Farms	www.sapelofarms.com
Chickamauga	CoLyCo	www.colycofarm.com
Cumming	Cane Creek Farm	www.canecreekfarm.net
East Point	Truly Living Well Center	www.trulylivingwell.com
Elberton	Broad River Pastures	www.broadriverpastures.com
Gordon	Babe and Sage Farm	www.babeandsagefarm.com
Jeffersonville	Rag & Frass Farm CSA	www.ragandfrassfarm.com
Lookout Mountain	Lookout Homestead	www.lookouthomestead.org
Sparta	Elm Street Gardens	www.elmstreetgardens.com
Toccoa	K and H Farms	www.k-and-hfarms.com
Waycross	Lady Bug Farm CSA	www.ladybugfarmcsa.com
Winterville	Collective Harvest	www.collectiveharvestathens.com

ON-FARM MARKETS

Blairsville	7M Family Farms	www.7mfamilyfarms.com
Box Springs	Findley Farms	www.findleyfarm.com
Cedartown	Jumping Frog Farm	www.jumpingfrogfarm.com
Chatsworth	Freedom Farms	www.freedomfruit.net
Ellijay	Ellijay Mushrooms	www.ellijaymushrooms.com
Ellijay	Red Apple Barn	www.redapplebarn.com
Jonesboro	Atlanta Harvest	www.AtlantaHarvest.com
Omega	Weeks Honey Farm	www.weekshoneyfarm.com
Pine Mountain	Jenny Jack Sun Farm	www.jennyjackfarm.com
Powder Springs	Two by Two Farms	www.twobytwofarmsga.com
Saint George	Homestead Basket	www.homesteadbasket.com
Sylvania	Savannah River Farms	www.savannahriverfarms.com
Tifton	Berry Good Farms	www.berrygoodfaems.com

FOOD HUBS

Atlanta	Puravii Foods	www.PuraviiFoods.com
Atlanta	Royal Food Service	www.royalfoodservice.com
Atlanta	The Common Market	www.thecommonmarket.org
Atlanta	The Turnip Truck of Georgia	www.turniptruckatlanta.com
Conyers	One Source Foods	www.onesourcefoods.net
Jeffersonville	Middle Georgia Growers	www.middlegeorgiagrowers.com
Stone Mountain	Global Growers Network	www.globalgrowers.net

HAWAII

AGRIHOODS

Hōkūnui
Maui
www.hokunui.com

Hōkūnui is a regenerative farming community comprised of 258 acres in Makawao. Nestled between two gulches, Hōkūnui was once a diverse native forest, and designed to integrate soil regeneration, water conservation, culture, native reforestation, and food production. Less than 10% of the land is dedicated to housing, leaving over 230 acres in permanent agricultural and cultural operations. Walking trails lead residents from their backyard through the green pastures alongside cattle, sheep, and chickens, to the community area and Farm Store, offering fresh produce, meat, and ready-to-eat meals. Hōkūnui Maui incorporates green building materials and technologies, alternative energy, and self-sufficient water sources. Housing consists of 21 agriculturally zoned lots with 2 residential homes on each lot. All homes are built with off-grid photovoltaic energy, generators, and private, potable water systems, along with rain catchment and surface water harvesting for agricultural water.

Kukui'ula
Kauai
www.kukuiula.com

Kukui'ula is an upscale agrihood alongside a 20-acre lake where members enjoy canoeing, picnics, fishing, and exploring edible walking trails. Activities include golf, hiking, and watersport. Within walking distance is The Upcountry Farm, a 10-acre natural wonderland where residents can pick their own organic produce, help with harvesting, just relax, or partake in gardening lessons from the farm team. There are many luxury home models, each with breathtaking views and indoor-outdoor lanais. Homes are located steps from The Clubhouse and a wide range of restaurants and shops. The Lodge at Kukui'ula, operated by Two Roads Hospitality, offers luxury vacation homes that are available for rent by nonmembers.

COMMUNITY SUPPORTED AGRICULTURE (CSA) PROGRAMS

Hilo	Ho'olaha Ka Hua	www.hawaiifoodbasket.org
Honaunau	Lions Gate Kona Coffee	www.coffeeofkona.com
Honolulu	Wally's Farm, LLC	www.wallysfarm.biz
Kealakekua	Adaptations Fresh Feast CSA	www.adaptationsaloha.com
Kilauea	Kauai Kunana, Dairy and Farm	www.kauaikunanadairy.com
Mountain View	Ginger Ridge Farms	www.gingerridgefarms.com
Volcano	Aloha Happy Ranch	www.alohahappyranch.com
Waimanalo	FarmRoof	www.farmroof.com

ON-FARM MARKETS

Captain Cook	Edge of the World	www.konaedge.com
Captain Cook	Love Family Farms	www.hawaiifruit.net
Mountain View	Hilo Coffee Mill Market	www.hilocoffeemill.com

FOOD HUBS

Hilo	The Food Basket, Inc.	www.hawaiifoodbasket.org
Honolulu	Oahu Fresh	www.oahufresh.com
Kealakekua	Adaptations Inc	www.adaptationsaloha.com
Waialua	Farm Link Hawaii	www.farmlinkhawaii.com

IDAHO

AGRIHOODS

Dry Creek Ranch
Boise
www.drycreekranch.com

Dry Creek Ranch is set on 1,400 beautiful acres, featuring open spaces, trail systems, a community farm, and a commitment to sustainability. A professionally managed on-site farm utilizes natural growing methods for seeding, growing, and harvesting. Residents can enjoy weekly produce delivered to their door. 25% of the developed acreage consists of one-half to one-acre sized lots. Larger lots can be purchased to accommodate recreational vehicles, boats, and horse stables. Dry Creek Ranch accommodates customized building designs and floor plans. The community features an equestrian facility, where residents can enjoy dressage, western pleasure riding, lessons, and competitions. Groomed trails are located throughout the neighborhood. Dry Creek Ranch has donated land to build an elementary school in the West Ada district.

Hidden Springs
Boise
www.hiddensprings.com

Winner of the Best Smart Growth Award from the National Association of Home Builders, Hidden Springs is located 10 miles north of Boise on a homesteading site of 1,844 acres. Created around an agricultural heritage on the site of a 135-year-old farmstead, Hidden Springs offers access to 800 acres of open space conservation land. In addition to the Dry Creek Mercantile and restaurant, schools, fire department, and saltwater swimming pool, the development centers around an organic farm that produces vegetables and herbs for CSA members and customers of the Mercantile. The founding vision for Hidden Springs was to build a rural community in the tradition of Idaho's small towns, while carefully preserving the natural surroundings of Dry Creek Valley. Hidden Springs maintains a 40-acre working farm and a small-town neighborhood design. Homes are designed with traditional characteristics reflecting the area's rural character and farming traditions, while utilizing responsible and efficient energy and resources.

COMMUNITY SUPPORTED AGRICULTURE (CSA) PROGRAMS

Boise	Earthly Delights Farm	www.earthlydelightsfarm.com
Boise	Cunningham Pastured Meats	www.cunninghampasturedmeats.com
Boise	Field Goods Farm	www.fieldgoodsfarm.com
Boise	Global Gardens CSA	www.idahorefugees.org/globalgardens
Clark Fork	Moose Meadow Farm	www.moosemeadoworganic.com
Lewiston	River City Farm	www.rivercityfarm.wordpress.com
Meridian	True Roots Organics	www.TrueRootsOrganics.com
Meridian	Spyglass Gardens	www.spyglassgardens.com
Rathdrum	Grateful Plate Farmstead	www.gratefulplatefarmstead.com
Shelley	Shelley's Fresh Produce	www.shelleysproduce.com

ON-FARM MARKETS		
Carmen	Mountain Valley Farmstead	www.MountainValleyFarmstead.com
Downey	Brady's Plant Ranch	www.bradysplantranch.com
Emmett	Richardson Farm	www.idahoberry.wordpress.com
Kuna	Cabalo's Orchard & Gardens	www.cabalosorchard.com
Kuna	Goshen Farm,	www.goshenfarm.weebly.com
Pocatello	Giving Ground Farm	www.givinggroundseeds.com
Weiser	Kelley Orchards	www.kelleyorchards.com
FOOD HUBS		
Bellevue	Kraay's Market & Garden	www.kraaysmarketgarden.com

ILLINOIS

Prairie Crossing

Grayslake
www.prairiecrossing.com

Founded in 1987, Prairie Crossing is a conservation community consisting of 400 homes on 675 acres and includes a 100-acre organic farm and CSA. The community was designed to combine responsible development, the preservation of open land, and easy commuting by rail. Residents have access to an array of indoor and outdoor amenities and recreation. The stunning centerpiece of Prairie Crossing is the 20-acre Lake Aldo Leopold, named after the great Wisconsin conservationist and author, it is exclusively for residents and guests to swim, canoe, sail, or ice skate. Prairie Crossing features an edible landscape and orchards where residents are invited to harvest fruit. Prairie Crossing offers a wide variety of housing choices, all designed in the midwestern style of architecture, with energy-efficient features and old-fashioned porches. Home designs are consistent with the U.S. Department of Energy (DOE) green construction and energy conversation initiatives. The community's Station Square condominium development and retail/office buildings were awarded LEED-ND status.

Serosun Farms

Hampshire
www.serosunfarms.com

Serosun Farms is an innovative, sustainable, conservation community situated on over 400 acres of picturesque countryside. Estate members of Serosun Farms enjoy high-performance, custom homes with superior craftsmanship utilizing the latest technology and green building practices, complemented by breathtaking views. Lots consist of approximately one acre of land. Homes groupings create small intimate neighborhoods, and feature architectural designs that include Prairie, Victorian, and Craftsman homes. The community is centered around a 160-acre working farm that supplies fresh produce, flowers, farm-raised meat, and a variety of specialty items. Serosun Farms includes eight miles of trails, an equestrian center, fishing ponds, a playground, and a community center with a swimming pool, a game room, and event facilities. Serosun Farms serves as a tranquil oasis for weekend or second homeowners and equestrians. Winter activities include opportunities to snowshoe or cross-country ski through 40 acres of woodlands.

COMMUNITY SUPPORTED AGRICULTURE (CSA) PROGRAMS

Assumption	August Creek Farm	www.augustcreekfarm.com
Aurora	Renewed Roots Initiative	www.renewedroots.org
Bloomington	Browns Fresh Produce	www.brownsproduce.com
Caledonia	Angelic Organics	www.AngelicOrganics.com
Chicago	Growing Home Inc	www.growinghomeinc.org
Chicago	Tomato Mountain Farm	www.tomatomountain.com
Golconda	The Ryder Family Farm CSA	www.harvestofdailylife.com
Grayslake	Midnight Sun Farm	www.midnightsunfarm.com
Grayslake	Prairie Wind Family Farm	www.prairiewindfamilyfarm.com
Grayslake	Sandhill Family Farms	www.sandhillfamilyfarms.com

Harvard	Fair Share CSA	www.fairsharecsa.com
Harvard	Freedom Organix	www.freedomorganix.com
Libertyville	Radical Root Organic Farm	www.radicalrootfarm.com
McLeansboro	Thunder 5 Ranch Members Club	www.thunder5ranch.com
Morris	Bray Grove Farm	www.braygrovefarm.com
Old Mill Creek	Tempel Farms Organics	www.tempelfarmsorganics.com
Paris	L&A Family Farms	www.lafamilyfarms.com
Poplar Grove	Trogg's Hollow	www.troggshollow.com
Richmond	Green Earth Farm	www.greenearthfarm.org
Rockford	Roots & Wings Youth Farm	www.learngrowconnect.org
Stewardson	Triple S Farms	www.triplesfarms.com
Streator	Santorineos Family Farm	www.santofamfarm.com
Tunnel Hill	LEAF Food Hub	www.leaffoodhub.com
Walnut	Walnut Acres Family Farm	www.walnut4meat.com
Watseka	Gray Farms	www.grayfarmsproduce.com
Wheaton	Wellhausen Farms	www.wellhausengroup.com
Winfield	Three Plaid Farmers	www.blog.threeplaid.com
Winnebago	Harrison Market Gardens	www.harrisonmarketgardens.com
Woodstock	M's Organic Sustainable Farm	www.localharvest.org/farms

ON-FARM MARKETS

Alpha	Country Corner Farm	www.country-corner.com
Alto Pass	Rendleman Orchards Farm	www.rendlemanorchards.com
Beason	Gail's Pumpkin Patch	www.gailspumpkinpatch.com
Carbondale	McNitt Growers	www.mcnittgrowers.com
Carlyle	Voss Pecans	www.vosspecans
Champaign	Curtis Orchard & Pumpkin Patch	www.curtisorchard.com
Chicago	Eden Place Farms	www.edenplacefarms.org
Chicago	Growing Home, Inc.	www.growinghomeinc.org
Chicago	PCC Austin Farm	www.pccwellness.org
Coal Valley	Crandall Farms	www.crandallfarms.com
Davis	Raines Honey Farm	www.raineshoneyfarm.com
Edwardsville	Liberty Apple Orchard	www.libertyappleorchard.com
Harvard	Royal Oak Farm Orchard	www.royaloakfarmorchard.com
Hurst	Big Muddy Hogs	www.bigmuddyhogs.com
Lake Zurich	Natural Environments	www.robertcboyce.com
Lee Center	Stone Home Farm	www.stonehomefarm.com
Leland	Larson's Country Market	www.larsonscountrymarket.com
Loda	Mulberry Lane Farm	www.MulberryLaneFarm.com

Marengo	Thornpaw Lea Farm	www.thornpawleafarm.com
Marine	Mills Apple Farm	www.millsapplefarm.com
McHenry	Willies Honey Company	www.willieshoneyco.com
Monee	Gorman Farm Fresh Produce	www.gormanfarmfreshproduce.com
Paris	L&A Family Farms	www.lafamilyfarms.com
Paxton	Cow Creek Farm	www.cowcreekorganicfarm.com
Plainfield	Bronkberry Farms	www.bronkberryfarms.com
Lincolnshire	Didier Farms	www.didierfarms.com
Sandoval	Fox River Farm,	www.foxriverfarm.net
South Beloit	Sunrise Market Farm, Inc.	www.sunrisemarketfarm.com
Sterling	Northland Farms	www.northlandfarms.net
Union	Prairie Sky Orchard	www.prairieskyorchard.com
Wilmington	Tammen Treeberry Farm	www.tammentreeberryfarm.net
Winnebago	Edwards Apple Orchard West	www.edwardsorchardwest.com
Woodstock	All Seasons Orchard	www.allseasonsorchard.com
Woodstock	Grace Farm Studios	www.gracefarmstudios.com
Woodstock	Madoli Farms	www.madolifarms.com

FOOD HUBS

Chicago	Healthy Food Hub	www.healthyfoodhub.org
Chicago	Local Foods	www.localfoods.com
Chicago	The Mandolini Co.	www.mandolinico.com
Lyons	Moss Funnel Farms	www.joesblueberries.com
Martinsville	Illiana Ag Alliance	www.illianaagalliance.com
Niles	Irv & Shelly's Fresh Picks	www.freshpicks.com
Tunnel Hill	LEAF Food Hub	www.leaffoodhub.com

INDIANA

AGRIHOODS

Tryon Farms
Michigan City
www.tryonfarm.com

Tryon Farms is a community of smart, modern country weekend homes on historic Lake Michigan, one hour from Chicago and 1.5 miles from Lake Michigan beaches. Residents enjoy healthy, wide-open spaces on 120 acres of preserved meadows, dunes, oakwood forests, and roaming cows and chickens. Homes are designed to blend seamlessly with the land and are low-maintenance and environmentally sensitive. Community includes over 5 miles of nature trails, freshwater swimming, ponds and streams for fishing, and birding. A historic dairy barn serves as the community hall, and the Tryon Farm institute offers workshops such as beekeeping, habitat restoration, and fish stocking, as well as environmental education and guided hikes. The original farm family's brick farmhouse serves as bed and breakfast and guest house. Tryon Farm includes community gardens and is convenient to the Michigan City Farmers' Market, Pavolka Fruit Farm, Garwood Orchard, wineries, and many varied restaurants.

COMMUNITY SUPPORTED AGRICULTURE (CSA) PROGRAMS

Colfax	Stillhaven Farms	www.stillhavenfarms.com
Colfax	This Old Farm, Inc.	www.thisoldfarminc.com
Columbia City	Old Loon Farm	www.oldloonfarm.com
Daleville	Landess Farm	www.landessfarm.com
Evansville	Seton Harvest	www.setonharvest.org
Freedom	Freedom Valley Farm	www.freedomvalleyfarm.com
Goshen	Clay Bottom Farm	www.claybottomfarm.com
Greenfield	Tuttle Orchards	www.tuttleorchards.com
Indianapolis	Center for Urban Ecology (CUE) Farm at Butler University	www.butler.edu/urban-ecology/urban-farm
Oaktown	Melon Acres CSA	www.melonacres.com
Patoka	Kolb Homestead	www.kolbhomestead.com
St. Mary of the Woods	White Violet Center for Eco-Justice	www.whiteviolet.org
Upland	Victory Acres Farm and CSA	www.victoryacres.org
Westfield	Farming Engineers Market Shares	www.Farmingengineers.com

ON-FARM MARKETS

Bloomington	Sunny Branch Farm	www.sunnybranchfarm.com
Bloomington	The Chile Woman	www.thechilewoman.com
Clinton	Aris Farm Alpacas	www.ArisFarmAlpacas.com
Dale	Steckler Grassfed	www.StecklerGrassfed.com
Evansville	Bud's Farm Market	www.budsfarm.com
Fishers	Aggressively Fresh Fishers	www.aggressivelyfresh.com

Lafayette	Wea Creek Orchard	www.weacreekorchard.com
Lanesville	Deere Farms	www.deerefarms.com
Michigan City	Radke Orchards	www.radkeorchards.com
Michigan City	Scherf Farms Dairy & Creamery	www.scherffarms.com
New Carlisle	Rainfield Farm	www.rainfieldfarm.com
New Haven	Bruick Brothers Produce	www.advancedtree.com
New Salisbury	Bryant's Blueberries	www.bryantsblueberries.com
North Manchester	J.L. Hawkins Family Farm	www.hawkinsfamilyfarm.com
Peru	McClures Orchard/Winery	www.mccluresorchard.com
Plymouth	Childs' Farm	www.childsfarm.net
South Bend	Matthys Farm Market	www.matthysfarmmarket.com
Sunman	Fork Right Farm	www.forkrightfarm.com
Terre Haute	Richmond Acres	www.richmondacres.weebly.com
Vallonia	Kamman's Greenhouse & Farm	www.kammansfarmmarket.com
Whiteland	Whiteland Orchard	www.whitelandorchard.com

FOOD HUBS

Aurora	Fresh Local Food Collaborative	www.ginnfarms.org
Colfax	This Old Farm, Inc.	www.thisoldfarm.com
Greenfield	Hoosier Harvest Market	www.hoosierharvestmarket.com
Trafalgar	Hickoryworks	www.Hickoryworks.com

133

IOWA

AGRIHOODS

Dows Farm Agri-Community

Ames
www.linncounty.org/930/10760/Dows-Farm-Agri-Community

Proposed development. The Dows Farm Agri-Community, consisting of mixed-use housing units and a farm, will be constructed on 179 acres of land, formerly the Dows Farm. The concept for Dows Farm stemmed from Linn County's purchase of 485 acres from the Dows family in 2016, where 306 acres would expand the conservation footprint of the county-owned Squaw Creek Park. The separate 179 acres is designated for urban development based on the agrihood model. Dows Farm will include vineyards, orchards, pastures, education centers, a farmers' market and CSA, restaurants, daycare centers, and other services in the village commons. Trails will link to the neighborhoods and agricultural features. The north 306 acres is adjacent to the Dows Farm and will include a 43-acre working farm to grow healthy foods using sustainable farming practices. 88 acres is reserved for conservation and 48 acres for development. Mixed-use residential units will include commercial space, 186 single-family homes, 94 multi-family homes, and 101 apartment units.

Middlebrook

Cumming (Des Moines)
www.middlebrookfarms.com

Middlebrook is Iowa's first official agrihood, located 20 minutes from downtown Des Moines. With more than 100 acres of land dedicated to agricultural endeavors, Middlebrook includes a town farm, neighborhood gardens, a community farm, orchards, edible landscapes, and animal pastures. Community trails lead to the existing Great Western Bike Trail. The heart of the town center is the Town Farm, where residents gather, attend educational events, and shop at a retail farm stand. A 20-acre community farm produces organic vegetables, herbs, fruit, and flowers for Middlebrook residents and the broader community. Middlebrook provides over 1,000 dwellings, with a wide variety of housing options that include single-family homes, town homes, apartments, senior living, and high-end estate homes. A wide range of models is offered, reflecting the region's traditional architecture and pedestrian-oriented streetscape.

URBAN AG

Walker Homestead, Iowa City

Farming and culinary education, CSA, Muddy Miss Farm, Winery, Event Venue
www.www.walker-homestead.com

COMMUNITY SUPPORTED AGRICULTURE (CSA) PROGRAMS

Ames	ISU Student Organic Farm	www.isustudentorganicfarm.weebly.com
Atlantic	Rolling Acres Farm	www.rollingacres.wordpress.com
Cedar Rapids	Matthew 25 Urban Farm	www.hub25.org
Chariton	Blue Gate Farm	www.bluegatefarmfresh.com
Decorah	Sweet Earth Farm	www.sweetearthfarmdecorah.com
Earlham	Heirloom Farm LLC	www.hlfarm.com/
Elkhart	New Family Farm	www.newfamilyfarm.com
Everly	Good Eetens Produce Farm	www.goodeetens.weebly.com

134

Granger	Wabi Sabi Farm	www.wabisabi-farm.com
Grinnell	Grinnell Heritage Farm	www.GrinnellHeritageFarm.com
Hancock	Botna Burrow	www.botnaburrow.com
Hancock	Loess Hills CSA	www.loesshillccsa.com
Maxwell	7 Pines Farm	www.7pinesfarm.com
Minburn	Small Potatoes Farm	www.smallpotatoesfarm.com
Mt. Vernon	Abbe Hills Farm	www.abbehills.com
Nevada	Berry Patch Farm	www.berrypatchfarm.com
Nevada	TableTop Farm	www.tabletopfarm.com
Oakland	Nishnabotna Naturals	www.NishnabotnaNaturals.com
Pleasant Hill	Balance Autism Farm	www.balanceautism.com
Redfield	Raccoon Forks Farm	www.raccoonforks.com
Waukee	L.T. Organic Farm	www.ltorganicfarm.org
Waverly	Kaiser Farm	www.kaiserfarmfresh.com

ON-FARM MARKETS

Amana	Oldhaus Fibers	www.oldhausfibers.com
Carlisle	North River Adventure Farm	www.nnorthrivercornmaze.com
Cedar Rapids	Baumhoefeners Red Barn	www.redbarnmarket.net
Donnellson	Appleberry Orchard	www.appleberryorchard.com
Dunlap	Dunham Bee Farm	www.dunhambeefarm.com
Gilmore City	JoKir's Wild Black Angus	www.jokirswild.com
Honey Creek	Doe's and Diva's Dairy	www.doesanddivas.com
Muscatine	Anderson Farm	www.grassfedrecipes.com
Nashua	Apples on the Avenue	www.applesontheavenue.com
Nevada	Black Cat Acres	www.blackcatacres.com
Nevada	Produce farm	www.blackcatacres.com
Oakland	Honey Creek Farms	www.neverendingharvest.com
Winterset	Burr Oak Farm	www.burroakfarm.com
Winterset	Randol Honey Farm	www.randolhoney.com
Woodward	Picket Fence Creamery	www.picketfencecreamery.com

FOOD HUBS

Clermont	Grown Locally	www.grownlocally.com
Davenport	Quad Cities Food Hub	www.qcfoodhub.com
Des Moines	Iowa Food Coop	www.iowafood.coop
Harlan	Farm Table Procurement	www.farmtabledelivery.com
Iowa City	Field to Family	www.fieldtofamily.org
Marshalltown	Iowa Choice Harvest	www.iowachoiceharvest.com
West Union	Iowa Food Hub	www.iowafoodhub.com

KANSAS

COMMUNITY SUPPORTED AGRICULTURE (CSA) PROGRAMS

Atchison	Atchison Area Farmer's Alliance	www.atchisonlocalproduce.com
Basehor	Prairie Garden Farm	www.prairiegardenfarm.com
Lawrence	Mellowfields Urban Farm	www.mellowfields.com
Lawrence	Rolling Prairie Farmers Alliance	www.rollingprairiecsa.com
McCune	Schenker Family Farms/ Farm to Fork Workplace Wellness	www.csa.schenkerfarms.com
Wakarusa	Good Ground Gardens	www.goodgroundgardens.com

ON-FARM MARKETS

El Dorado	Tubby Fruits Orchard	www.tubbyfruits.com
El Dorado	Boondocker Farms	www.boondockerfarms.com
Hesston	Fanska Farms	www.FanskaFarms.com
Manhattan	Kalaya Emu Estates	www.KalayaEmuEstate.com
Parker	Christy's Farm	www.christysfarm.org
Pleasanton	Synergistic Acres	www.synergisticares.com
Rose Hill	Skyview Farm and Creamery	www.skyviewfarm.net
Stilwell	Meadowlark Farm	www.themeadowlarkfarm.com
Stilwell	Meadowlark Acres	www.meadowlarkacres.com

FOOD HUBS

McCune	Schenker Family Farms	www.schenkerfarms.com

COMMUNITY SUPPORTED AGRICULTURE (CSA) PROGRAMS

Bloomfield	Coulter's Good Earth Farm	www.coulterfarm.com
Covington	Rains and Sun Hilltop Farm	www.rainsandsun.com
Crestwood	Meadowview Farm	www.meadowviewfarmandgarden.com
Edmonton	Blueberry Hills Farm	www.blueberryhillsnursery.com
Gravel Switch	Rolling Fork Organic Farm	www.rollingforkorganicfarm.com
Harned	Brooks Farm	www.brooksfarmky.com
Lexington	Crooked Row Farm	www.crookedrowfarm.com
London	Sustainable Harvest Farm	www.harvie.mx/lizfarmshare
Manchester	Old Homeplace Farm	www.oldhomeplacefarm.com
Payneville	Misty Meadows Farm	www.mistymeadowsfarm.vpweb.com
Turners Station	A Place on Earth CSA Farm	www.aplaceonearthcsa.com

ON-FARM MARKETS

Goshen	Woodland Farm	www.woodlandfarm.com
Paint Lick	Halcomb's Knob	www.halcombsknob.com
Winchester	Brookview Beef	www.brookviewbeef.com

FOOD HUBS

Covington & Newport	Ohio Valley Food Connection	www.ohiovalleyfood.com
Louisville	New Root's Fresh Stop	www.newrootsproduce.org
Salvisa	Four Hills Farms	www.fourhillsfarm.com

LOUISIANA

COMMUNITY SUPPORTED AGRICULTURE (CSA) PROGRAMS

Alexandria	Inglewood Farm CSA	www.inglewoodfarm.com
Covington	Tomkins Farm CSA	www.tomkinsfarms.com
DeRidder	Southern Pastures Farm LLC	www.southernpasturesfarm.com
Lafayette	Earthshare Gardens	www.earthsharegardens.com
Lafayette	Mark and Mary's City Farm	www.cityfarmjournal.blogspot.com
Opelousas	Thy Bounty Farms	www.thybountyfarms.com
Oscar	Loup Farms	www.loupfarms.com
Ponchatoula	Super Natural Organic Farms of America	www.snofa.net
Pride	Luckett Farms	www.luckettfarms.com
Scott	Gotreaux Family Farms	www.gofamilyfarms.com
Scott	Earthshare Gardens	www.earthsharegardens.org

ON-FARM MARKETS

Abbeville	Brookshire Farm Grassfed Beef	www.brookshirefarm.com
Alexandria	Rosalie Pecans	www.shop.rosaliepecans.com
Church Point	Robin Farms	www.robinfarms.com
Franklinton	3D Blueberry Farm	www.3dblueberries.com
Moreauville	WesMar Farms Goat Dairy	www.WesMarFarms.com
New Orleans	Nola Tilth	www.nolatilth.com
Pollock	Butterfield Farms	www.butterfieldfarm.net

FOOD HUBS

Lafayette	Acadiana Food Hub	www.acadianafoodhub.com
New Orleans	Hollygrove Market and Farm	www.hollygrovemarket.com
New Orleans	Sankofa Fresh Stop Market	www.sankofanola.org

Community Supported Agriculture (CSA) Programs

Auburn	Valley View Farm	www.valleyviewfarmme.com
Brunswick	Sound Pine Farm	www.soundpinefarm.com
Chelsea	Olde Haven Farm	www.oldehavenfarm.com
Farmington	Porter Hill Farm	www.porterhillfarm.com
Knox	New Beat Farm	www.newbeatfarm.com
Lisbon Falls	Little Ridge Farm	www.littleridgefarm.com
Newport	Lakeside Family Farm	www.lakesidefamilyfarm.com
Porter	Alma Farm	www.almafarm.com
Portland	Fresh Start Farms	www.cultivatingcommunity.org
Sabattus	Willow Pond Farm	www.willowpf.com
Scarborough	Frith Farm	www.frithfarm.net
Turner	Nezinscot Farm Store CSA	www.nezinscotfarm.com

On-Farm Markets

Auburn	Whiting Farm	www.whitingfarm.org
Buxton	Snell Family Farm	www.snellfamilyfarm.com
Cape Elizabeth	Alewive's Brook Farm	www.alewivesbrookfarm.com
Caribou	Circle B Farms	www.circlebfarmsinc.com
Casco	Murramarang Farm	www.almostafarmer.com
Dennysville	Smith Ridge Farm	www.smithridgefarm.com
Farmington	Fleur de Lis Farm	www.cotswoldsofmaine.com
Freeport	Wolfe's Neck Farm	www.wolfesneckfarm.org
Hallowell	The Maine Accent Field Grown	www.themaineaccent.com
Harrison	High View Farm Dairy	www.high-view-farm.com
Hope	Hope Orchards	www.hopeorchards.com
Kingsbury Plantation	Perseverance Wild Blueberry Farm	www.perseverancefarm.com
Limerick	Libby & Son U-Picks	www.libbysonupicks.com
Livermore	Boothby's Orchard and Farm	www.mainehoneycrisp.com
Lyman	Tibbetts Family Farm	www.tibbettsfamilyfarm.com
Rumford	Gone Loco at No View Farm	www.noviewfarm.com
Springvale	McDougal Orchards	www.mcdougalorchards.com
Turner	Nezinscot Farm Store	www.nezinscotfarm.com
Unity	Northern Solstice Alpaca Farm	www.northernsolsticealpaca.com
Waldoboro	Beau Chemin Preservation	www.beaucheminpreservationfarm.com
Wells	Chick Farm	www.chickfarm.com

Food Hubs

Unity	Unity Food Hub Management	www.unityfoodhub.com
Van Buren	Northern Girl	www.northerngirlmaine.com

MARYLAND

AGRIHOODS

Cooke's Hope
Easton
www.cookeshope.com

Located in Talbot County, Cooke's Hope was part of a land grant to Major Miles Cooke in 1659 by Lord Baron of Baltimore. Comprised of more than 650 acres, Cooke's Hope offers five distinct neighborhoods with breathtaking vistas, natural wildlife sanctuaries, and over five miles of walking trails. Amenities include tennis courts, private post office, fitness center, dog park, gift shop, and more. A service-oriented community, residents can customize yard and maintenance services. One of the neighborhoods, called Llandaff, includes both waterfront and inland sites that range from 2 to 57 acres, allowing for private farming and hunting opportunities. Llandaff has a covered bridge and miles of walking trails connected to Cooke's Hope.

COMMUNITY SUPPORTED AGRICULTURE (CSA) PROGRAMS

Baltimore	Whitelock Community Farm CSA	www.whitelockfarm.org
Bel Air	Wilson's Farm Market	www.wilsonfarmmarket.net
Bethesda	Spiritual Food CSA	www.spiritualfoodcsa.org
Cecilton	Priapi Gardens	www.priapigardens.com
Clarksburg	Citizens of Earth	www.thecitizensofearth.org
Cockeysville	Moon Valley Farm	www.moonvalleyfarm.net
Elkton	Fair Weather Farm at Fairhill	www.organiceducationfarm.org
Federalsburg	Blades Orchard, Friendship Farms	www.bladesorchard.com
Frederick	Sycamore Spring Farm	www.sycamorespringfarm.org
Freeland	Oak Spring Farm	www.oakspring-farm.com
Galena	Colchester Farm CSA	www.colchesterfarm.org
Germantown	Chocolates and Tomatoes Farm	www.chocolatesandtomatoes.com
Hampstead	Two Boots Farm	www.twobootsfarm.com
Monkton	Little Gunpowder Farm	www.littlegunpowderfarm. com
Oakland	Garrett Growers Cooperative	www.garrettgrowers.com
Pisgah	Karl's Farm	www.Karls-Farm.com
Poolesville	Rocklands Farm	www.RocklandsFarmMD.com
Rising Sun	Flying Plow Farm CSA	www.flyingplowfarm.com
Rocky Ridge	Stony Branch Growers	www.stonybranchgrowers.com
Thurmont	Shadows of Catoctin Farm	www.shadowsofcatoctinfarm.com
Upper Marlboro	Cabin Creek Heritage Farm	www.cabincreekheritagefarm.com
Waldorf	Zekiah Farms	www.zekiahfarms
Westminster	Chestnut Creek Farm	www.chestnutcreekfarm.com
Westminster	Evermore Farm	www.evermorefarm.com
Westminster	Sparkling Star Farm	www.SparklingStarFarm.com
White Hall	One Straw Farm	www.onestrawfarm.com

On-Farm Markets

Accokeek	Accokeek Foundation - Ecosystem	www.accokeekfoundation.org
Adamstown	Nick's Organic Farm	www.nicksorganicfarm.com
Baltimore	Whitelock Community Farm	www.whitelockfarm.org
Chestertown	Tag Along Alpacas	www.tagalongalpacas.com
Church Hill	Unity Church Hill	www.unitynursery.com
Clarksburg	Citizens of Earth	www.thecitizensofearth.org
Dickerson	Jehovah Jireh Farm	www.Jehovahjirehfarm.com
Ellicott City	Clark's Elioak Farm	www.clarklandfarm.com
Emmitsburg	Whitmore Farm	www.whitmorefarm.com
Germantown	Butler's Orchard	www.butlersorchard.com
Hurlock	Pop's Old Place	www.PopsOldPlace.com
Middletown	Karen's Kountry Store	www.southmountaincreamery.com
Mount Airy	Rock Hill Orchard	www.rockhillorchard.com
Mount Airy	Wagon Wheel Ranch	www.wagonwheelranch.org
Mount Airy	Gaver Farm	www.gaverfarm.com
Potomac	Nick's Organic Farm	www.nicksorganicfarm.com
Severn	Willow Oak Flower & Herb Farm	www.willowoakherbs.com
Tyaskin	Habanera Farm	www.habanerafarm.com
Upper Marlboro	Cabin Creek Heritage Farm	www.cabincreekheritagefarm.com
Westminster	Baugher's Orchard & Farm	www.baughers.com
Westminster	Cultivale Farm	www.cultivale.com
Westminster	Evermore Farm	www.evermorefarm.com
Westminster	Thorne Farm	www.thornefarm.com
White Hall	Shaw Orchards	www.shaworchards.com
Williamsport	Columbine Manor	www.cm-longhornbeef.com

Food Hubs

Beltsville	From the Farmer	www.fromthefarmer.com
Capitol Heights	Washington's Green Grocer	www.washingtonsgreengrocer.com
Easton	Chesapeake Harvest	www.chesapeakeharvest.com
Frederick	Hometown Harvest	www.hometownharvest.com
Jessup	Hungry Harvest	www.hungryharvest.net
Middletown	South Mountain Creamery	www.southmountaincreamery.com
Oakland	Garrett Growers Coop.	www.garrettgrowers.com
Sparks Glencoe	Chesapeake Farm to Table	www.chesapeakefarmtotable.org

MASSACHUSETTS

AGRIHOODS

37 Interlaken
Stockbridge

Proposed development. A destination resort and residential development will occupy 100 acres of the 320-acre site, aimed to preserve the history, views, and cottage-era estate characteristics. The initial 37 Interlaken project includes a hotel with 40-50 guest rooms and suites, 139 condominium units, and 34 single-family residences. Restaurants, event space, and amenities expected in a full-service resort will be open to the public. 15 to 20 acres of sustainable farmland will be open for the use of all residents. The project will incorporate an agrihood. Final project plans are pending approval by the Stockbridge planning board.

URBAN AG

Fenway Farms
Boston
www.greencitygrowers.com/fenway-farms/

Fenway Farms provides fresh, organically grown vegetables and fruit to Red Sox fans at Fenway Park's restaurants and concessions. The 5,000 square foot rooftop farm utilizes a unique modular milk crate growing system, allowing easier contained growing throughout the season. A state-of-the art weather-sensitive drip irrigation system monitors soil moisture and supplies water only when needed. The 10,600-square-foot farm has a total growing space of 2,400 square feet, and yielded 5,980 pounds of produce in 2018. Designed and maintained by Green City Growers, a mission-driven company transforming underutilized spaces into biodiverse productive landscapes. The farm is located on the third base side of the Dell EMC Level, and can be viewed by the general public at the Gate A staircase.

COMMUNITY SUPPORTED AGRICULTURE (CSA) PROGRAMS

Amherst	Brookfield Farm	www.brookfieldfarm.org
Barre	Renaissance Farms	www.renaissance-farms.com
Canton	Pakeen Farm	www.pakeenfarm.com
Chelmsford	Jones Farm	www.jonesfarm.net
Chesterfield	Crabapple Farm	www.crabapplefarm.org
Concord	First Root Farm	www.firstrootfarm.com
Dover	The Dover Farm	www.doverfarmcsa.com
Dracut	Berube Farm, LLC	www.berubefarm.com
Hopkinton	Long Life Farm, LLC	www.longlifefarm.com
Ipswich	Marini Farm	www.marinifarm.com
Lanesborough	Red Shirt Farm	www.redshirtfarm.com
Leicester	Cotyledon Farm	www.cotyledonfarm.com
Lincoln/Lexington	Busa Farm	www.busafarm.com
Lowell	World Peas CSA	www.nesfp.org/world-peas-food-hub
Medford	Plough & Stars Project	www.ploughandstarsproject.com
Montague	Red Fire farm	www.redfirefarm.com
North Easton	Langwater Farm	www.langwaterfarm.com
Natick	Natick Community Farm	www.natickfarm.org

Needham	Needham Community Farm	www.needhamfarm.org
Plympton	Billingsgate Farm	www.billingsgatefarm.com
Rehoboth	Anawan Farm	www.anawanfarm.com
South Hamilton	Green Meadows Farm	www.gmfarm.com
Uxbridge	Chockalog Farm	www.localharvest.org/chockalog-farm
Waltham	Waltham Fields	www.communityfarms.org
Wendell	Stone's Throw Farm	www.stonesthrowgrown.com
West Bridgewater	C&C Reading Farm, LLC	www.billingsgatefarm.com
West Newbury	Long Hill Orchard	www.longhillorchard.com
Westborough	Heirloom Harvest Farm	www.heirloomharvestcsa.com
Weston	Land's Sake Farm	www.landsake.org
Whately	Enterprise Farm CSA	www.enterprisefarmcsa.com

ON-FARM MARKETS

Acushnet	Acushnet Farmers Market	www.acushnetfarmersmarket.com
Ashburnham	Odd Pine Farm	www.oddpinefarm.com
Canton	Pakeen Farm	www.pakeenfarm.com
Concord	Pete and Jen's Backyard Birds	www.peteandjensbackyardbirds.com
Groton	Autumn Hills Orchard	www.autumnhillsorchard.com
Ipswich	Chicken Little Farm	www.chickenlittlefarm.webs.com
Lexington	Meadow Mist Farm	www.meadow-mist.com
Lexington	Wilson Farm	www.wilsonfarm.com
Marlborough	Spring Hill Farm	www.farmsteadusa.com/spring-hill-farm
Nantucket	Bartlett's Ocean View Farm	www.bartlettsfarm.com
North Attleboro	Miller's Family Farm	www.millersfamilyfarm.net
North Easton	Langwater Farm	www.langwaterfarm.com
South Amherst	Atkins Farms Country Market	www.atkinsfarms.com
South Lancaster	George Hill Orchards	www.yourfavoritefarm.com
Whately	Nourse Farms	www.noursefarms.com
Woods Hole	Nobska Farms, Inc.	www.nobskafarms.com

FOOD HUBS

Charlestown	Boston Organics	www.bostonorganics.com
Dalton	Berkshire Organics Market	www.berkshireorganics.com
Gardner	Massachusetts Local Food	www.masslocalfood.org
Greenfield	Western MA Food	www.fccdc.org
Lowell	World PEAS Food Hub	www.nesfp.org/world-peas-food-hub
Nantucket	Community Farm Institute	www.sustainablenantucket.org
Plainville	Red Tomato	www.redtomato.org
Richmond	Marty's Local	www.martyslocal.com
Shrewsbury	Worcester Regional Food	www.worcesterfoodhub.org

MICHIGAN

URBAN AG

Michigan Urban Farming Initiative
Detroit
www.miufi.org/

The Michigan Urban Farming Initiative is the nation's first urban agrihood and is located in Detroit's North End community. The MUFI Urban Ag Campus is nearly 3 acres, with one-third of the campus dedicated to production farming, another third to interactive agriculture, and the remaining third to buildings and structures. MUFI has been operating at this location since 2011, and with the help of over 10,000 volunteers, has been able to grow and distribute over 50,000 pounds of produce (grown using organic methods) to 2,000 local households at no cost to the recipients. The campus itself has become an international tourist destination, receiving thousands of tourists from all over the world each year. Individual households subscribe to a pay-what-you-can model. MUFI also supplies to local markets, restaurants, vendors, food pantries, churches, and shelters.

COMMUNITY SUPPORTED AGRICULTURE (CSA) PROGRAMS

Ada	Green Wagon Farm	www.greenwagonfarm.com
Albion	Nelsfarm Produce	www.nelsfarmproduce.com
Ann Arbor	Dyer Family Organic Farm	www.dyerfamilyorganicfarm.com
Battle Creek	Green Gardens	www.greengardensfarm.com
Belding	Chimney Creek Farm	www.chimneycreekfarm.com
Belding	Full Hollow Farm	www.fullhollowfarm.com
Belleville	Sunset Harvest Farm	www.sunsetharvestfarm.net
Brighton	Stone Coop Farm LLC	www.stonecoopfarm.com
Cedar	Clean Plate Farm	www.cleanplatefarm.com
Cedar Lake	Good News FarmBox	www.GoodNewsFarm.org
Central Lake	Providence Organic Farm	www.providenceorganicfarm.com
Clare	Central Michigan CSA	www.MichiganFarmFreshProduce.com
Coleman	Middleton Farm CSA	www.middletonfarmcsa.com
Columbiaville	Three Roods Farm	www.threeroodsfarm.com
Detroit	City Commons CSA	www.citycommonscsa.com
East Lansing	Foodshed Farm	www.foodshedfarm.com
Elwell	Monroe Family Organics	www.mforganics.com
Felch	Slagle's Family Farm	www.slaglesfamilyfarm.com
Grand Rapids	New City Urban Farm	www.newcityneighbors.org
Holland	Crisp Country Acres	www.crispcountryacres.com
Houghton	Osma Acres Farm CSA	www.osmaacresfarm.com
Kalamazoo	Long Valley Farm	www.longvalleyfarm.com
Lansing	Hunter Park Garden House	www.allenneighborhoodcenter.org
Leslie	Titus Farms	www.titusfarms.com
Metamora	Decker Farm and Orchard	www.deckerfarmandorchard.com
Milan	Zilke Vegetable Farm	www.zilkevegetablefarm.com
Muskegon	McLaughlin Grows Urban	www.communityencompass.org
Oxford	Upland Hills CSA	www.uplandhillscsa.org

Romulus	Old City Acres Urban Farm	www.oldcityacres.com
Tipton	Needle-Lane Farms	www.needlelanefarms.com
Willis	Honest Eats Farm	www.honesteatsfarm.com
Zeeland	Groundswell Comm. Farm	www.groundswellfarm.org

ON-FARM MARKETS

Almont	Brookwood Fruit Farm	www.brookwoodfruitfarm.com
Benton Harbor	Piggott's Farm Market	www.piggottsfarmmarket.com
Benton Harbor	The Extraordinary Berry	www.theextraordinaryberry.com
Berrien Center	Frank Farms	www.frankfarms.com
Caledonia	Vertical Paradise Farms	www.vpfarms.com
Cass City	Battel's Sugar Bush & Farm	www.battelsyrup.weebly.com
Clare	Crawford Farms	www.MichiganFarmFreshProduce.com
Coleman	Coon's Berry Farm	www.coonsberryfarm.com
Coloma	Fruit Acres Farm U-Pick	www.fruitacresfarms.com
Dryden	Brandywine Farm Nursery	www.brandywinefarmnursery.com
Fennville	Evergreen Lane Farm	www.evergreenlanefarm.com
Fennville	Pleasant Hill Farm	www.pleasanthillblueberryfarm.com
Grand Rapids	Moelker Orchards & Farm	www.moelkerorchards.com
Grand Rapids	Wells Orchards	www.wellsorchards.com
Grass Lake	Witamy Farm	www.witamyfarm.com
Greenville	Good Land Growers	www.goodlandgrowers.com
Greenville	Klackle Orchards	www.klackleorchards.com
Hickory Cnrs.	Hickory Corners Homestead	www.hickorycornershomestead.com
Holland	Shady Side Farm	www.shadysidefarm.com
Holly	Mitchell Farm	www.mitchellfarm.biz
Ionia	Hanulcik Farm Market	www.farm-grown.com
Kent City	Fruit Ridge Hayrides	www.fruitridgehayrides.com
Laingsburg	Peacock Road Family Farm	www.peacockrff.com
Lake City	Friends Farm	www.friendsministry.net
Lakeview	Fresh Whole Rabbit	www.catalayarabbitry.weebly.com
Lansing	Peckham Farms	www.peckham.org
Lowell	Happy Buddha Farm,	www.happybuddhafarm.com
Lowell	Two Sparrows Farm	www.twosparrowsfarm.com
Lyons	KlineKrest Certified Organic	www.klinekrestcertifiedorganicproduce.com
Marshall	The Blue Barn	www.thebluebarninmarshall.com
Mason	Swallowtail Farm	www.swallowtailfarm.net
Melvin	Speaker Lone Oak Orchard	www.speakerorchard.com
Metamora	Brass Ring Beef	www.parksshowcattle.com
Middleville	Origins Hobby Farm	www.orriginshobbyfarm.com
Milan	Wasem Fruit Farm	www.wasemfruitfarm.com
Mt. Pleasant	GCC Organics	www.gccorganics.com
New Era	Lewis Farm & Petting	www.lewisfarmmarket.com
New Era	Oceana Winery & Vineyard	www.oceanawinery.com
Niles	Lavender Hill Farm	www.thelavenderhill.com
Northville	Michigan Flower Farm	www.michiganflowerfarm.com
Omena	New Mission Organics	www.newmissionorganics.com
Otter Lake	Blueberry Lane Farms	www.blueberrylanefarms.com

Petoskey	Coveyou Scenic Farm	www.coveyouscenicfarm.com
Pinckney	Michigan Garlic Farm	www.michigangarlicfarm.com
Quincy	Greener Grass Farms	www.greenergrassfarms.com
Quincy	Orchard Beach Farm	www.farmermaps.com
Ravenna	Creswick Farms	www.CreswickFarms.com
Rockford	Grange Fruit Farm	www.grangefruit.com
Rosebush	Graham's Organics	www.grahamsorganics.com
Saint Johns	Phillips Orchards Cider Mill	www.phillipsorchards.com
Saint Joseph	Nye's Apple Barn and Farms	www.nyesapplebarn.com
South Haven	A.W. Overhiser Orchards	www.overhiserorchards.com
St. Louis	Madison Road Produce	www.madisonroadproduce.com
Stephenson	Immerfrost Farm	www.ImmerfrostFarm.com
Stockbridge	Zatkovich Pastures	www.zatkovichpastures.com
Sturgis	Borderline Farm	www.borderline.farm
Suttons Bay	Black Star Farms	www.blackstarfarms.com
Three Oaks	Kaminski Farms Meats	www.kaminskifarmsmeats.com
Webberville	Spartan Country Meats	www.spartancountrymeats.com
Zeeland	Woodland Enterprises, Inc.	www.woodlandberries.com

FOOD HUBS

Ann Arbor	Washtenaw Food Hub	www.washtenawfoodhub.com
Detroit	Eastern Market Corporation	www.easternmarket.com
Grand Rapids	WM Farm Link	www.wmfarmlink.com
Kalamazoo	KVCC FIC Food Hub	www.kvcc.edu/healthyliving
Lansing	Allen Market Place	www.allenmarketplace.org
Marquette	Upper Peninsula Food	www.upfoodexchange.com
Pontiac	Harvest Michigan	www.HarvestMichigan.com
Traverse City	Cherry Capital Foods	www.cherrycapitalfoods.com

COMMUNITY SUPPORTED AGRICULTURE (CSA) PROGRAMS

Apple Valley	Pahl Farms	www.pahls.com
Big Lake	Brown Family Farm, LLC	www.brownfamilyproduce.com
Big Lake	Culinary Delights Farm	www.culinarydelightsfarm.com
Cambridge	Country Taste Farm	www.countrytastefarm.com
Duluth	Uncle Herman's Farm	www.unclehermansfarm.com
Ellendale	Hilltop Greenhouse Farm	www.hilltopgreenhouse.com
Felton	Kragnes Family Farms CSA	www.kragnesfamilyfarms.com
Finland	Round River Farm CSA	www.round-river.com
Foreston	Salad Days at Webster Farm	www.websterfarmorganic.com
Hastings	Fresh Earth Farms	www.freshearthfarms.com
Iron	Owl Forest Farm	www.owlforestfarm.com
Kasota	Cedar Crate Farm	www.cedarcratefarm.com
Mankato	Minnesota Valley Action Council Food Hub	www.mnvac.org
Minneapolis	Growing Lots Urban Farm	www.growinglotsurbanfarm.com
Minneapolis	Shared Ground Farmers	www.sharedgroundcoop.com
Minnetrista	Gale Woods Farm	www.galewoodsfarm.org
Mountain Lake	Jubilee Fruits & Vegetables	www.jubilee.mtlake.org
Nerstrand	Simple Harvest Farm	www.simpleharvestfarm.com
North Branch	Frost Farms	www.frostfarmsmn.com
Northfield	Spring Wind Farm	www.springwind.org
Oakdale	Jon's Market Garden	www.jonsmarketgarden.yolasite.com
Pelican Rapids	Lida Farm	www.lidafarm.com
Pine City	Rolling Thunder Farms	www.RTFGreen.com
St. Paul	The HAFA CSA	www.hmongfarmers.com
St. Paul	Garden Fresh Farms	www.gardenfreshfarms.org
Stillwater	FruitShare.com	www.fruitshare.com
Waverly	Untiedt's Vegetable Farm	www.untiedtswegrowforyou.com
Wrenshall	Food Farm	www.foodfarm.us
Wrenshall	Stone's Throw Farm	www.stonesthrowfarm.com

ON-FARM MARKETS

Brainerd	Nelson-Shine Produce	www.nelsonshineproduce.com
Buffalo	Woods' Edge Apples	www.localharvest.org/woods-edge-apples-orchard
Chatfield	Ward Hilltop Farm	www.wardhilltopfarm.shutterfly.com
Deer River	Living Food Farm	www.livingfoodfarm.com
East Bethel	Minnesota Fresh Farm	www.minnesotafreshfarm.com
Faribault	Straight River Farm	www.straightriverfarm.com
Finland	Minnesota Syrup Co.	www.mnsyrup.com
Forest Lake	Covered Bridge Farm	www.coveredbridgefarm.net
Frazee	Maple Hills Orchard,	www.maplehillsorchard.com
Grand Rapids	Blueberry Meadows	www.blueberrymeadows.com
Grey Eagle	Cornerstone Pines	www.cornerstonepineschristmastrees.com

Hastings	Fischers Croix Farm Orchard	www.fischerscroixfarmorchard.com
Hastings	Sam Kedem Nursery	www.kedemgarden.com
Howard Lake	Crow River Nursery	www.crowrivernursery.com
Lake Shore	Jake and Scout's Berry Farm	www.jakeandscoutsberryfarm.com
Lamberton	Omega Maiden Oils	www.omegamaidenoils.com
Nerstrand	Simple Harvest Farm	www.simpleharvestfarm.com
Northfield	Fireside Orchard	www.firesideorchard.com
Northfield	Little Hill Berry Farm	www.littlehillberryfarm.com
Pequot Lakes	Brambleberry Farm	www.brambleberryfruitfarm.com
Pine City	Peaceful Pines Farm	www.peacefulpinesfarm.com
Pine Island	Byrne Farm	www.byrnefarm.com
Pine River	Pine Winder Blueberry Farm	www.pinewinder.com
Pine River	Red Barn Orchard	www.redbarnorchard.com
Sunrise	Sunrise Sheep & Wool	www.sunrisesheep.com
Webster	Sweetland Orchard	www.sweetlandorchard.com

FOOD HUBS

Brainerd & Little Falls	Sprout MN	www.sproutmn.com
Falcon Heights	The Good Acre	www.thegoodacre.org
Fergus Falls	Fresh Connect Food Hub	www.lcsc.org/freshconnect
St. Paul	Shared Ground Farmers	www.sharedgroundcoop.com

MISSISSIPPI

Community Supported Agriculture (CSA) Programs

Ashland	Tubby Creek Farm	www.tubbycreekfarm.com
Dennis	Happy Trails Flower Farm	www.happytrailsflowerfarm.com
Lucedale	Sweet Grass Pastures	www.sweetgrasspastures.com
Saucier	Farmer Browns Southern Farm	www.farmerbrownssouthernfarmcsa.com
Starkville	Bountiful Harvest Farms	www.bountifulharvestfarms.com

On-Farm Markets

Dumas	Hays Berry Farms	www.haysberryfarms.com
Lena	Reyer Farms	www.reyerfarms.com
Macon	New Grass Farms	www.newgrassfarms.com

Food Hubs

Hernando	4Rivers Fresh Foods	www.4RiversFoods.com
Jackson	Up in Farms Food Hub	www.upinfarms.com
Ocean Springs	Ocean Springs Fresh Market	www.oceanspringsfreshmarket.com

MISSOURI

AGRIHOODS

Farmers Park   Rental Community
Springfield
www.farmersparkspringfield.com

Farmers Park is a mixed-use, connective-space community that blends Queen City retail, business, art, green space, and luxury living into a single, vibrant hub. Farmers Park is an open-air neighborhood that incorporates local food, community gardens, micro-orchards, low water irrigation systems and drought-resistant vegetation, white membrane roofing, walkable and bikeable trails. The park installed 120 solar panels that provide approximately 42,000 kilowatt hours of renewable electricity annually, or a carbon footprint reduction equivalent to planting 771 trees. There are 58 rental apartments that are EPA energy star rated, and designed for natural lighting. The site includes 13 community garden beds and three miles of greenway walking trails. Residents can shop for fresh produce and other farm-fresh foods at the nearby Farmers Market of the Ozarks, representing small local farmers.

COMMUNITY SUPPORTED AGRICULTURE (CSA) PROGRAMS

Augusta	Sunflower Hill Farm	www.sunflowerhillfarm.com
Boonville	Fed from the Farm	www.fedfromthefarm.com
Bowling Green	Organian's Bounty	www.organiansbounty.com
Cape Girardeau	Laughing Stalk Farmstead	www.laughingstalk.com
Centerview	Corn Acres	www.cornacres.com
Centralia	Sunnydale Farms	www.sunnydalefarmbox.com
Eolia	Hart Beet Farm	www.hartbeetfarm.com
Fort Leonard Wood	FLW Fresh CSA	www.flwfarmersmarket.com
Granby	Oakwoods Farm	www.oakwoodsfarm.com
Jamestown	Happy Hollow Farm	www.happyhollowfarm-mo.com
Nelson	Bacon Acres Ranch	www.baconacresranch.com
Spanish Lake	Seeds of Hope Farm	www.seedsofhopefarm.org
Springfield	Millsap Farm	www.millsapfarms.com
Springfield	Urban Roots Farm	www.UrbanRootsFarm.com

ON-FARM MARKETS

Ashland	Blue Fox Farm	www.bluefoxfood.com
Augusta	Centennial	www.centennialfarms.biz
Boonville	Fed from The Farm	www.fedfromthefarm.com
Brashear	Lost Branch Blueberry Farm	www.lostbranchblueberries.com
Camdenton	Canyon Goat Company, Inc.	www.canyongoat.comindex.html
Dittmer	Stone-Leady Farms	www.stoneleadyfarms.com
Eolia	Thistle Hill Plantation	www.thistlehillplantation.com
Forsyth	Beyond Eden	www.vintagepoultry.com
Granby	OakWoods Farm	www.oakwoodsfarm.com
Gray Summit	Seven Gables Farm	www.sevengablesfarm.com
Hartville	Greenhill Vineyard	www.greenhillgrapes.com
Hermann	Schneider Farms	www.schneiderfarms.com

150

Hermann	Wil farm	www.wilfarm.org
Jefferson City	Lage Farms	www.lagefarms.com
Koshkonong	Missouri's Best Beef Co-Op	www.mobest beef.com
Lampe	Heritage Farm and Ranch	www.heritageranch.com
Leasburg	Ozark Berry Farm	www.Ozarkberryfarm.com
Lonedell	Hart Apiaries	www.hartapiaries.com
Louisiana	Lil' Sprouts Farm	www.EarthSprouts.com
Napoleon	Play Haven Farm	www.playhavenfarm.com
New Melle	Wind Ridge Farm	Www.windridgefarm.net
Rolla	The Blue Hill Company	www.thebluehio.com
Salem	Meramec Bison Farm	www.meramecbison.com
Seymour	Rachel's Goat & Chicken Farm	www.rachelsgoatfarm.com
Spickard	Homestead Hill Farm	www.homesteadhillfarming.com
St. Charles	Benne's Best Meat	www.bennesbest.com
St. Charles	Hermans Farm Orchard	www.hermansfarmorchard.com
Sullivan	Northern Prairie Alpacas	www.northernprairiealpacas.com
West Plains	Jolliff Farm	www.jollifffarm.wordpress.com
West Plains	Lucky Falling Star Ranch	www.luckyfallingstarranch.com
West Plains	Peace Valley Poultry	www.freshchickenandturkey.com
Wright City	Palme Acres Farms	www.palmeacres.com

FOOD HUBS

Kansas City	Kansas City Food Hub	www.thekcfoodhub.com
Warrenton	Farmer Girl Grassfed Meats	www.farmergirlmeats.com

MONTANA

AGRIHOODS

Orchard Gardens
Rental Community

Missoula
www.orchardgardens.tamarackpm.com

Orchard Gardens is a sustainable community situated on 4.6 acres near the urban-rural fringe of Missoula's western side, an area still deeply rooted in agricultural traditions. There are 35 affordable rental units that include all utilities, patio or balcony, appliances, air conditioners, laundry facilities, parking spaces, and storage areas for every tenant. Orchard Gardens is close to public transportation, shopping and medical facilities, and has wheelchair access. The site includes a community barn, playground, and offers garden plot rentals for its residents. A bike trail connects Orchard Gardens with the central Missoula valley and its services. Community Gardens sponsors farmers' markets and community events.

COMMUNITY SUPPORTED AGRICULTURE (CSA) PROGRAMS

Arlee	Harlequin Produce	www.harlequinorganicproduce.com
Belgrade	Kokoro Flowers	www.kokoroflowers.com
Belgrade	SpringHill Organic Farms	www.springhill-organic farms.appspot.com
Belgrade	Amaltheia Organic Dairy	www.amaltheiadairy.com
Belgrade	Serenity Sheep Farm Stay	www.serenitysheepfarmstay.com
Billings	Kate's Garden	www.scentsofbalance.com
Bozeman	Gallatin Valley Botanical	www.gallatinvalleybotanical.com
Bozeman	Running Strike Farms	www.runningstrikefarms.com
Bozeman	Foxglove Flower Farm	www.foxgloveflowerfarm.com
Bozeman	Three Hearts Farm	www.threeheartsfarm.com
Cascade	Bird Creek Ranch	www.birdcreekranch.com
Fort Shaw	Groundworks Farm	www.groundworksfarmmt.com
Melstone	Kyhl Farms	www.kyhlfarms.com
Missoula	Western Montana Growers Co-op	www.wmgcoop.com/csa
Stevensville	KT-Farms	www.ktfarms.com

ON-FARM MARKETS

Baker	Starvation Flats Boer Goats	www.starvationflatsboergoats.com
Bozeman	Northern Rocky Mountain Alpacas	www.NRMAlpacas.com
Eureka	Cranky Carl's Farm	www.wwww.crankycarlsfarm.com
Joliet	Carbonado Farm	www.mtlamb.com
Kalispell	Going to the Sun Fiber Mill	www.gttsfibermill.com
Kalispell	Cherry Creek Gardens & Farms	www.cherrycreekgardens.com
Melstone	Kyhl Farms	www.kyhlfarms.com

FOOD HUBS

Missoula	Western Montana Growers	www.wmgcoop.com
Polson	Montana Co-op	www.montanacoop.com

NEBRASKA

AGRIHOODS

Garden View
Lincoln
www.gardenviewcommunity.com

Garden View is a 62.5-acre community of single-family homes. The site includes a farm, orchard, and community gardens. Storefronts are built to blend naturally into the landscape. Garden View is a neighborhood designed with nature in mind, with carefully tended green space, beautiful paths, community gardens, water features, and abundant natural landscapes that highlight the beauty of southeast Nebraska. Garden View is also a community designed to live in harmony with nature. Sustainable practices in lawn care and water management are made a priority, and shared composting areas and proximity to farming facilities blend the traditions of rural Nebraska with the modern amenities of urban life.

COMMUNITY SUPPORTED AGRICULTURE (CSA) PROGRAMS

Colon	Terrapin Acres	www.terrapinacresne.com
Columbus	Country Lane Gardens	www.countrylanegardens.org
Firth	Bright Hope Family Farm	www.brighthopefamilyfarm.locallinesites.com
Norfolk	Wolff Farms Produce	www.wolfffarmsproduce.com
Omaha	Fork N Farm	www.forknfarm.com
Omaha	Tomato Tomato	www.tomatotomato.org
Plymouth	West End Farm	www.westendfarm.ne.com
Randolph	Pfanny's Farm	www.pfannysfarm.com
Raymond	Common Good Farm	www.commongoodfarm.com
Schuyler	Theilen Produce Gardens	www.theilenproduce.com
Scottsbluff	Meadowlark Hearth	www.meadowlarkhearth.org

ON-FARM MARKETS

Avoca	Bloom Where You're Planted	www.BloomPumpkinPatch.com
Ceresco	Darby Springs Farm	www.darbysprings.wordpress.com
Columbus	Country Lane Gardens	www.countrylanegardens.org
Omaha	Sun Natural Open Air Market	www.sunnatural.org
Unadilla	Chisholm Family Orchard	www.chisholmfamilyfarm.com

FOOD HUBS

Omaha	Nebraska Food Cooperative	www.nebraskafood.org
Omaha	No More Empty Pots	www.nmepomaha.org

NEVADA

AGRIHOODS

Carson Valley
Douglas County

Douglas County has multiple projects under consideration, including the development of agrihoods in Carson Valley. An Agrihood Interest Group was formed in 2019 by the county's Economic Vitality Division. Plans would include lifestyle residential developments that leave a large portion of open space for agricultural or ranch use.

Farmstead at Corley Ranch
Over 55 Community
Gardnerville
www.farmsteadatcorleyranch.com

The Farmstead at Corley Ranch is a farm-to-table, master-planned community set on the historic Corley Ranch in Douglas County, Nevada. The Farmstead clusters eco-friendly artisan studios, commercial space, and cottage and ranch homes around a community garden, greenhouse, orchard, and iconic barn. Designed for active adults 55 and older, residents can live, work, shop, and grow their own food. Utilizing the Farmstead's farm, greenhouse, and orchard, an expert cultivator will masterfully plan and grow seasonal harvests for residents and the community. The Farmstead at Corley Ranch has capped the number of units to 250, and housing options include the craftsman/bungalow architectural style, artisan studios, cottages, and ranch homes.

COMMUNITY SUPPORTED AGRICULTURE (CSA) PROGRAMS

Dayton	Nancy's Green Barn Farm	www.nancysgreenbarnfarm.com
Dayton	Holley Family Farms	www.holleyfamilyfarms.com
Fallon	Workman Farms	www.workmanfarmsproduce.com
Las Vegas	Trish and Ed's Organics at Etheridge Farms	www.trishandedsorganics.com
Moapa	Meadow Valley Farm	www.meadowvalleycsa.com
Overton	Quail Hollow Farm	www.quailhollowfarmcsa.com

ON-FARM MARKETS

Las Vegas	Cowboy Trail Farm	www.cowboytrailfarms.com
Las Vegas	Gilcrease Orchard	www.thegilcreaseorchard.org
Stagecoach	Iron Mountain Nursery & Farm	www.imnandf.com

FOOD HUBS

Fallon	Fallon Food Hub	www.fallonfoodhub.com

AGRIHOODS

The Village at Stone Barn
Peterborough
www.conducivelife.com/projects

The Village at Stone Barn is the nation's first "regenerative agrihood," located in historic Peterborough, NH. The Village at Stone Barn sits on a 32-acre hillside near Mount Monadnock, with walking trails, wetlands, yoga space, farm-to-table café, and working farm, surrounded by orchards, berry patches, vegetable and flower gardens, and small livestock. The Village at Stone Barn grows food that is "beyond organic," building healthy ecosystems to improve the nutrition in the crops, while reversing climate change by using practices that actually draw down CO_2 and improve water and nutrient cycling in the natural landscape. All condominiums are solar-powered and designed to maximize natural light and air circulation.

COMMUNITY SUPPORTED AGRICULTURE (CSA) PROGRAMS

Brentwood	Willow Pond Community Farm	www.willowpondfarm.org
Canterbury	Brookford Farm CSA	www.brookfordfarm.com
Charlestown	Hemingway Farms	www.hemingwayfarms.com
Chesterfield	Mad Radish CSA	www.madradishcsa.com
Concord	Lewis Farm & Greenhouses	www.lewisfarmnh.com
Concord	Local Harvest CSA	www.localharvestnh.com
Dublin	Farmer John's Plot	www.farmerjohnsplot.org
Fitzwilliam	Tracie's Community Farm	www.traciesfarm.com
Gilford	Beans and Greens Farm	www.beansandgreensfarm.com
Litchfield	Steve Normanton	www.stevenormanton.com
Peterborough	Walkabout Farm	www.walkaboutfarm.org
Stratham	Orange Circle Farm LLC	www.orangecirclefarm.com
Wilton	Bee Fields Farm	www.beefieldsfarm.com
Wilton	Hungry Bear Farm	www.hungrybearfarm.com
Wilton	Ledge Top Farm LLC	www.ledgetopfarm.com
Winchester	Picadilly Farm CSA	www.picadillyfarm.com

ON-FARM MARKETS

Bradford	Cornucopia Farm	www.cornucopiafarmnh.com
Bradford	Elior Acres	www.EliorAcres.com
Canterbury	Running Fox Farm	www.runningfoxfarmnh.com
Charlestown	Hemingway Farms	www.hemingwayfarms.com
Concord	Rossview Farm	www.rossviewfarm.com
Danbury	Huntoon Farm	www.huntoonfarm.com
Dublin	Farmer John's Plot	www.farmerjohnsplot.org
East Kingston	Windcrest Tree Farm	www.windcrestfarm.info
Eaton	Berry Knoll	www.BerryKnoll.com

Farmington	Butternut Farm	www.Butternutfarm.net
Fitzwilliam	Tracie's Community Farm	www.traciesfarm.com
Francestown	Rocky Meadow Farm	www.rockymeadowfarm.com
Hopkinton	Gould Hill Farm	www.gouldhillfarm.com
Jackson	Windy Hill Natural Beef	www.windyhillbandb.com
Lee	Demeritt Hill Farm	www.demeritthillfarm.com
Litchfield	Wilson Farm	www.wilsonfarm.com
Lyndeborough	Paradise Farm	www.Paradisefarmnh.com
Marlborough	Gap Mountain Goats	www.GapMountainGoats.com
Meredith	Arbutus Hill Farm	www.ladyfarmer.com
Milan	Six Acre Farm	www.sixacrefarm.com
Sanbornton	Broadview Farm	www.broadviewfarm.com
Stewartstown	Apple Haven Farm	www.applehavenfarm.com
Tamworth	Remick Country Doctor Museum	www.remickmuseum.org
Walpole	Walpole Valley Farms	www.walpolevalleyfarms.com

FOOD HUBS

Colebrook	North Country Farmers Coop.	www.ncfcoop.com

AGRIHOODS

Pendry Natirar Residences
Peapack
www.pendryresidencesnatirar.com

Pendry Natirar is a residential resort on 500 wooded acres in Somerset County, New Jersey, one hour west of New York City. Natirar originated in 1912, and today 400 acres is conserved by the county surrounding Pendry Natirar's 90-acre domain, with trails for hiking, biking, and horseback riding. The 100-year-old restored Tudor-style mansion includes a restaurant, cooking school, Spa Pendry, farm, and private club. Residents can enjoy turnkey living with personalized residential services and property management. The 12-acre Natirar Farm sustainably grows the produce served in Pendry Natirar's dining establishments. Pendry Residences will be comprised of up to 24 Estate Villas and Farm Villas. The aesthetic and design boast natural wood and stone finishes, handcrafted millwork, spacious balconies and outdoor living, full kitchens, high ceilings, gas fireplaces, and contemporary design and functionality.

Urby
Harrison
www.urby.com/harrison

Rental Community

Urby is a 409-unit rental community in Harrison, located near the PATH train, enabling a 20-minute commute to Manhattan. Apartments are light-filled, open floor plans with ceiling-high windows. Apartments feature keyless entry, bamboo floors, huge windows, and built-in closets. The complex includes community garden plots for residents. Expansive outdoor green spaces are connected by strolling paths, heated saltwater pool and patio, outdoor lounges, fire pits, bocce ball, and ping pong. Indoor features include a woof garden, a 30-foot "treehouse" library, the Urby Blues recording studio with resident musician, a communal kitchen, and a two-story fitness center. Urby Kitchen is the collective kitchen for classes and events around food, and the Coperaco Café serves residents seven days a week, operating as Le Bar in the evening with live music. Urby's culture committee hosts monthly tastings and events. Urby Harrison is one of four NY-area developments designed and built by the Dutch firm, Concrete, and one of two that include an on-site farming facility.
(See Urby, Staten Island, New York, in this resource directory.)

COMMUNITY SUPPORTED AGRICULTURE (CSA) PROGRAMS

Blairstown	Genesis Farm	www.csgatgenesisfarm.com
Chester	Highlands Harvest Club	www.alstedefarms.com
Far Hills	Uncle Bill's Farm	www.unclebillsfarm.org
Hopewell	Ralston Farm	www.ralstonfarm.com
Lawrenceville	Z Food Farm	www.zfoodfarm.com
Manalapan	Silver Forge Farm	www.silverforgefarm.com
New Brunswick	Rutgers Gardens Student Farm CSA	www.agriurban.rutgers.edu/StudentSustainableFarm.html
Newark	Greater Newark Conservancy	www.citybloom.org

Pennington	Chickadee Creek Farm	www.chickadeecreekfarm.com
Pennington	Honey Brook Organic Farm	www.honeybrookorganicfarm.com
Raritan	Hand Picked Farm CSA	www.handpickedfarm.com
Stockton	Sandbrook Meadow Farm	www.sandbrookmeadowfarm.com
Warren	Windsong Farm	www.windsongorganicfarm.com

ON-FARM MARKETS

Elk Township	The McCanns Farm	www.themccannsfarm.com
Flemington	Burjans Pumpkin Festival	www.burjansfarm.com
Forked River	Argos Farm	www.argosfarm.com
Glen Gardner	Grochowicz Farm Market	www.grofarms.com
Hammonton	DiMeo Farms & Blueberry	www.DiMeoFarms.com
Hampton	Dancing Waters Farm	www.mohair-fiber.com
Lafayette	C & R Perfect Pick Farm	www.perfectpickfarm.com
Lawrenceville	Cherry Grove Farm	www.cherrygrovefarm.com
Manahawkin	Beach View Farms	www.beachviewfarms.com
Manalapan	Happy Day Farm	www.happydayfarmnj.com
Milford	Bobolink Dairy	www.cowsoutside. com
Monmouth Junct.	Von Thuns Country Farm Market	www.vonthunfarms.com
Monroeville	Hayniczs Orchardview Farm	www.hayniczorchardviewfarm.com
Moorestown	Little Hooves Romneys	www.LittleHoovesRomneys.com
Morristown	Grow It Green Morristown	www.growitgreenmorristown.org
Mullica Hill	Hill Creek Farms	www.Hireekfarms.com
Newark	Greater Newark Conservancy	www.citybloom.org
Newton	Brodhecker Farm	www.brodheckerfarms.com
Newton	Windy Brow Farms	www.windybrowfarms.com
Pennington	Blue Moon Acres Cert. Organic	www.bluemoonacres.com
Phillipsburg	Perfect Christmas Tree Farm	www.perfectchristmastree.com
Plumsted	My Poppy's Alpacas	www.mypoppysalpacas.com
Robbinsville	Oasis Family Farm	www.oasisfamilyfarm.com
Vernon	Mount Vernon Farms	www.njtreefarmer.com

Agrihoods

Mesilla Vineyards Estates
La Cruces
www.mesillavineyardestates.com

Mesilla Vineyards Estates offers ready-to-build, one-acre residential lots located within the boundaries of La Mancha Subdivision and approved for City of Las Cruces water, Zia Natural Gas, and individual septic tanks. Bordered by vineyards, Mesilla Vineyards Estates is located in the heart of Mesilla Valley, close to historic Old Mesilla and the Rio Grande, with incredible views of the Organ Mountain range. Mesilla Vineyards Estates features a 14-acre working farm managed by a professional horticulturist. Residents of Mesilla Vineyards Estates will enjoy the beauty of a farm having access to freshly grown produce. The farm will provide a relaxing environment for walks, and will feature a community gazebo for private use.

Community Supported Agriculture (CSA) Programs

Albuquerque	Red Tractor Farm	www.redtractorfarm.net
Albuquerque	Abundia Farms	www.abundiafarms.weebly.com
Albuquerque	Skarsgard Farms	www.skarsgardfarms.com
Albuquerque	Old Town Farm	www.oldtownfarm.com
Cerro	Cerro Vista Farm CSA	www.cerrovistafarm.com
Fallon	NanaDewHarb Farm	www.NanaDewHerbFarm.com
Moriarty	Schwebach Farm	www.schwebacharm.com
Pecos	Molino de la Isla Organics LLC	www.molinodelaisla.com
Santa Fe	Beneficial Farms	www.beneficialfarm.com
Tijeras	East Mountain Organic Farms	www.eastmountainorganicfarms.com
Williamsburg	Las Palomas Heirloom Farms	www.palomasfarm.com

On-Farm Markets

Clovis	Windrush Alpacas	www.windrushalpacas.com
Corrales	Wagner Farms	www.wagnerfarmscorrales.com
Espanola	J&L Gardens	www.jandlgardens.com
Magdalena	Dunhill Ranch	www.dunhillranch.com

Food Hubs

Las Cruces	True Food	www.elpasotruefood.com

NEW YORK

AGRIHOODS

Arbor House
Affordable Rental Community

Bronx
www.centerforactivedesign.org/arbor-house

Arbor House is an eco-friendly and health-promoting residential building in the South Bronx. The 120,000-square-foot building provides 124 units of affordable housing for families earning 60% of the area medium income. Twenty-five percent of the units give preference to New York City Housing Authority (NYCHA) residents and those on NYCHA's waitlist. Arbor House incorporates a variety of active design strategies to promote healthy lifestyles, with accessible indoor and outdoor fitness areas. Located on the roof is a 10,000-square-foot hydroponic farm that functions as a community supported agriculture (CSA) arrangement where Arbor House residents can purchase shares of healthy food produced by the farm. About 40% of the produce is made available to the local community schools, hospitals, and markets. Arbor House serves as a national model for healthy affordable housing and was developed by Les Bluestone and team at Blue Sea Development.

Urby
Rental Community

Staten Island
www.www.urby.com/staten-island

Urby sits on the North Shore waterfront, offering a 5,000-square-foot urban farm (with a farmer-in-residence), a communal gourmet kitchen (with chef-in-residence), and a rooftop apiary. There are 570 rental units in three distinct housing blocks and another 430 units planned. Studio, one-, and two-bedroom apartments are light-filled, and feature open layouts and ceiling-high windows for sweeping views of lower Manhattan and the harbor. Urby is located in the Stapleton neighborhood, overlooking downtown Manhattan and two train stops from the Staten Island Ferry. Residents enjoy a double-decker gym and many common spaces including the Urby Kitchen, an all-day café, and restaurants such as Coperaco. The apartment building hosts gourmet cooking classes, chef tastings, and empanada and sushi making. Urby Staten Island is one of four NY-area developments designed and built by the Dutch firm, Concrete, and one of two that include an on-site farm.

(See Urby, Harrison, New Jersey, in this resource directory.)

URBAN AG

Stonebarns Center – Farming Education, public/school tours, events.
www.stonebarnscenter.org

Brooklyn Grange, Brooklyn Navy Yard – 3 rooftop farms spanning 5.6 acres; store; CSA, education; consulting. www.brooklyngrangefarm.com

COMMUNITY SUPPORTED AGRICULTURE (CSA) PROGRAMS

Bergen	Northwoods Alpacas	www.NorthwoodsAlpacas.com
Brewster	SPACE on Ryder Farm	www.spaceonryderfarm.org
Brookhaven	HOG Farm	www.hamletorganicgarden.org
Brooklyn	Prospect Lefferts Gardens	www.plgcsa.org
Brooklyn	Brooklyn Grange	www.brooklyngrangefarm.com
Brooktondale	Nook & Cranny Farm	www.nookandcrannyfarm.com

Cato	1860 Organics	www.1860organics.com
Chester	Peace and Carrots Farm	www.peaceandcarrotsfarm.com
Claryville	Neversink Farm	www.neversinkfarm.com
Cold Spring	Glynwood CSA	www.glynwood.org
Collins	Choose Your Own Basket	www.creeksideproduce.com
Deposit	Catskill Cattle Co.	www.catskillfresh.com
Earlton	Hiddenview Farm	www.hiddenviewfarmNY.com
Elba	Sinemus Farms	www.sinemusfarms.com
Erieville	Dizzy Lizzie's Farm	www.dizzylizziesfarm.com
Fenner	Hartwood Farm	www.hartwoodfarm.com
Forestville	Hanova Hills Farm Lake Cty.	www.lakecountrybeef.com
Gasport	Becker Farms CSA	www.beckerfarms.csaware.com
Germantown	Hearty Roots Community Farm	www.heartyroots.com
Ghent	Common Hands Farm	www.commonhandscsa.com
Ghent	Hawthorne Valley Farm	www.hawthornevalleyfarm.org
Goshen	J&A Farm	www.jafarm.org
Groton	Buried Treasures Organic Farm	www.buriedtreasuresorganicfarm.com
Herkimer	Jones Family Farm	www.anotherjonesfamilyfarm.com
Highland	Healthway Farms	www.healthwayfarms.com
Honeoye Falls	Bubbaloo Farm	www.bubbaloofarm.com
Hopewell Junction	Fishkill Farms	www.fishkillfarms.com
Keeseville	Fledging Crow Vegetables	www.fledgingcrow.com
Kinderhook	Katchie Farm	www.katchiefarm.com
Kingston	Solid Ground Farm	www.solidground.farm
Lee Center	Iron Hoof Farm	www.ironhooffarm.com
Livingston Manor	Root 'N Roost Farm	www.rootnroost.com
Livonia	Fire Creek Farms	www.thefirecreekfarms.com
Lockport	McCollum Orchards	www.oldfarmnewlife.com
Mattituck	Browder's Birds	www.browdersbirds.com
New Hampton	Bialas Farms	www.bialasfarms.com
New Lebanon	Abode Farm CSA	www.abodefarmcsa.com
New Paltz	Huguenot St Farm	www.Huguenotfarm.com
New York	Fulton Stall Market CSA	www.fultonstallmarket.org
New York	Prince George-Norwich CSA	www.princegeorgecsa.com
Ovid	Crosswinds Farm & Creamery	www.crosswindsfarmcreamery.com
Ovid	Daring Drake Farm	www.daringdrake.com
Pine Plains	Full Circus Farm	www.fullcircusfarm.wordpress.com
Poughkeepsie	Poughkeepsie Farm Project	www.farmproject.org
Pulaski	Freedom Rains Farm	www.freedomrainsfarm.com
Riverhead	Garden of Eve Organic Farm	www.GardenofEveFarm.com
Rock Stream	Ever Green Farm	www.evergreenfarmonline.com
Saranac	Woven Meadows	www.wovenmeadows.com
Schaghticoke	Denison Farm	www.denisonfarm.com
Schenectady	Lansing Farm Market	www.lansingfarmmarket.com
Schoharie	Fox Creek Farm	www.foxcreekfarmcsa.com
Schuylerville	9 Miles East Farm	www.9mileseast.com
Shortsville	Pachamama Farm CSA	www.PachamamaFarmNY.com

South Cairo	Stoneledge Farm	www.stoneledge.farm
Southampton	Quail Hill Farm/Peconic Trust	www.peconiclandtrust.org
Stuyvesant	Fatstock Farm	www.fatstockfarm.com
Troy	Edible Uprising Farm	www.edibleuprisingfarm.com
Trumansburg	Plowbreak Farm	www.plowbreakfarm.com
Victor	Mud Creek Farm CSA	www.mudcreekfarm.com
Voorheesville	Patroon Land Farm	www.regionalfoodbank.net
Walton	East Brook Farm CSA	www.eastbrookfarm.com
Walworth	G and S Orchards CSA	www.gandsorchards.com
Yorktown Heights	Hilltop Hanover Farm & Environmental Center	www.hilltophanoverfarm.org

ON-FARM MARKETS

Baldwinsville	Abbott Farms	www.abbottfarms.com
Baldwinsville	Reeves Farms	www.reevesfarms.com
Ballston Spa	Dakota Ridge Farm	www.dakotaridgefarm.com
Brooktondale	Shelterbelt Farm	www.shelterbeltfarm.com
Canton	Annie's Garlic	www.anniesgarlic.com
Cazenovia	Critz Farms	www.critzfarms.com
Collins	Creekside Market	www.creeksideproduce.com
Cortland	Halls Hill Blueberry Farm	www.hallshillblueberryfarm.com
Deposit	Catskill Fresh Farmstand	www.catskillfresh.com
East Hampton	Food Pantry Farm	www.foodpantryfarm.org
East Meadow	East Meadow Farm	www.ccenassau.org
Erin	Stoneyridge Orchard	www.stoneyridgeorchard.com
Fort Edward	Hidden Nest Farm	www.hiddennestfarm.com
Frankfort	Windecker's Grassy Knoll	www.windeckerfarm.com
Fultonviille	Bellinger's Orchard	www.bellingersorchard.com
Gardiner	Full Moon Farm	www.fullmoonfarmny.com
Gasport	Librock Beef	www.librockbeef.com
Ghent	Hawthorne Valley Farm	www.hawthornevalleyfarm.org
Ghent	Made in Ghent	www.madeinghent.com
Hamden	The Lucky Dog Farm Store	www.luckydogorganic.com
Hollowville	Scarecrow Farm	www.scarecrowfarmny.com
Jamesville	Rocking Horse Farm	www.rockinghorsefarmcny.com
Jefferson	Cowbella at Danforth Farm	www.cowbella.com
Keene Valley	Rivermede Farm Market	www.rivermedefarm.com
Kingston	Kingston YMCA Farm	www.kingstonymcafarmproject.org
Lowville	Herrdale Acres Beef	www.herrdaleacres.com
Marcy	Candellas Farm	www.candellasfarm.com
Martville	Happy Hooves Farm	www.betterbeef4u.com
Medina	Teasel Meadow Farms	www.teaselmeadowfarms.com
Memphis	Gillie Brook Farm	www.gilliefarms.com
Millbrook	Walbridge Farm Market	www.walbridgefarm.com
Millerton	Dashing Star Farm	www.dashingstarfarm.com
New Paltz	Dressel Farms	www.dresselfarms.com
Newark	The Apple Shed	www.theappleshed.com
Newport	MAWS Farm	www.MAWSFarm.com

Oswego	Ontario Orchards	www.ontarioorchards.com
Pomona	The Orchards of Concklin	www.theorchardsofconcklin.com
Poughkeepsie	Sprout Creek Farm	www.sproutcreekfarm.org
Remsen	Heywoods Blueberries	www.heywoodsblueberries.com
Rochester	Brighton Honey	www.BrightonHoney.com
Scottsville	Stokoe Farms	www.stokoefarms.com
Sherburne	Cook's Maple Products	www.cooksmaple.com
Syracuse	Navarino Orchard	www.navarinoorchard.com
Ulster Park	Apple Bin Farm Market	www.theapplebinfarmmarket.com
Waddington	Harmony Farm Apiary	www.harmonyfarm.net
Walworth	G and S Orchards	www.gandsorchards.com
Warwick	Lowland Farm	www.lowlandfarm.com
West Charlton	Arnold's Farm	www.arnoldsproduce.com
Yorktown Heights	Hilltop Hanover Farm	www.hilltophanoverfarm.org
Yorktown Heights	The Meadows Farm	www.Meadowsfarmmarket.com

Food Hubs

Athens	Field Goods	www.field-goods.com
Bronx	Farm Fresh	www.farmfreshny.com
Brooklyn	Happy Valley Meat	www.happyvalleymeat.com
Delhi	Delaware Bounty	www.delawarebounty.com
Essex	The Hub on the Hill	www.thehubonthehill.org
Hamden	Lucky Dog Local Food Hub	www.luckydogorganic.com
Liberty	Catskills Food Hub	www.catskillsfoodhub.org
Oceanside	Schare & Associates	www.juicedeals.com
Rochester	Foodlink Food Hub	www.foodlinkny.org
Rochester	Headwater Foods, Inc	www.thegoodfoodcollective.com
Schoharie	Corbin Hill Food Project	www.corbinhillfoodproject.org
Syracuse	Farmshed Harvest Food	www.farmshedharvest.com

NORTH CAROLINA

AGRIHOODS

Balsam Mountain Preserve
Sylva
www.balsammountainpreserve.com

Own or Cabin Fractional Program

Set on 3,000 acres of preservation land under the stewardship of the Balsam Mountain Trust, the Nature Center serves as a community discovery center, with three full-time naturalists who manage the Birds of Prey program, and provide education to residents, their children and grandchildren. The 3,700-foot-high site includes an Arnold Palmer golf course, a practice park, mountain views, and wildlife, camping, dining, fitness, and wellness. Equestrian center has 34 miles of groomed trails, offers lessons, pony rides. Kids camp includes trout fishing and horseback riding. Groomed hiking trails created on 34 miles of former logging roads meandering to the Nantahala National Forest. Home styles include homesteads on 1-2 acres bordering conservation land, various styles of custom-built homes, including a model with a private crow's nest. Cottages in the heart of the community. Cabin fractional program provides full membership of amenities and two guaranteed weeks per season for eight years. Future plans include the Ruby City Farm to provide food and educational opportunities for owners.

Creekside Farm, at the Cliffs at Walnut Cove
Arden
www.www.creeksidefarmwc.com

Creekside Farm is a new neighborhood of 18 home sites situated along the Cliffs signature Jack Nicklaus Golf Course. Developed on a 100-year-old farm, residents can enjoy a 360-degree view of the golf course, the farm, pastures, and the beautiful Blue Ridge Mountains that surround Walnut Cove. Six acres have been set aside for a Community Supported Agriculture (CSA) program. Creekside Farm uses organic farming techniques, and the gardens are a mix of flowers, vegetables, and herbs. Beehives produce flavorful honey as well as pollinate the wide variety of flowers and crops on the farm. The livestock and free-range chickens play an important role in the life and ecosystem of the farm. The farm includes fruit orchards, a hops farm, and the Cliffs Tavern Restaurant. A repurposed red schoolhouse built in 1920 serves as the neighborhood hub, education center, and a place for farm

Olivette Riverside Community and Farm
Asheville
www.olivettenc.com

Olivette is a 346-acre planned community and historic farm, located along the French Broad River, just 6.7 miles from downtown Asheville. An agrihood community, Olivette is home to a vibrant vegetable, fruit, and flower farm. The community also provides seven acres of riverfront beach, a large private river island, several miles of walking trails, community-wide geothermal heating and cooling, community gardens, a pavilion and a fire-circle amphitheater, Little Free Libraries, a bike-sharing program, and fiber-to-home broadband internet access. The farm grows salad greens, specialty produce, flowers, and fruit and collects honey for local farmers' markets and restaurants, as well as CSA memberships to the Olivette and the Asheville community. Olivette Farm uses methods such as crop rotation, cover cropping, and thoughtful tillage, as well as a wide variety of both traditional and modern growing practices. The award-winning Riverside homes offer superior craftsmanship and exceptional energy efficiency in partnership with Christopher Fox Builders.

River Bluffs

Castle Hayne
www.riverbluffsliving.com

River Bluffs is a unique waterfront community of beautiful homes built among tall trees. The 313-acre community includes a working farm, CSA, and farmers' market. The 10-acre community farm utilizes sustainable growing methods. Community amenities include a pool, café, fitness center, walking trails, numerous parks, and a dog park. The beautiful Riverwalk is the longest, privately funded overwater river walk in the country, measuring in at 2,700 feet long. River Bluffs is situated along the scenic Cape Fear River, 10 minutes from downtown Wilmington. Water is a large part of the community's lifestyle, and the marina complex has an average water depth of 35', includes 188 boat slips, state-of-the-art floating docks, and two gazebos on the Riverwalk. The River Club provides a warm and inviting gathering space with a restaurant, lounge, widescreen TVs, and a large stone fireplace, with breathtaking riverfront views. River Bluffs offers a wide range of residential home designs, including quaint cottages, plantation-style and historically inspired homes, expansive water-view homes, and homes tailored to the active-adult lifestyle.

The Urban Farm at Aldersgate

Over-55 Community

Charlotte
www.urbanfarmataldersgate.org

Under development. The Urban Farm at Aldersgate spans 6.7 acres and will serve as a food source and learning lab for the eastside community and beyond. Designed by the Carolina Farm Trust and managed by a farmer, the farm will feature traditional farming beds, an aquaponics garden, mobile kitchen, beehives for pollination, and a hoop garden with culturally relevant produce for sale. It will have a farm stand year-round with seasonal produce grown on the farm and other products from local farms (within 100 miles). It is designed to be a hub of community engagement with entertainment, special events, and cooking demonstrations. The Urban Farm at Aldersgate will include a farmstand and CSA program. Aldersgate is a 231-acre nonprofit retirement care community with 450 residents founded in 1943 as the Methodist Home.

Wetrock Farm

Durham
www.wetrockfarm.com

Under development. Nestled in the pastoral foothills of North Carolina, the 230-acre solar-powered community will be the first net-zero, and the first agrihood in the vibrant Triangle area. Located 15 minutes north of Durham's downtown center, residents will enjoy 100+ acres of walking trails and natural open spaces. Wetrock Farm's 141 homes are LEED-certified. The Farmstead will operate all seasons using sustainable practices on 15 acres of active farming space, offering residents access to fresh, seasonal food grown in their neighborhood. Amenities include: weekly food share deliveries, sustainable farming practices, a full-time farm manager, heated year-round greenhouses, educational programs, partnerships with neighboring farms, rotating vegetable fields, heirloom-variety fruit tree orchards, vineyards of muscadine grapes, fields of blueberries, and pick-your-own strawberries. Fruit tree orchards will be beautifully landscaped with native perennials to accompany and complement the fruit trees. Hundreds of trees include peach, cherry, apple, pear, persimmons, pawpaw, and pecan.

Community Supported Agriculture (CSA) Programs

Burlington	Keck Farms CSA	www.keckfarms.com
Burnsville	Tractor Food and Farms	www.tractorfoodandfarms.com
Candor	Hope Farms	www.hopefarms.co
Charlotte	Small City Farm CSA	www.smallcityfarm.com
Concord	Cold Water Creek Farms	www.coldwatercreekfarms.com
Ellerbe	Sandhills Farm to Table	www.sandhillsfarm2table.com
Fairview	Cane Creek Asparagus	www.canecreekcsa.com
Fairview	Hickory Nut Gap Farm	www.hickorynutgapfarm.com
Kernersville	Seed 2 Seed	www.seed2seed.org
Marshall	Long Valley Eco-Biotic Farm CSA	www.localharvest.org/long-valley-eco-biotic-farm
Oxford	Healthy Hen Farms	www.healthyhenfarms.com
Raleigh	Rare Earth Farms	www.rareearthfarms.com
Staley	Heartstrong Farm	www.growheartstrong.com
Waxhaw	Poplar Ridge Farm	www.poplarridgefarmnc.com
Willow Spring	Hilltop Farms	www.hilltopfarms.org
Zionville	North Fork Farm	www.northforkfarmbeef.com

On-Farm Markets

Angier	Ronnie's Berry Farm	www.ronniesberryfarm.com
Albemarle	Muddy Boots Farms	www.muddybootsfarms.com
Angier	In Theory Farm	www.intheoryfarm.com/
Benson	Wood Family Farm	www.woodfamilyfarmnc.com
Burlington	Buttermilk Creek Farm	www.buttermilkcreek.net
Carthage	Karefree Produce	www.karefreeproduce.com
Cedar Grove	Captain John's Lamb	www.dorperscedargrovenc.com/
Charlotte	Scallys Natural Beef	www.scallysnaturalbeef.com
Chocowinity	Southside Farms	www.southsidefarms.com
Dunn	Twin Oaks Heritage Farm	www.graysonspremiumpork.com
Germanton	Buffalo Creek Farm	www.buffalocreekfarmandcreamery.com
Gibsonville	Blueberry Thrill Farm	www.blueberrythrillfarm.com
Gibsonville	Grove Winery	www.GroveWinery.com
Granite Falls	Johnny Wilson Farm	www.johnnywilsonfarm.com
Greensboro	Bernies Berries	www.BerniesBerries com
Hayesville	Walnut Hollow Ranch	www.walnuthollowranch.com
Hendersonville	Grandads apples	www.grandadsapples.com
Hendersonville	Justus Orchard	www.justusorchard.com
Hillsborough	Ramble Rill Farm	www.ramblerillfarm.com
Iron Station	Gilcrest Natural Far	www.gilcrestnc.com
Leland	Shelton Herb Farm	www.SheltonHerbFarmNC.com
Louisburg	Cypress Hall Farms	www.CypressHallFarms.com

Lowgap	Davis Boxwood & Daylily	www.davisdaylilynursery.com
Madison	Tucker's Farm and Nursery	www.tuckersfarmnc.com
Maple	Coinjock Creek Farms	www.coinjockcreek.com
Olin	Prevette Family Farm	www.prevettefamilyfarm.com
Pelham	Sleepy Goat Cheese	www.sleepygoatfarm.com
Pittsboro	Cohen Farm	www.cohenfarm.com
Raleigh	Inter-Faith Food Shuttle	www.foodshuttle.org
Red Springs	Hawkeye Farms	www.hawkeyeindianculturalcenter.com
Roanoke Rapids	Happy Acres Farm	www.happyacresfarm.net
Salisbury	Cauble Creek Vineyard	www.caublecreekvineyard.com
Selma	Creekside Farm	www.creeksidefarmberries.com
Sherrills Ford	Bird Brain Ostrich Ranch.	www.birdbrainranch.com
Stanley	Apple Orchard Farm	www.appleorchardfarmnc.com
Vale	Helms Christmas Trees	www.HelmsChristmasTreeFarm
Vale	Windy Wool Windings	www.saintsandstars.powweb.com
Whitsett	Foust Family Farms	www.FoustFamilyFarms.com
Willow Spring	Adams Vineyards	www.adamsvineyards.com
Winterville	Renston Garden Market	www.renstongardenmarket.com

FOOD HUBS

Beaufort	Walking Fish Cooperative	www.walking-fish.org
Bethel	CHE Community Food Hub	www.checfh.org
Boone	High Country Food Hub	www.highcountryfoodhub.org
Burgaw	Feast Down East Food Hub	www.feastdowneast.org
Burnsville	Tractor Food and Farms	www.tractorfoodandfarms.com
Charlotte	Freshlist	www.freshlist.com
Durham	Eastern Carolina Organics	www.easterncarolinaorganics.com
Raleigh	Foster-Caviness Food Hub	www.foster-caviness.com
Raleigh	The Produce Box	www.theproducebox.com
Salisbury	SEED Foundation of NC	www.SEEDFoundationNC.com
Warrenton	Working Landscapes	www.workinglandscapesnc.org
Wilmington	Down East Connect	www.downeastconnect.com

167

NORTH DAKOTA

COMMUNITY SUPPORTED AGRICULTURE (CSA) PROGRAMS

Bottineau	Bartlett Farms	www.bartlettfarms.us
Bottineau	Four Seasons CSA	www.4seasonscsa.tumblr.com
Buxton	Dundadun Acres	www.dundadunacres.com
Carpio	North Star Farms	www.northstarorganic.com
Carrington	Ostlie's Sunnyside Acres	www.ostlieacres.com
Fargo	Prairie Faith Homegrown	www.prairiefaith.webs.com
Grandin	Heart and Soil Farm	www.heartandsoilfarm.com
Mandan	Riverbound Farm	www.riverbound.com
New Salem	Lo-Green Acres	www.logreenacrescsa.blogspot.com
Ruso	Ruso Ranch	www.rusoranch.com
Streeter	Forager Farm	www.foragerfarm.com
Valley City	Llama Trax Gardens	www.llamatrax.com
West Fargo	Hildebrant Farm	www.hildebrantfarm.com

AGRIHOODS

Aberlin Spring
Morrow
www.aberlinsprings.com

Ohio's first agrihood, Aberlin Springs opened in late 2018 and was originally developed by the Aberlin family in the early 1990s. The community is set among acres of preserved forests and meadows where homes and hamlets are connected by looping country roads and a network of footpaths. Located in the heart of Warren County just 45 minutes from a major urban center, Aberlin Springs is a conservation community and the 141-acre site will house 140 homes clustered around common land. The Swiss-style timber frame chalet serves as the community clubhouse, with a fitness area and demonstration kitchen. The community market hosts farm and partner products, and a wellness center. The fishing pond is fully stocked for residents, community court-yard hosts gatherings, special events, and concerts. The farm includes over 100 chickens, a small herd of sheep, rabbits, goats, and a donkey. A wide variety of greens and microgreens are pro-duced at the greenhouse. Custom residential homes are offered, with a wide range of styles and sizes.

Elliott Farm
Loveland
www.dreeshomes.com

Under development. The 100-acre Elliott Farm will include 200 homes designed to reflect the com-munities of yesteryear. The community features community gardens, a historical barn that serves as a community center, paved walking trails, a fishing pond, and parks. Residents can garden on their own community garden plot. The Little Miami scenic bike trail is a mile away.

COMMUNITY SUPPORTED AGRICULTURE (CSA) PROGRAMS

Adamsville	Bush Valley Farm	www.bushvalleyfarm.com
Auburn	Sirna's Farm & Market	www.sirnasfarm.com
Beavercreek	Oasis Aqua Farm	www.oasisaquafarm.com
Centerburg	Granny B Farms	www.grannybfarm.com
Centerburg	Veggies and Eggs by Dan	www.veggiesandeggs.com
Cincinnati	Our Harvest Cooperative	www.ourharvest.coop
Cincinnati	Triple L Acres	www.triplelacres.com
Cincinnati	Turner Farm Inc.	www.turnerfarm.org
Cincinnati	Urban Greens	www.urbangreenscinci.com
Danville	Toad Hill Organic Farm	www.toadhill.tripod.com
Dayton	Patchwork Gardens	www.patchworkgardens.net
Eaton	Boulder Belt Farm Share Initiative	www.boulderbelt.com
Fremont	Wayward Seed Farm	www.waywardseed.com
Granville	Bird's Haven Farms	www.birdshavenfarms.com
Marysville	Burnt Toast Farms	www.burnttoastfarms.com
Marysville	Sunnyside Mini-Farm	www.sunnysideminifarm.com

Morrow	Kruthaup Family Farm	www.kruthaupfarm.com
New Lebanon	Mile Creek Farm	www.milecreekfarm.com
Oberlin	City Fresh	www.cityfresh.org
Peninsula	Greenfield Berry Farm	www.greenfieldberryfarm.com
Spencer	Bindel Farms	www.bindelfarms.com
Stoutsville	Paiges' Produce	www.paigesproduce.com
Wauseon	Meant to Be Farms	www.meanttobefarms.weebly.com
Waynesville	Carroll Creek Farms	www.carrollcreekfarms.com
Weston	Schooner Farms	www.shoonerberries.com
Wooster	Farm Roots Connection Co-op	www.farmrootsconnection.com
Wooster	Muddy Fork Farm	www.muddyforkfarm.com
Youngstown	Farm to You	www.growyoungstown.org

ON-FARM MARKETS

Amsterdam	Rax and Trax Farms	www.raxandtraxfarms.com
Auburn Twp	Voytko Berry Farm	www.voytkofarms.com
Auburn Twp.	Sirna's Farm & Market	www.sirnasfarm.com
Bellefontaine	Wishwell Farms	www.wishwellfarms.com
Berlin Heights	Quarry Hill Orchards	www.quarryhillorchards.com
Berlin Heights	The Stem Shire	www.stemshire.com
Canfield	White House Fruit Farm	www.whitehousefruitfarm.com
Centerburg	Granny B Farms	www.grannybfarm.com
Centerville	Foster's Farmhouse	www.fostersfarmhouse.com
Chardon	Maple Valley Sugarbush	www.maplevalleysugarbush.com
Chillicothe	Hirsch Fruit Farm	www.hirschfruitfarm.com
Cincinnati	Turner Farm Inc.	www.turnerfarm.org
Clarksville	Bonnybrook Farms	www.BonnybrookFarms.com
Clarksville	Messuri Family Farm	www.messurifamilyfarm.com
Clyde	Eshleman Fruit Farm	www.EshlemanFruitFarm.com
Conneaut	Northridge Blueberries	www.northridgeblueberries.com
Copley	Jacobs Heritage Farm	www.JacobsHeritageFarm.com
Covington	Adams Greenhouse & Produce	www.adamsgreenhouse.com
Eaton	Boulder Belt Eco-Farm	www.boulderbelt.com
Grand Rapids	Thurmans' Farm Market	www.Thurmansfarmmarket.com
Hinckley	Weymouth Farms & Orchard	www.weymouthfarms.com
Hinckley	Family Roots Farm	www.familyrootsfarm.com
Hiram	Polecat Pines Mushroom Farm	www.polecatpines.com
Homeworth	Breezy Hill Farm	www.breezyhillfarmohio.com
Jeromesville	Malabar Peach Orchard	www.ohiopeaches.com
Lancaster	Ruffwing Farms	www.ruffwingfarms.com
Leetonia	Dandelion Lane Farm	www.DandelionLaneFarm.com
Lisbon	W Bench Farms, LLC	www.wbenchfarms.com
Lodi	Marian Kay Berry Farm	www.mkberryfarm.com
Madison	Rainbow Farms	www.rainbowfarmsonline.com

Mantua	Carlton Farm Produce	www.carltonfarmproduce.com
Mantua	Goodell Family Farm	www.goodellfamilyfarm.com
Marietta	Lane's Farm Market and Orchard	www.lanesfarmmarket.com/
Marion	Lawrence Orchards	www.lawrenceorchards.com
Mechanicsburg	Folck Family Farm	www.folckfamilyfarm.net
Medina	Schmidt Family Farms	www.SchmidtFamilyFarms.org
Medina	Tim's Turkeys/Stein Farm	www.timsturkeys.com
Middlefield	Ridgeview Farm	www.ridgeviewfarm.com
Mogadore	Rufener Hilltop Farms	www.rufeners.com
Mount Vernon	4R Angus Farm	www.4RAngusFarm.weebly.com
Mount Vernon	Double 8 Cattle Company	www.double8cattle.com
Napoleon	Hetrick Honey Bees	www.hetrickhoneybees.com
New Lebanon	Cook's Garden	www.cooksgardennewlebanon.com
Newark	Charlie's Apples at Windy Hill	www.charliesapples.com
N. Royalton	Purple Skies Homestead	www.purpleslieshomestead.com
Orient	Folsom & Pine Farm	www.folsomandpine.com
Paris	Arrowhead Orchard	www.arrowheadorchard.com
Plain City	The Orchard & Company	www.theorchardandcompany.com
Sardinia	Jaybird Farms	www.jaybirdfarms.com
S. Bloomfield	Blueberry Valley	www.columbusblueberry.com
Springfield	Root Down Acres	www.RootDownAcres.com
Stewart	Vest Berries and Produce	www.vestberries.com
Stryker	R Farm of Northwest Ohio	www.rfarmnwo.com
Sunbury	Glass Rooster Cannery	www.glassroostercannery.com
Tipp City	Angry Hippie Farms, LLC	www.angryhippiefarms.com
Trenton	Schaefers Farm Market	www.schaefersfarmmarket.com
Wapakoneta	Hilltop Harvest Farm	www.hilltopharvestfarm.com
Waverly	Way Farms	www.way-farms.com
Williamsport	Honeyrun Farm	www.honeyrunfarm.com
Yellow Springs	Wild Hare Natural Farm	www.whnf.biz

FOOD HUBS

Athens	Shagbark Seed & Mill	www.shagbarkmill.com
Bexley	Bexley Natural Market	www.bexleynaturalmarket.org
Bryan	All Things Food	www.allthingsfood.com
Cincinnati	Our Harvest Cooperative	www.ourharvest.coop
Cleveland	Cleveland Food Hub	www.Clevelandfoodhub.com
Oberlin	Oberlin Food Hub	www.oberlinfoodhub.com
Wooster	Local Roots Wooster	www.localrootswooster.com

OKLAHOMA

AGRIHOODS

Carlton Landing   Own or Rent
Lake Eufaula
www.carltonlanding.com

Carlton Landing is Oklahoma's newest town. Grant and Jen Humphreys, the lakeside community's first residents, founded the community in 2011. The town occupies one of Lake Eufaula's most picturesque areas, with sandy beaches, towering cliffs, beautiful woodlands, and some of the lake's finest water quality. The master plan includes schools, a waterfront chapel, nature center, community parks, trails, and a town center with restaurants and shops. Plans call for more than 3,000 homes and a private residence club. Residents can choose from a wide range of home styles and sizes. The Farm is the centerpiece of the Agricultural Neighborhood and the heart of Carlton Landing's sustainable community. The Town Farmer delivers fresh produce to residents and guests through the farmers' market and farm-to-table menus at the Town Center restaurants. The CSA program enables residents to acquire farm shares and receive a steady delivery of seasonal food, herbs, and flowers.

COMMUNITY SUPPORTED AGRICULTURE (CSA) PROGRAMS

Bennington	Buy Homestead Fresh	www.buyhomesteadfresh.com
Blanchard	Berry Creek Farm CSA	www.berrycreekfarm.us
Edmond	Doodles & Blooms Flowers	www.doodlesnblooms.com
Fort Cobb	Acadian Family Farm	www.acadianfamilyfarm.com
Guthrie	Grace Family Farm	www.GraceFamilyFarm.com
Newcastle	TG Farms CSA	www.tgfarms.com
Oaks	Three Springs Farm	www.threespringsfarm.com
Okeene	Freed Family Farm	www.freedfamilyfarm.com
Oklahoma City	Guilford Gardens	www.kamskookery.com
Woodward	Anichini Moore Ranch Farm	www.anichinimoore.com
Yukon	Jesko Farms CSA	www.jeskofarms.com

ON-FARM MARKETS

Anadarko	Woods & Waters Winery	www.woodsandwaterswinery.com
Broken Bow	Honey Bear Ranch	www.honeybear-ranch.com
Cyril	Forbidden Fruits Farm	www.forbiddenfruitsfarm.com
Guthrie	Vision Farms	www.vision-farms.org
Harrah	Wind Drift Orchards	www.winddriftorchards.com
Liberty-Mounds	Endicott Farms	www.endicottfarms.com
Pink	ZaKK Farms,OK Belties	www.okbelties.weebly.com
Pocola	Wild Things Farm	www.wildthingsfarm.com
Roff	Real-Ranch LLC	www.real-ranch.com
Thomas	Crispin Murray Grey Beef	www.crispin-grassfedbeef.com
Tuttle	Chisholm Trail Farm	www.chisholmtrailfarm.com

FOOD HUBS

Oklahoma City	Earth to Urban Local Food	www.urbanagrarian.com
Oklahoma City	Oklahoma Food Co-op.	www.okalahomafood.coop

Edwards Addition

Monmouth

www.olsencommunities.com/home/olsen-communities/edwards-addition/

Edwards Addition, a "new traditional neighborhood," is inspired by neighborhoods found throughout the Pacific Northwest. Each house has a welcoming front porch, tree-shaded sidewalks, pocket parks, community agriculture, and gardening. Edwards Addition includes a village farm that grows around five tons of organic local fruits and vegetables each year, permanent irrigation, and a 3-acre community garden. Interested Edwards Addition residents can work on the farm in exchange for produce or they can buy a share of what the farm produces. The Village Green is at the heart of the neighborhood and available for gathering with neighbors and events. The first home was sold in 2002 and as of the summer of 2017, most of the 200 lots have occupied homes. There is a wide range of housing types and lot sizes: tiny 700-square-foot homes, 3,000-square-foot multigenerational houses, and many more traditional small, medium, and large plans.

Fairview Addition

Salem

www.olsencommunities.com/home/olsen-communities/fairview-addition/

Called Salem's urban "front porch community," homes are built with garages in the back, situated on a 275-acre development of tree-lined streets, pocket parks, and community agriculture. The master plan includes an amphitheater, oak grove, commercial and residential space, and woodlands. A wide range of home styles and floor plans is available.

Pringle Creek

Salem

www.pringlecreek.com/

Pringle Creek Community is a fully sustainable, 32-acre residential development located in the heart of Oregon's Willamette Valley. The community offers build-ready lots, custom home plans, and a selection of newly constructed homes, all developed to the highest build quality and green certifications. Plans include 137 lots, a 1-acre community garden, and a 12-acre orchard with berry patches and glasshouses. Residents can enjoy all the modern amenities of urban living in a beautiful natural setting filled with thoughtfully planned outdoor spaces, walking and biking paths, gardens and orchards, and community gathering places. The namesake, Pringle Creek, runs through the length of the community, where 35% of the community is shared green space. The creek has been restored and certified as Salmon Safe, with watershed clean enough for native salmon to spawn and thrive. Residents can grow their own produce in the community garden or subscribe to the CSA program with porch delivery. Home designs include a "net-zero" home, and various styles and sizes ranging from modern to cottage, attached and detached.

COMMUNITY SUPPORTED AGRICULTURE (CSA) PROGRAMS

Baker City	Val's Veggies	www.valsveggies.com
Beaverton	Dinihanian's Farm Market	www.yourcsa.com
Bend	Fields Farm	www.fieldsfarm.org
BORING	Aslan's How Organics	www.aslans-how-organics.com
Cornelius	Blooming Junction	www.bloomingjunction.com
Cornelius	Unger Farms	www.ungerfarms.com
Forest Grove	Adelante Mujeres CSA	www.adelantemujeres.org
Forest Grove	Sun Gold Farm	www.sungoldfarm.com
Forest Grove	Tangle Wood Farms	www.tanglewoodfarmtofork.com
Gresham	Full Cellar Farm	www.fullcellarfarmoregon.com
Hood River	Hood River Organic	www.hoodriverorganic.com
Langlois	Valley Flora	www.valleyflorafarm.com
Lebanon	Pitchfork & Crow	www.pitchforkandcrow.com
McMinnville	Even Pull Farm	www.evenpullfarm.com
Molalla	Diggin' Roots Farm	www.digginrootsfarm.com
Noti	Winter Green Farm	www.wintergreenfarm.com
Oregon City	Moomaw Family Farm	www.moomawfarm.com
Portland	Able Farms	www.ablefarms.org
Portland	Rockwood Urban Farm	www.rockwoodurbanfarm.com
Redmond	Dome Grown Produce	www.domegrown.org
Salem	Fairy Godmother's Garden	www.fairygodmothersgarden.com
Salem	Marion-Polk Food Share Youth Farm	www.marionpolkfoodshare.org
Salem	Minto Island Growers	www.mintogrowers.com
Stayton	Fresh to You Produce & Garden	www.ftyp.com
Sweet Home	Sweet Home Meats	www.swmeats.com
Troutdale	Dancing Roots Farm	www.dancingrootsfarm.com
Yamhill	Kookoolan Farms	www.kookoolanfarms.com
Yamhill	Wicked Wahine Farm CSA	www.wickedwahinefarm.com
Yoncalla	Helios Farms	www.heliosfarms.com

ON-FARM MARKETS

Albany	Bose Family Farm	www.bosefamilyfarm.com
Ashland	Restoration Seeds	www.restorationseeds.com
Beaverton	Hoffman Farms Store	www.hoffmanfarmsstore.com
Boring	Liepold Farms	www.liepoldfarms.com
Boring	Aslan's How Organics	www.aslans-how-organics.com
Corbett	Klock Farm	www.klockfarm.com
Cornelius	Blooming Junction Garden	www.bloomingjunction.com
Cornelius	Unger Farms	www.ungerfarms.com
Corvallis	Sunset Valley Organics	www.SunsetValleyOrganics.com
Elgin	PD Farms	www.greifsgourmetgarlic.com
Forest Grove	Love Farm Organics	www.lovefarmorganics.com

Hermiston	K & K Blueberries	www.kandkblueberries.com
Hillsboro	Easy Go Farm	www.easygofarm.net
Hillsboro	New Earth Farm	www.newearthfarm.net
Hood River	Hood River Lavender Farm	www.hoodriverlavender.com
Jacksonville	Rogue Artisan Foods	www.rogueartisanfoods.com
Junction City	Thistledown Farms	www.thistledownfarms.net
Langlois	Valley Flora	www.valleyflorafarm.com
Lebanon	Berkey's Blueberries	www.Berkeysblueberries.com
Milwaukie	Justys Produce and Flowers	www.justysproduce.com
Monroe	Crooked Gate Ranch	www.greatgrassbeef.com
Mount Hood	Mt. Views Orchards Fruit	www.mtvieworchards.com
Mt. Hood	Mt Hood Organic Farms	www.mthoodorganicfarms.com
Newberg	Bide a Wee Farm	www.bideaweefarm.com
Newberg	Oregon Dream Ponies	www.OregonDreamPonies.com
Parkdale	Kiyokawa Family Orchards	www.kiyokawafamilyorchards.com
Salem	Minto Island Growers	www.mintogrowers.com
Salem	Thank You Berry Much Farms	www.thankyouberrymuchfarms.com
Sandy	Fungi Farm Shiitake	www.fungifarm.com
Selma	Ronan Country Fibers	www.ronanfibers.com
Sherwood	Baggenstos Farm Store	www.baggenstosfarms.com

FOOD HUBS

Burns	Country Natural Beef	www.countrynaturalbeef.com
Eugene	Organically Grown Company	www.organicgrown.com
Forest Grove	Adelante Mujeres	www.adelantemujeres.org
Fossil	Painted Hills Natural Beef	www.paintedhillsnaturalbeef.com
Springfield	Lane Local Foods	www.localfoodmarketplace.com

PENNSYLVANIA

AGRIHOODS

Amblebrook

Over 55 Community

Gettysburg
www.amblebrookgettysburg.com

Under development. Amblebrook is a new 55+ community in Straban Township, Pennsylvania, near Gettysburg. Plans call for approximately 2,000 single-family homes on nearly 800 acres of gently rolling Central Pennsylvania hills. Community residents can gather at the Town Center, with a clubhouse, bar and grill, farm stand, and coffee shop. Plans include an outdoor pool, tennis courts, and walking trails that weave through acres of beautifully preserved, natural space.

Buckwalter Farm

Warwick Township

Proposed development. 100-acre plan for mixed-use 320 residential units, with 50 percent open space. Agriculturally themed plan includes apartments, homes, shops, markets, farming, and dining. The farm is owned by the Buckwalter family, and is located on Lititz Pike and East Millport Road. The project is based on the agrihood model, will be pedestrian-friendly, and retain the natural appeal of streams, ponds, trees, meadows, and woodlands.

Willowdale Station

Unionville

Under development by Montchanin Builders. Willowdale Station will include 17 custom single-family homes. Home sites will feature 2-story, quaint cottage-style architecture and 2-car garages on 10,000 square foot lots. Located on 26 acres at the crossroads of Routes 82 and 926, the community will feature abundant open space, communal gardens, working agricultural fields, a community harvest barn, fire pits, and the Sovan Bistro.

URBAN AG

Hilltop Urban Farm

Pittsburgh
www.www.hilltopurbanfarm.org

Hilltop Urban Farm is located on 107 acres of land, with 23 acres dedicated to farming. The community is a multipronged initiative that produces locally grown crops, provides agriculture-based education, generates entrepreneurial opportunities, and strengthens communities. Hilltop Urban Farm is set to become the largest urban farm in the United States. The three core programs include youth-centered education, workforce training for new adult urban farmers, and an active, accessible farmers' market. The Farmer Incubation Program (FIP) is a 3-year workforce development program for new small-scale organic urban farm enterprises.

Bellefonte	Healthy Harvest Farm	www.healthyharvestfarmcsa.com
Bensalem	Phoenix Farms	www.phoenixfarms.us
Carlisle	Earth Spring Farm	www.earthspringcsa.com
Chester Springs	Yellow Springs Far	www.yellowspringsfarm.com
Coatesville	Vollmecke Orchards	www.csachestercounty.com
Cochranville	North Star Orchard	www.northstarorchard.com
Duncannon	Yeehaw Farm Whole Diet	www.yeehawfarms.com
East Earl	Wimer's Organics	www.wimersorganics.com
Emmaus	Kneehigh Farm	www.kneehighfarm.com
Gap /Glenmoore	Adragone Aeroponics	www.adragonegrows.com
Gardners	Orchard Country Produce	www.orchardcountryproduce.com
Gardners	Piney Mountain Orchard	www.pineymountainorchard.com
Greensburg	Sarver's Hill Organic Farm	www.sarverhillfarm.org
Harford	Harford Farm	www.harfordfarmpa.com
Hulmeville	Phoenix Farms	www.phoenixfarms.us
Huntingdon	Plowshare Produce	www.plowshareproduce.com
Irvona	Hickory Ridge Natural	www.hrnaturalharvest.com
Linesville	Lisk's Heritage Farm	www.lisksheritagefarm.com
Manheim	Creekside Farm Market	www.thecreeksidemarket.com
Mifflintown	Village Acres Farm	www.villageacresfarm.com
Millersville	Homefields Farm	www.homefields.org
Monaca borough	Kohser Farms	www.kohserfarms.WordPress.com
Newport	North Mountain Pastures	www.NorthMountainPastures.com
Noxen	Fertile Grounds	www.FertileGroundsCSA.com
Philadelphia	Greensgrow Farms	www.greensgrow.org
Philadelphia	West Philly Foods CSA	www.westphillyfoods.com
Phoenixville	Charlestown Farm	www.charlestownfarm.org
Phoenixville	Sankanac CSA	www.sankanaccsa.com
Pittsburgh	Penn's Corner Farm Alliance	www.pennscorner.com
Rochester	Kretschmann Farm	www.kretschmannfarm.com
Shoemakersville	Taproot Farm	www.taprootfarmcsa.com
Stoneboro	Old Time Farm	www.OldTime.Farm
Susquehanna	Hemlock Creek CSA	www.hemlockcreekcsa.com
Three Springs	Star Hollow Farm	www.starhollowfarm.com
Tyler Hill	The Multi-Farm Meat CSA	www.twinbrookfarmsandlivestock.com
Valencia	Harvest Valleys Farms	www.harvestvalleyfarms.com
Warfordsburg	Farm of Peace CSA	www.farmofpeace.com
Waynesboro	Yesterday's Favorite Farm	www.yesterdaysfavoritefarm.com
Worthington	Five Elements Farm	www.fiveelementsfarm.com
Zelienople	Brenckle's Organic Farm	www.brencklesfarm.com

177

ON-FARM MARKETS

Apollo borough	Kistaco Farm Market	www.kistacofarm.com
Avella	Weatherbury Farm	www.weatherburyfarm.com
Bedford	Foxtail Farmstead	www.foxtailfarmstead.com
Bethlehem	Scholl Orchards	www.schollorchards.com
Biglerville	Swartz's Pumpkin Patch	www.swartzspumpkinpatch.com
Biglerville	Yellow Hill Farm	www.yellowhillfarm.com
Brockway	Windy Hill Farm	www.windyhillfarmnaturals.com
Buckingham	Blue Moon Acres	www.bluemoonacres.com
Catawissa	Rohrbach's Farm Market	www.rohrbachsfarm.net
Coopersburg	Flint Hill Farm Education Ctr.	www.flinthillfarm.org
Douglassville	Wholesome Dairy Farms	www.wholesomedairyfarms.com
Duncannon	Yeehaw Farm Store	www.yeehawfarms.com
Edinboro	Hulings Blueberries and Farm	www.hulingsblueberries.com
Enon Valley	Enon Valley Garlic	www.EnonValleyGarlic.com
Fleetwood	Gauker Farms	www.gaukerfarms.com
Forest City	Mount Pleasant Herbary	www.mountpleasantherbary.com
Halifax	Small Valley Milling	www.smallvalleymilling.com
Hulmeville	Phoenix Farms	www.phoenixfarms.us
Kittanning	Acorn Hollow Farm	www.acornhollowfarm.com
Manheim	Creekside Farm Market	www.thecreeksidemarket.com
Monongahela	Triple B Farms	www.triplebfarms.com
Montrose	Foxy Farms	www.localharvest.org/foxy-farms
Nazareth	Fairman Farm	www.fairmanfarm.com
New Castle	McConnell's Christmas Trees	www.mcconnellsnursery.com
New Hope	Solebury Orchards	www.soleburyorchards.com
Oakdale	Beccari's Farm Market	www.beccaris.com
Pottstown	Four Sisters Farm	www.foursisters.farm
Pottstown	Hill Creek Farm	www.hillcreekfarmpa.com
Robesonia	Meadow Mountain Farm	www.meadowmountainfarm.com
Saylorsburg	Stryker Farm	www.strykerfarm.com
Solebury	Manoff Market Gardens	www.manoffmarketgardens.com
Sunbury	Owens Farm	www.owensfarm.com
Tamaqua	Valley Road Farm	www.valleyroadfarm.com
Tarentum	Normans Orchard	www.normansorchard.com
Tidioute	Riverview Farms	www.riverviewfarmspa.com
Tyler Hill	Twin Brook Farms	www.twinbrookfarmsandlivestock.com
Waterford	Glenn Troyer Farms	www.glenntroyerfarms.com
Waynesboro	TLM Hillside Farm	www.tlmhillsidefarm.com
Waynesboro	Yesterday's Favorites Farm	www.yesterdaysfavoritesfarm.com
Westfield	Brookfield Maple Products	www.brookfieldmapleproducts.com
Wexford	Soergel Orchards	www.soergels.com
Whitehall	Mondjack Apiaries	www.Mondjackapiaries.com
York	Flinchbaughs Orchard	www.flinchbaughsorchard.com
Zelienople	Brenckle's Organic Farm	www.brencklesfarm.com

Dillsburg	South Central PA Harvest	www.scpafood.com
Halifax	Small Valley Milling	www.smallvalleymilling.com
Harrisburg	Radish & Rye Food Hub	www.radishandryefood.com
Honey Grove	Voulter Farms	www.coulterfarms.net
Hustontown	Tuscarora Organic Growers	www.tog.coop
Philadelphia	Fair Food Farmstand	www.fairfoodphilly.org
Philadelphia	Philadelphia Wholesale	www.pwpm.net
Philadelphia	Philly Cow Share	www.phillycowshare.com
Philadelphia	The Common Market	www.thecommonmarket.org
Pittsburgh	Penn's Corner Farm Alliance	www.pennscorner.com
Sligo	Clarion River Organics	www.clarionriverorganics.com

RHODE ISLAND

COMMUNITY SUPPORTED AGRICULTURE (CSA) PROGRAMS

Charlestown	Sweet Pea Farm	www.sweetpeafarmri.com
Cranston	Blue Skys Farm	www.blueskysfarm.com
Cranston	Four Fiends Farm CSA	www.fourfriendscsa.com
Cranston	Scratch Farm	ww.scratchfarm.com
Coventry	Bella Farms	www.bellafarm15.wordpress.com
East Greenwich	Ledge Ends CSA	www.LedgeEndsProduce.com
Exeter	Hallene Farm	www.hallenefarm.com
Hope	The Good Earth Organic CSA	www.goodearthri.com
Hope Valley	Arcadian Fields Organic Farm	www.arcadianfields.com
Hopkinton	Stonyledge Farm	www.studiofarmproducts.com
Little Compton	Cluck & Trowel	www.cluckandtrowel.com
Newport	Garman Farm	www.garmanfarm.com
Portsmouth	DaSilva Farm	www.DasilvaFarm.com
Portsmouth	The Local Patch	www.localpatchri.com
Saunderstown	Casey Farm	www.historicneweng-land.org/visit/homes/casey.htm

ON-FARM MARKETS

Hope	The Good Earth Organic Farm	www.goodearthri.com
Matunuck	Browning Homestead Farm	www.browninghomesteadfarm.com
Warwick	Rocky Point Farm	www.rockypointblueberries.com

FOOD HUBS

North Kingstown	American Mussel Harvesters	www.americanmussel.com
Providence	Brown Market Shares	www.brownmarketshares.com

AGRIHOODS

Palmetto Bluff
Bluffton
www.www.palmettobluff.com

Own or Vacation Stay

Palmetto Bluff is an expansive 20,000-acre resort community that offers a range of neighborhoods including luxury homes, wellness centers, sporting, outdoor recreation, restaurants, and vacation lodging. With 32 miles of waterfront, Palmetto Bluff is dedicated to nature conservation and the history of low-country life. A working farm with a full-time farmer offers fresh produce to residents, and serves the community's nine restaurants, food-based events, educational events, community farm stand, and partnership with local food banks.

The Cliffs at Mountain Park
Marietta
www.cliffsliving.com/community/the-cliffs-at-mountain-park/

The Cliffs is a collection of seven private luxury residential mountain and lake club communities encompassing more than 20,000 acres in the Blue Ridge Mountains. One membership at The Cliffs grants access to an unparalleled suite of amenities, including seven clubs, seven nationally acclaimed golf courses, seven wellness centers, boating and water sports, a Beach Club, full-service marina, paddle sports, cycling, tennis, an equestrian center, miles of hiking trails, more than a dozen dining and private event venues, an organic farm, and more than 2,000 year-round programs and social activities. The Cliffs has its own five-acre farm, Broken Oak Organics, and estate lots next to Creekside Farm. Creekside Farm is a 60-acre 100-year-old working farm that produces over 300 varieties of heirloom vegetables, herbs, and flowers. At the heart of the farm is a historic barn for neighbors to gather.

COMMUNITY SUPPORTED AGRICULTURE (CSA) PROGRAMS

Bamberg	Maynard Family Farm	www.maynardfarm.com
Blair	Gypsy Wind Farms	www.barbadosblackbelly.com
Charleston	Legare Farms	www.legarefarms.com
Chester	Wild Hope Farm	www.wildhopefarm.com
Clemson	Clemson Student Organic Farm	www.clemson.edu/sustainableag/student_farm.html
Columbia	City Roots	www.cityroots.org
Gable	Dorr Farms	www.dorrfarms.com
Gilbert	Humble Farm	www.thehumblefarrm.com
Salem	Sweet Appalachian Farms	www.sweetappalachianfarms.weebly.com
Wagener	Bear Bottom Honey	www.bearbottomhoney.com
Williston	A Carolina Harvest	www.ACarolinaHarvest.com
York	Bush-N-Vine Farm	www.bushnvinefarm.com

On-Farm Markets

Abbeville	The Twenty-eight Eleven	www.the2811.com
Blythewood	Blythewood Beef	www.blythewoodbeef.com
Chester	Watson Farms Meats	www.watsonfarmsbeef.com
Edisto Island	Geechie Boy Market Mill	www.geechieboymill.com
Fort Mill	Springs Farm	www.springsfarm.com
Fort Mill	The Peach Stand	www.peachstand.com
Georgetown	Millgrove Farms	www.millgrovefarms.com
Lancaster	The Ivy Place	www.ivyplaceevents.com
Long Creek	Chattooga Belle Farm	www.ChattoogaBelleFarm.com
McBee	McLeod Farms Market	www.macspride.com
McClellanville	Blue Pearl Farms	www.bluepearlfarms.com
N. Myrtle Beach	Natural Grown Meats	www.NaturalGrownMeats.com
Pelzer	Hurricane Creek Farms	www.hurricanecreekfarms.com
St. Helena Island	Dempsey Farms U-Pick	www.dempseyfarmsupick.com
Six Mile	The Happy Berry	www.thehappyberry.com
Smyrna	Roger Ridge Ranch	www.rogerridgeranch.com
Sumter	Sunny Cedars Farm	www.sunnycedars.com
Travelers Rest	Carolina Honey Bee Co.	www.carolinahoneybeecompany.com
Trenton	Cook's Farm	www.cooksfarm.com

Food Hubs

Charleston	Grow Food Carolina	www.growfoodcarolina.com
Charleston	Lowcountry Street Grocery	www.lowcountrystreetgrocery.com
Greenville	Swamp Rabbit Cafe	www.swamprabbitcafe.com

COMMUNITY SUPPORTED AGRICULTURE (CSA) PROGRAMS

Ashton	CDP Farm	www.cdpfarms.com
Beresford	Mary's Kitchen and Gardens	www.maryskitchenandgardens.com
Britton	Coteau Sunrise Farm	www.coteausunrisefarm.com
Brookings	Good Roots Farm and Gardens	www.goodrootsfarmandgardens.com
Brookings	Hillside Prairie Gardens	www.prairiegrown.com
Bruce	Haroldson Farms	www.haroldsonfarms.com
Chester	Linda's Gardens	www.lindasgardens.com
Montrose	Warner's Produce	www.warnersproduce.weebly.com
Nisland	Nisland Farm	www.nislandfarm.com
Oacoma	Muddy Pumpkin Farms	www.muddypumpkin.com
Pierre	B and G Produce	www.bgproduce.wordpress.com
Sioux Falls	Glory Garden	www.glorygarden.org
Spearfish	Cycle Farm	www.cyclefarm.net
Vermillion	Heikes Family Farm	www.heikesfamilyfarm.com
Worthing	Deep Root Gardens CSA	www.deeprootgardens.net

ON-FARM MARKETS

Brandon	Fruit of the Coop	www.fruitofthecoop.com
Marion	Berrybrook Organics & U-Pick	www.berrybrookorganics.com
Pierpont	Better Roots Farm, LLC	www.betterrootsfarm.com
Raymond	Purity Seeds	www.purityseedsUSA.com
Vermillion	Ufford Hills Pumpkin Patch	www.uffordhills.net

TENNESSEE

AGRIHOODS

Berry Farms
Franklin
www.berryfarmstn.com

Berry Farms is a mixed-use master-planned community where work, shopping, and leisure blend seamlessly with front-porch living on pedestrian-friendly streets. Located on 600 acres in the heart of Williamson County, Berry Farms offers a preserved history that dates back to the early 1800's, centered around connecting people to work, shopping, restaurants, and meaningful open space. The Berry Farms Community Garden is a program of the Rural Plains Association of Owners and features 46 raised beds that are 4 feet by 8 feet. The community garden is an organics-only garden open only to Berry residents, and includes compost and mulch areas, a tool shed, irrigation, and necessary watering hoses.

Harvest Point
Spring Hill
www.harvestpointliving.com

Harvest Point is a value-oriented, master-planned development located 20 minutes from Cool Springs. The organic community garden is open to residents, and is free of herbicides, pesticides, and commercial fertilizers. Water, compost areas, and tool storage are provided. Outdoor recreation includes a resort-style swimming pool, picnic areas, pocket parks, seating, 5 miles of walking trails, biking trails, all surrounded by woods, wildlife, tranquil ponds, and streams near the Walden Branch of Carter's Creek. Residents can choose from a number of recognized and reputable builders.

Springbrook Farm
Alcoa
www.springbrookfarmtn.com

Under development. Springbrook Farm is a master-planned development consisting of a retail lifestyle center, multi-family residential, commercial office space, a hotel and conference center, and a new city administrative center. Site of the former Alcoa, Inc. West Plant, the plan includes single-family homes, town homes, senior living, multifamily homes, and community gardens.

COMMUNITY SUPPORTED AGRICULTURE (CSA) PROGRAMS

Clarksville	Giving Thanks Farm	www.givingthanksfarm.com
College Grove	Tavalin Tails	www.tavalintails.com
Corryton	Care of the Earth Farm	www.careoftheearthcommunityfarm.com
Crab Orchard	Wild Things Farm	www.wildthingscsafarm.com
Dover	Black Family Farms	www.blackfamilyfarms.net
Franklin	Herron Family Pastures	www.herronfamilypastures.com
McKenzie	Coldwater Bottom Gardens	www.coldwaterbottomgardens.com
Memphis	Baba's Oasis	www.babasoasis.org

Milan	Milan Farmers Market	www.farmersmarketmilan.com
Morrison	Southland Farms	www.southlandfarmstn.com
Nashville	Fresh and Local	www.freshandlocalnashville.com
Nashville	Green Door Gourmet	www.greendoorgourmet.com
Nunnelly	Pinewood Farms	www.thepinewoodfarm.com
Pikeville	Dazi Acres	www.daziacres.com
Rockvale	Triple A Farms	www.tripleafarms3.com
Springfield	White's Family Farm	www.whitesfamilyfarm.org
Stanton	Oak Hill Farm	www.oak-hill-farm.org
Toone	Falcon Ridge Farm	www.farmatfalconridge.com
Tracy City	White City Produce	www.wcproducegreenhouses.weebly.com
White House	Hill Family Farm	www.hillfamilyfarm.wordpress.com

ON-FARM MARKETS

Alexandria	Folsom Farms	www.folsomfarms.com
Antioch	Local Living Farm	www.locallivingfarm.com
Cedar Hill	Woodall Farm Strawberries	www.Picktnproducts.com
Clarksville	Cook's Ranch Beef	www.cooksranchbeef.com
Cookeville	Hidden Springs Orchard	www.hiddenspringsorchard.com
Cookeville	Little Creek Produce	www.littlecreekproduce.com
Corryton	Clear Springs Farm	www.Clearspringsfarm.org
Cottage Grove	Crum Farms Market	www.crumfarms.com
Dandridge	Brewers Mushrooms	www.brewersmushrooms.com
Franklin	Herron Family Pastures	www.herronfamilypastures.com
Granville	Bell Point Farms	www.bellpointfarms.weebly.com
Jonesborough	Clover Creek Farm	www.clovercreekhairsheep.com
Lewisburg	Bee Sweet Berry Farm	www.beesweetberryfarm.com
Morrison	Farmer Brown's Hydroponics	www.mcminnville.locallygrown.net
Nashville	Green Door Gourmet	www.greendoorgourmet.com
Southside	J&J Century Farm	www.jandjcenturyfarm.com
Spencer	Baker Mountain Farm	www.BakerMountainFarm.com

FOOD HUBS

Chattanooga	Harvested Here Food Hub	www.harvestedhere.org
Memphis	Bring It Food Hub	www.bringitfoodhub.com
Memphis	New South	www.newsouthcoop.com
Memphis	Roots Memphis Farm	www.rootsmemphis.com
Nashville	Nashville Grown	www.nashvillegrown.org

TEXAS

AGRIHOODS

Elgin Agrarian Community
Elgin
www.pegasusatx.com/development

Under development. Elgin Agrarian Community is a mixed-use community situated on 24 acres that will include 80 cottage-style homes, off-the-grid water and energy resources, forested trails, a recreation and training center, and a 5-acre organic farm. The farm will produce fresh food for residents through a community-supported agriculture program. The site is located less than 1 mile from the historic Downtown of Elgin. Developed by Pegasus Corporation in partnership with a rural historic preservation organization.

Harvest
Argyle (North Lake)
www.harvestbyhillwood.com

Harvest is a 1,150-acre master-planned, mixed-use development in Northlake, Texas, and home to approximately 3,200 energy-efficient, single-family houses. A shared focus on farming and gardening provides homeowners with ample opportunities to grow their own produce, pitch in to harvest community crops, share surplus food with the North Texas Food Bank, or deepen their agricultural knowledge through on-site gardening classes. Homebuyers may choose from a wide variety of architectural styles, offered by David Weekley Homes, Highland Homes, Plantation Homes, and D.R. Horton Homes.

Harvest Green
Richmond
www.harvestgreentexas.com

Harvest Green is Houston's first agrihood, built on 280 acres of greenbelts and open space. The on-site 12-acre Village Farm is designed to be a working educational experience for Harvest Green residents, and encompasses fields, a greenhouse, goats, chickens, and plots where residents can grow produce for their own use. Residents also are able to pick berries, herbs, and other produce from several designated gardens throughout the community. The Farmhouse serves as a recreation center, with a resort-style pool, fitness center, and studio. Homebuyers have the option to have their builder add a ready-to-grow backyard garden, and also works in partnership with Enchanted Nurseries & Landscapes of Richmond to install the gardens and help new homeowners set up up soil and seeds. Harvest Green has also partnered with Messina Hof Wine Cellars, Inc. to bring the Messina Hof Harvest Green Winery to the agrihood, with a 130-seat restaurant and venue for hosting events.

Millican Reserve
College Station
www.millicanreserve.com

Millican Reserve is a 2,700-acre community with 2,000 planned home sites located in Brazos Valley. Several distinct ecosystems define Millican Reserve, including deep yaupon thicket, spring-fed creeks, and expansive post-oak savannah. Oak trees meander throughout, as do cypress, cedar elms, and eastern red cedar. The Farm at Millican Reserve implements sustainable practices to provide families with locally sourced, chemically free produce and eggs. Millican Reserve offers a CSA and farmers' market on the green. Home site options include large acreage lot sizes surrounded by a conservation lane, natural woodlands, and wildlife habitat.

Orchard Ridge
Liberty Hill
www.liveorchardridge.com

Located north of Austin, Orchard Ridge is a thoughtfully designed "vital community," where homes are front-porch friendly, inspired by farmhouse architecture of the past. The community is surrounded by creeks, ponds, and an abundant collection of trails and scenic expanses. Orchard Ridge offers garden spaces that include fruit and nut orchards, community garden plots, terraced landscaping, preserved habitat, and parks for families and neighborhood gatherings. Orchard Ridge's recreational opportunities include an extensive trail system and expansive amenity center with resort-style pools and fitness center. Land development, stewardship, and home-building practices adhere to green principles. Orchard Ridge's new homes are meticulously designed by award-winning builders, with a mix of floor plans that can be tailored to suit the homebuyer.

Village Farm
Austin   Tiny Homes
www.villagefarmaustin.com

Village Farm is a tiny home community based in East Austin, about 8 miles from downtown Austin. Village Farm offers low-cost, free-standing tiny homes, rooted in sustainable design. The initial phase comprises 42 tiny home lots, followed by an additional 112 lots. Village Farms is a short walk from a general store, cafe, amphitheater, community gardens, and pocket parks, and offers a variety of activities and events. Village Farm Austin is centered around Green Gate Farms, a USDA-certified organic farm established in 2006. Green Gate offers a Community Supported Agriculture (CSA) program.

Whisper Valley
Austin
www.whispervalleyaustin.com

Under development. Whisper Valley is a 2,000-acre master-planned, eco-friendly development committed to sustainability, affordability, and cutting-edge technology. Homebuyers are eligible for tax credits due to geothermal energy, solar photovoltaic power, high-efficiency appliances, and Nest smart home technology. Whisper Valley offers creatively designed residential neighborhoods and business districts, nestled into 700 acres of beautiful parks, scenic trails, rolling hills, meandering streams, quiet meadows, and pristine forests. Future neighborhood services, village-type restaurants, retail, office areas, two school campuses, an emergency services center, and transportation center will make it a convenient place to live, work, shop, and play.

COMMUNITY SUPPORTED AGRICULTURE (CSA) PROGRAMS

Alvarado	Walnut Creek Farm	www.Walnutcreekfarmtexas.com
Austin	Green Gate Farms	www.greengatefarms.net
Austin	Johnson's Backyard Garden	www.jbgorganic.com
Cameron	Sand Creek Farm	www.sandcreekfarm.net
Dallas	Fisher Family Farm & Ranch	www.fisherfarmandranch.com
El Paso	True Food Buying Club	www.elpasotruefood.com
Elm Mott	World Hunger Relief, Inc.	www.worldhungerrelief.org
Eustace	Penny's Pastured Poultry	www.pennyspasturedpoultry.com
Frisco	Booster Club Foods	www.boosterclubfoods.com
Harlingen	Yahweh's All Natural Farm	www.yahwehsallnaturalfarm.com
Houston	Plant It Forward	www.plant-it-forward.org
Iola	Texas US Farms	www.texasusfarms.com
Lindale	Beth's Little Farm Market	www.bethslittlefarmmarket.com
Manor	Munkebo Farm	www.munkebofarm.com
Manor	Tecolote Farm	www.tecolotefarm.net
McKinney	Squeezepenny Sustainable Farm	www.squeezepenny.com
Richmond	Loam Agronomics	www.loamagronomics.com
Thrall	Blessing Falls Family Farm	www.blessingfalls.com
Waco	The Home Grown Farm	www.thehomegrownfarm.com

ON-FARM MARKETS

Abilene	Grapevine Farms	www.grapevinefarms.com
Alto	Ruby-Farm	www.ruby-farm.com
Alvin	Funky Monkey Farms, LLC	www.funkymonkeyfarms.com
Amarillo	Honey's Farm Fresh	www.honeysfarmfresh.com
Bandera	A Garden in Every Home	www.agardenineveryhome.com
Brownsboro	Echo Springs Blueberry Farm	www.echospringsblueberyfarm.com
Campbell	Texas A&M University-Commerce Twin Oaks Blueberry Farm	www.tamuc.edu/blueberry
Decatur	SB Longhorns	www.sblonghorns.com
Elgin	Coyote Creek Organic Farm	www.CoyoteCreekFarm.com
Hallettsville	The Herb Cottage	www.theherbcottage.com
Hico	Liberty Farms Dairy	www.libertdairyfarms.com
Hockley	Partybarn Farm	www.partybarnfarm.com
Houston	Hope Farms Market	Www.hopefarmshtx.org
Iola	Texas US Farms	www.texasusfarms.com
Italy	Mill Creek Meat Company	www.millcreekmeatcompany.com
Kemah	Gardenkids of Kemah	www.gardenkidskemah.org
Ladonia	Flohas Farms	www.flohasfarms.com
Lexington	Dewberry Hills Farm	www.dhfarms.com
Lexington	Taylor Farm	www.Taylor farm.org
Lubbock	Wolf Creek Farms	www.wolfcreekfarmsonline.com
Magnolia	Bar M Ranch	www.bmrcattle.com

Manor	Munkebo Farm	www.munkebofarm.com
Montgomery	P-6 Farms	www.p-6farms.com
Oglesby	Punkin Center Berry Farm	www.punkincenterberryfarm.com
Plantersville	Jollisant Farms	www.Jollisantfarms.com
Roanoke	Henrietta Creek Orchard	www.Henriettacreekorchard.com
Troy	JZJ Natural Beef	www.jzjnaturalbeef.com
Weimar	Cuts of Color	www.cutsofcolor.com

FOOD HUBS

Austin	Farm to Table	www.farmtotabletx.com
Austin	Farmhouse Delivery	www.farmhousedelivery.com
Brackettville	The Montalvo House	www.themontalvohouse.org
Brookshire	Custofoods	www.custofoods.com
Dallas	The Provision House	www.Theprovisionhouse.com
Lorena	Texas Cheese House	www.texascheesehouse.com
San Antonio	Truckin' Tomato	www.truckintomato.com

UTAH

COMMUNITY SUPPORTED AGRICULTURE (CSA) PROGRAMS

Benson	Johnson Family Farms	www.johnsonfamilyfarms.com
Draper	Bell Organic Gardens	www.bellorganic.com
Jensen	Heritage Family Gardens CSA	www.heritageefamilygardens.com
Layton	Zoe's Garden	www.zoegarden.com
Pleasant View	Sunshine Family Farms	www.sunshinefamilyfarms.com
Provo	La Nay Ferme	www.lanayferme.com
Salt Lake City	Backyard Urban Garden Farms	www.bugcsa.com
Salt Lake City	3 Squares Produce Farms	www.3squaresproduce.com
South Salt Lake	The Green Urban Lunch Box	www.thegreenurbanlunchbox.com
Syracuse	Black Island Farms	www.BlackIslandFarms.com
Vernon	Christiansen's Family Farm	www.christiansenfarm.com
Washington	Staheli Family Farm	www.stahelifamilyfarm.com
Wellsville	Longbourn Farm	www.longbourn.com
West Point	East Farms	www.eastfarmscsa.com

ON-FARM MARKETS

Hyde Park	Mt. Naomi Farms	www.mtnaomifarms.com
Logan	Phoenix Tears Nursery	www.phoenixtearsnursery.com
New Harmony	Little America Organic Orchard	www.littleamericaorganicorchard.com

VERMONT

AGRIHOODS

Cobb Hill Cohousing
Hartland
www.cobbhill.org

Cobb Hill Cohousing is an eco-friendly community in Hartland Four Corners, built on 270 acres of forest, pasture, and agriculture soils, with 26 varieties of vegetables grown on the farm. Members own their own homes plus a share in the commonly owned land, barns, the Hunt House, wood-shop, and common house. The common house is for dining, gathering, and recreation. The Hunt House is a farmhouse converted to office spaces, currently rented to the Sustainable Food lab. Cobb Hill is home to Cedar Mountain Farm and CSA, Cobb Hill Cheese and Frozen Yogurt, Cobb Hill Icelandics, a shiitake mushroom CSA, a maple syrup enterprise, a group of beekeepers, a soap business, an active 4H club, and more. Homes feature solar hot water, south-facing passive-solar orientation, triple-pane windows, green-building design, a high-efficiency central heating system, composting toilets, and electric car-charging stations. Residents can enjoy garden spaces, hiking trails, and groomed cross-county ski trails.

South Village
South Burlington
www.southvillage.com

South Village is Vermont's first agrihood and conservation community offering traditional housing designs combined with 50% open spaces on 220 acres. The community includes a 12-acre organic farm, 40 acres of protected wetlands, and features paths for cycling and cross-country skiing. Other amenities include community gardens, chickens and bees, and abundant habitat for wild-life. The Farm at South Village operates with a 528-panel photovoltaic solar array that produces 150kw of carbon-free electricity. Residents may participate in land stewardship programs, volun-teer with the farm and garden, and subscribe to the farm's CSA. South Village participates with the Intervale Food Hub, providing farm fresh and locally made foods year round. Residents can choose from a range of single-family homes or town homes. South Village is Vermont's first Tra-ditional Neighborhood Development (TND), and homes are clustered in pedestrian-friendly nar-row streets with wide sidewalks. Single-family homes are farmhouse style, featuring high ceilings, front porches, and conform to LEED-certified, Energy Star, and the National Green Building Stand-ard.

COMMUNITY SUPPORTED AGRICULTURE (CSA) PROGRAMS

Bradford	Honey Locust Farm	www.HoneyLocustFarmVT.com
Brattleboro	New Leaf CSA	www.newleafcsa.com
Brattleboro	Wild Carrot Farm	www.wildcarrotfarm.net
Brookline	Tanglebloom Flowers	www.tanglebloom.com
Castleton	Dutchess Farm	www.dutchessfarmvt.com
Craftsbury	Pete's Greens Good Eats	www.petesgreens.com
Dummerston	The Scott Farm Orchard	www.scottfarmvermont.com
Fairfax	River Berry Farm	www.riverberryfarm.com
Fairlee	Your Farm	www.yourfarmonline.com

Monkton	Last Resort Farm	www.lastresortfarm.com
Northfield	Green Mountain Girls Farm	www.eatstayfarm.com
Norwich	Hogwash Farm	www.hogwashfarm.com
Tinmouth	Breezy Meadows Orchard	www.breezymeadowsorchards.com
West Topsham	Sugar Mountain Farm	www.sugarmtnfarm.com

ON-FARM MARKETS

Berlin	Burelli Farm	www.burellifarm.com
Bristol	The Last Resort Farm	www.lastresortfarm.com
Cabot	Burtt's Apple Orchard	www.burttsappleorchard.com
Cabot	Gozzard City at Provender Farm	www.getyourgoose.com
Calais	Random Gardens	www.randomgardens.com
Franklin	Wandering Moose Farms	www.wanderingmoosefarms.com
Mansfield	The Farm at Morrison Corner	www.WoolAndFeathers.com
Montgomery	Creamery Bridge Farm	www.Creamerybridgefarm.com
New Haven	Lester Farm and Market	www.lesterfarmmarket.com
Rochester	Mom & Pop's Maple Syrup	www.MomAndPopsMaple.com
South Royalton	Hurricane Flats	www.hurricaneflats.com
Walden	Square Deal Farm	www.squaredealfarm.org
Washington	The Farm of Milk and Honey	www.farmofmilkandhoney.com
Weathersfield	Goulden Ridge Farm	www.gouldenridgefarm.com
Westford	Morse Hillside Farm	www.MorseHillsideFarm.com
Wilmington	Adams Farm and Meat	www.adamsfamilyfarm.com
Windsor	Contented Butterfly Farm	www.contentedbutterflyfarm.com

FOOD HUBS

Barre	Farmers to You	www.farmerstoyou.com
Brattleboro	Food Connects	www.foodconnects.org
Burlington	The Intervale Food Hub	www.intervalefoodhub.com
Hardwick	Vermont Food Venture	www.hardwickagriculture.org
Middlebury	Middlebury Foods	www.middleburyfoods.com
Newport	Green Mountain Farm Direct	www.greenmountainfarmdirect.org
Rutland	Rutland Area Farm	www.rutlandfarmandfood.org
Waitsfield	Mad River Food Hub	www.madriverfoodhub.com

Bundoran Farm
North Garden
www.explorebundoranfarm.com

Under development. Bundoran Farm is a conservation community on 2,300 acres, with 99 planned single-family homes, located 15 minutes south of Charlottesville in the foothills of the Blue Ridge Mountains. The community is surrounded by 1,100 acres of pasture and 1,000 acres of managed forest, where home sites are tucked into the landscape and designed to protect agrarian character. Food elements include a farm, orchard, vineyard, and 15 miles of hiking and bridle trails. Residents also have access to two private lakes for fishing and kayaking. The Pippin Hill Farm and Vineyard is located on the farm.

Chickahominy Falls   Over 55 Community
Glen Allen
www.chickahominyfalls.com

Chickahominy Falls is a 400-home active adult community located less than 30 minutes from downtown Richmond. The community includes a professionally managed farm, farmhouse, farmers' market area, and areas for beekeeping. Residents can enjoy extensive walking trails, birdwatching, and fishing in ponds located along the Chickahominy River. Amenities include a clubhouse, outdoor pool and patio, and event space. The community features a 400 age-restricted attached homes clustered into small neighborhoods and connected by the walking trails.

Willowsford
Loudoun County
www.willowsford.com

Located in the heart of Loudoun County, Virginia, Willowsford spans over 4,000 acres and is comprised of four distinctive, interconnected "villages." More than half of the land is designated as open space under the stewardship of the non-profit Willowsford Conservancy. Out of the other half, 300 acres are used to raise several breeds of livestock and cultivate more than 150 varieties of vegetables, herbs, fruit, and flowers, many of which are distributed to the community through the CSA program and Farm Stand. Despite its agricultural setting, Willowsford is just 10 minutes from Dulles International Airport, and 40 minutes from downtown Washington D.C.

COMMUNITY SUPPORTED AGRICULTURE (CSA) PROGRAMS

Berryville	Cool Spring Farm	www.coolspringcsa.com
Bluemont	Great Country Farms	www.greatcountryfarms.com
Brightwood	Brightwood Vineyard	www.brightwoodvineyardandfarm.com
Chatham	Strawberry Creek Farm	www.strawberrycreekfarm.com
Check	Seven Springs Farm CSA	www.7sringscsa.com
Cologne	Dayspring Farm	www.dayspringfarm.org
Eastville	Mattawoman Creek Farms	www.mattawomancreekfarms.com
Fort Valley	H and H Farms	www.handhfarmsva.com
Great Falls	Amalthea Ridge, LLC	www.amalthearidge.com

Harrisonburg	Season's Bounty Farm	www.Seasonsbountyfarm.com
Kenbridge	Crickets Cove Organics	www.CricketsCove.net
Leesburg	HuckleBerry Fresh	www.huckleberryfresh.luluslocalfood.com
Locust Grove	Miller Farms Market	www.millerfarmsmarket.com
Lovettsville	Quarter Branch Farm	www.quarterbranchfarm.com
Lovettsville	Spring House Farm	www.SpringHouseFarmVA.com
Middleburg	Day Spring Farm	www.dayspringfarmva.com
Midlothian	Chesterfield Berry Farm	www.chesterfieldberryfarm.com
Mt. Jackson	Sinclair Farm	www.sinclairfarm.com
Nokesville	Yankey Farms	www.yankeyfarms.com
Richmond	Farm to Family	www.thefarmbus.csaware.com
Rixeyville	Bart & Sarah's at Great Oak	www.bartandsarahs.com
Shawsville	Leaping Waters Farm	www.leapingwatersfarm.com
Spout Spring	Lund Angus Farm	www.lundangus.com/
Verona	Malcolms Market Garden	www.malcolmsmarketgarden.com
Vienna	Potomac Vegetable Farms	www.potomacvegetablefarms.com
Virginia Beach	Cullipher Farm	www.cullipherfarm.com
Virginia Beach	Skipper Farms	www.Skipperfarms.com

ON-FARM MARKETS

Allisonia	Deer Haven Blueberry Patch	www.deerhavenblueberrypatch.com
Amelia	Avery's Branch Farms	www.averysbranchfarms.com
Bealeton	Messicks Farm Market	www.Messicksfarmmarket.com
Beaverdam	Alpaca Pastures of Virginia	www.AlpacaPasturesVA.com
Beaverdam	Dragonfly Farms	www.dragonflyfarms.com
Bedford	Johnsons Orchards	www.JohnsonsOrchards.com
Berryville	Mackintosh Fruit Farm	www.mackintoshfruitfarm.com
Blacksburg	3 Birds Berry Farm	www.3birdsberryfarm.com
Blue Grass	Puffenbarger Sugar Orchard	www.puffenbargersugarorchard.com
Catlett	Seven Oaks Lavender Farm	www.sevenoakslavenderfarm.com
Chantilly	Ticonderoga Farms	www.ticonderoga.com
Chesapeake	Mount Pleasant Farms	www.mountpleasantfarms.com
Chesapeake	Skipper Farms	www.Skipperfarms.com
Colonial Beach	Westmoreland Berry Farm	www.westmorelandberryfarm.com
Colonial Heights	Boulevard Flower Gardens	www.boulevardflowergardens.com
Culpeper	Saddle Ridge Farm	www.saddleridgefarm.net
Daleville	Ikenberry Orchards	www.Ikenberryorchards.com
Danville	Owen Farm Tours	www.owenfarmtours.com
Floyd	Riverstone Organic Farm	www.riverstoneorganicfarm.com
Fredericksburg	Botanical Bites	www.botanicalbitesandprovisionsllc.com
Gloucester	Life Enrichment Sciences	www.lifeenrichmentsciences.com
Gretna	Our Father's Farm	www.ourfathersfarmva.com
Hanover	Empress Farm	www.empressfarmfoods.com
Haymarket	Burnside Farms	www.burnsidefarms.com
King William	Pampatike Organic Farm	www.pampatike.com
Leesburg	Loudounberry Farm	www.loudounberryfarm.com
Locust Grove	Miller Farms Market	www.millerfarmsmarket.com
Lovettsville	Patowmack Farm	www.patowmackfarm.com

Middleburg	Ayrshire Farm	www.AyrshireFarm.com
Mount Jackson	Sinclair Farm	www.sinclairfarm.com
Newport	Bee Berry Farm	www.beeberryfarm.net
North Garden	Vintage Virginia Apples	www.albemarleciderworks.com
Purcellville	A Dozen Eggs	www.pastureraisedeggs.com
Richardsville	Digging Dog Farm	www.thediggingdogfarm.com
Richmond	Gallmeyer Farms	www.gallmeyerfarms.com
Roanoke	Jeter Farm	www.jeterfarm.com
Rockville	Keenbell Farm	www.keenbellfarm.com
Roseland	Dickie Bros. Orchard	www.dickiebros.com
Round Hill	Practically Country	www.practicallycountry.com
Ruther Glen	Mt Olympus Berry Farm	www.mtolympusfarm.com
Scottsville	Hope of Glory Farm	www.hopeofgloryfarm.com
Smithfield	Oliver Farms LLC	www.oliverproduce.com
Suffolk	Golden Eagle Alpaca Farm	www.goldeneaglealpacafarm.com
The Plains	Over the Grass Farm	www.overthegrassfarm.com
Vernon Hill	Sapphire Farms	www.sapphirefarmsva.com
Virginia Beach	Vaughan Farms Produce	www.vaughanfarmsproduce.com
Wakefield	Drewry Farm	www.drewryfarms.com
Weyers Cave	Harmony Harvest Farm	www.harmonyharvestfarm.com
Woodstock	Mowery Orchard	www.MoweryOrchard.com
Wytheville	Beagle Ridge Herb Farm	www.beagleridgeherbfarm.com

FOOD HUBS

Ashland	Produce Source Partners	www.producesourcepartners.com
Charlottesville	Local Food Hub	www.localfoodhub.org
Duffield	Appalachian Harvest	www.asdevelop.org
Elkwood	4P FOODS	www.4pfoods.com
Elkwood	Blue Ridge Local	www.blueridgeproduce.net
Floyd	Good Food - Good People	www.goodfoodgoodpeople.net
Glen Allen	Farm Table	www.thefarmtable.org
Moneta	Eco Friendly Foods	www.ecofriendly.com
Richmond	Milton's Local	www.miltonslocal.com
Williamsburg	Off the Vine Market	www.offthevinemarket.com
Windsor	Coastal Farms	www.coastalfarms.luluslocalfood.com

WASHINGTON

AGRIHOODS

Grow Community
Bainbridge Island
www.growbainbridge.com

Grow Community is an 8-acre development consisting of 132 residences, comprised of single-family homes, townhouses, and condominiums. All duplexes and single-family homes are powered by photovoltaics, and solar arrays are optional in all homes. Neighborhoods are designed according to One Planet principles: ultra-energy-efficient homes, zero emissions and waste, sustainable materials, locally grown food, resource conservation, wildlife habitat, and edible landscaping, culture, happiness, and health. The community is located within minutes of local merchants, grocers, town library, cafes, recreational venues, parks, health clinics, and schools.

Skokomish Farms
Shelton (Puget Sound)

Proposed development. Skokomish Farms is an environmental farming community built on a former hay farm in the Puget Sound area of Washington state. The community is designed to encourage the homesteading spirit, and includes a professionally managed organic farm, vineyards, orchards, grass-fed livestock, wetlands, and greenhouse-grown winter crops. Residents are encouraged to grow their own farm businesses.

Stackhouse Apartments   Rental Community
Seattle
www.stackhouseapartments.com

Stackhouse Apartments is a mixed-use, green-living community that includes a 188-unit apartment building, a 96-unit apartment building, and a commercial building. Buildings are LEED-certified. The development includes a professionally managed rooftop farm, community gardens, and an on-site farm stand that offers free produce for residents. Stackhouse is footsteps away from the Amazon campus, Westlake center, and many restaurants and cafes. Residents may choose from a variety of floor plans ranging from a studio, 1-, 2-, or 3-bedroom homes. In addition, Stackhouse features rare and unique town homes and lofts. Amenities include community guest suites, two community decks, a game room, and more.

Suzuki Farms
Bainbridge Island

Proposed development. Suzuki Farms is an island community with buildings that are designed with health in mind, with clean indoor air environments and net-zero energy. The project includes a community campus, a working farm, community gardens, and agricultural education. In partnering with Housing Resources Bainbridge and Housing Kitsap, a range of prices will be offered to income-qualified families and individuals.

COMMUNITY SUPPORTED AGRICULTURE (CSA) PROGRAMS

Bothell	Tonnemaker Family Orchard	www.tonnemaker.com
Brush Prairie	Hunters' Greens	www.huntersgreens.com
Carnation	Mezza Luna Farms	wwww.mezzalunafarms.com
Carnation	Snoqualmie Valley Farmers	www.snovalleycoop.com
Centralia	Coffee Creek Community	www.CoffeeCreekCommunityGardens.com
Clinton	Maha Farm and Forest	www.mahafarm.com
Curtis	Boistfort Valley Farm	www.boistfortvalleyfarm.com
Greenbank	Organic Farm School at Greenbank Farm	www.greenbankfarm.biz
Lake Stevens	Mother Nature's Farm	www.mothernatures.farm/
Olympia	Building Earth Farm	www.farmandfruitstand.com
Orting	Dropstone Farms	www.dropstonefarms.com
Port Angeles	Salt Creek Farm	www.saltcreekfarm.org
Rice	Winniford Family Farm	www.winnifordfamilyfarm.com
Ridgefield	Northwest Organic Farm	www.northwestorganicfarms.com
Ridgefield	Quackenbush Farm	www.quackenbushfarm.com
Rochester	Helsing Junction Farm	www.helsingfarmcsa.com
Rochester	Wobbly Cart Farm	www.wobblycart.com
Sequim	Nash's Organic Produce	www.nashsorganicproduce.com
Sultan	Boldbrook Farm	www.boldbrookfarm.com
Vancouver	Storytree Farm	www.storytreefarm.com
WallaWalla	Nothing's Simple Farm	www.nsfarm.org
White Salmon	Stonework Farm	www.stoneworkfarm.com

ON-FARM MARKETS

Addy	Simple Gifts Farm	www.simplegiftsfarm.net
Arlington	Biringer Farm	www.biringerfarm.com
Arlington	Bryant Blueberry Farm	www.bryantblueberries.com
Bow	A Man and His Hoe	www.amanandhishoe.com
Bow	Bow Hill Blueberries	www.bowhillblueberries.com
Burlington	Viva Farms	www.vivafarms.org
Camas	Conway Family Farms	www.conwayfamilyfarm.com
Carnation	First Light Farm	www.firstlightfarm.wordpress.com
Colbert	Hansen's Green Bluff Orchard	www.hansensgreenblufforchard.com
Colfax	Joseph's Grainery	www.josephsgrainery.com
Colfax	Maple K Farms	www.maplekhighlands.com
Coupeville	Lavender Wind Farm	www.lavenderwind.com
Deer Park	Fussy Hen Flower & Herb	www.fussyhen.com
Duvall	Misc. Farm	www.miscfarm.com
Enumclaw	Blue Dot Farm	www.bluedotfarm.com
Enumclaw	Boise Creek Boer Goats	www.boisecreekboers.com
Enumclaw	Rusty Plow Farm	www.rustyplowfarm.com
Everson	Washington Chestnut Co.	www.washingtonchestnut.com
Ferndale	Eastview Blueberry Farm	www.eastviewblueberryfarm.com
Ferndale	Sm'Apples Orchard	www.smapples.com
Ferndale	Triple Wren Farms	www.triplewrenfarms.com

Granger	Jones Farms Fruit	www.jonesfarmsinc.com
Greenbank	Farm Shop at Greenbank	www.greenbankfarm.biz
Longview	Lower Columbia School	www.lowercolumbiaschoolgardens.org
Lynden	Belle Wood Acres	www.bellewoodfarms.com
Maple Valley	Liberty Alpacas	www.libertyalpacas.com
Medical lake	Garden Gate Lavender	www.gardengatelavender.com
Mount Vernon	Dunbar Gardens	www.dunbargardens.com
Newman Lake	Carver Farms	www.carverfarms.com
Oak Harbor	Hunters Moon Farm	www.huntersmoonorganics.com
Oakville	Five Star Farm	www.fivestarfarmbeef.com
Olympia	Nelson Ranch	www.nelsonranch.com
Olympia	Steamboat Junction Farm	www.steamboatjunctionfarm.com
Olympia	Township 18 Farm	www.township18.com
Orondo	Orondo Cider Works	www.ciderworks.com
Port Townsend	Alpenfire Orchards	www.alpenfirecider.com
Poulsbo	Abundantly Green	www.abundantlygreen.com
Puyallup	Linbo Blueberry Farm	www.linboblueberries.com
Sedro Woolley	Skiyou Ranch	www.skiyouranch.com
Sequim	Annie's Flower Farm	www.anniesflowerfarm.com
Shelton	Skokomish Valley Farms	www.skokomishvalleyfarms.com
Snohomish	Canfield Farms	www.canfieldfarms.com
Tenino	Colvin Ranch	www.colvinranch.com
Tonasket	Heart of the Highlands	www.heartofthehighlands.net
Toppenish	Just Living Farm	www.justlivingfarm.org
Woodinville	21 Acres Farm Market	www.21acres.org
Woodland	Dobler Hill Dairy	www.doblerhilldairy.com
Yakima	Barrett Orchards	www.treeripened.com

FOOD HUBS

Chewelah	Northwest Farm Fresh	www.nwfarmfresh.com
Mount Vernon	Puget Sound Food Hub Coop.	www.pugetsoundfoodhub.com
Okanogan	Okanogan Producers	www.okanoganproducers.org
Seattle	Seattle Tilth Produce	www.seattletilth.org
Spokane	LINC Foods	www.LINCFoods.com
Spokane	Northwest Farm Fresh	www.nwfarmfresh.com
Tacoma	Terra Organics	www.terra-organics.com
Wenatchee	Wenatchee Valley Farmers	www.wenatcheefarmersmarket.com
Woodinville	Farmstand Local Foods	www.farmstandlocalfoods.com

AGRIHOODS

Broomgrass
Gerrardstown
www.broombrass.com

Broomgrass is a 320-acre community consisting of 16 residences, founded in 2003 with a commitment to sustainability, environmental stewardship, and a working farm. The Broomgrass farm plan, passed annually during the winter meeting, allows community members to coordinate the agricultural intentions for the coming year. Residents are free to do as much or as little as they wish regarding agricultural activity. Amenities include a pool, spa, pond, and looping trail. The community is located adjacent to Stauffer's Marsh, a 450-acre wildlife conservancy operated by the Potomac Valley Audubon Society that includes a network of biking and walking trails. About 10 miles north is Sleepy Creek Wildlife Management Area, which includes a 205-acre lake for boating and fishing, and extended-stay log cabins.

COMMUNITY SUPPORTED AGRICULTURE (CSA) PROGRAMS

Berwind	McDowell County Farms	www.mcdowellcountyfarms.com
Bruceton Mills	Evans Knob Farm	www.evansknobfarm.com
Chilton	Red Belly Farms	www.redbellyfarms.com
Morgantown	Mountain Harvest Farm	www.mountainharvestfarmllc.com
Pennsboro	Bonds Creek Farm	www.bondscreekfarm.com
Shenandoah Junct.	Moon on the Mountain	www.moononthemountain.com
Shepherdstown	Blue Morning CSA	www.bluemorningfarm.com
Shepherdstown	Green Gate Farm	www.greengatefarmwv.com
Terra Alta	Round Right Farm	www.roundrightfarm.com
Wheeling	Grow Ohio Valley	www.growov.org

ON-FARM MARKETS

Burlington	Green Family Farm	www.greenfamilyfarm.org
Clem	Garden Treasures WV	www.gardentreasureswv.com
Gay	Beeappy Farm	www.beeappy.com
Martinsburg	Shepherd's Whey Creamery	www.shepherdswheycreamery.com
Renick	Sunshine Farm & Gardens	www.sunfarm.com
Renick	White Oak Farm	www.whiteoakberryfarm.com
Shenandoah Junct.	Harmony Hill Farm	www.HarmonyHillFarmWV.com
Terra Alta	Possum Tail Farm	www.possumtailfarm.com
Terra Alta	Working H Farms	www.workinghfarms.com
Wardensville	Wardensville Garden	www.wardensvillegardenmarket.org
Williamsburg	Mountain Meadows Farm	www.mtmeadowsfarm.com
Williamstown	Ridge View Farm	www.ridgeviewfarmbeef.com

FOOD HUBS

Alderson	Alderson Community Food	www.aldersonfoodhub.org
Davis	Highland Market	www.phffi.org/highland-market
Huntington	Wild Ramp/Tri-State Foods	www.wildramp.org
Union	Monroe Farm Market Coop.	www.monroefarmmarket.com

WISCONSIN

AGRIHOODS

Agape
Mukwonago
www.agapeagrihood.com

Under development. Agape is a conservation community comprised of 10 single-family homes on 36 acres. The community includes an irrigated community garden, 16 acres of preserved open space, 1.2 miles of walking and horseback riding trails, and 1.1 miles of equine fencing. Residents have the opportunity to board a horse or other animal, with over 9 acres of pastureland and a barn. Plans include small farm animals, an apple orchard, and beehives.

COMMUNITY SUPPORTED AGRICULTURE (CSA) PROGRAMS

Arkansaw	Hog's Back Farm	www.hogsbackfarm.com
Bangor	Old Oak Family Farm	www.oldoakfamilyfarm.com
Belgium	Rare Earth Farm	www.rareearthfarm.com
Belleville	Winterfell Acres LLC	www.winterfellacres.com
Belmont	Two Onion Farm	www.twoonionfarm.com
Blue Mounds	Vermont Valley Comm. Farm	www.vermontvalley.com
Brooklyn	Tomato Mountain Farm	www.tomatomountain.com
Campbellsport	High Cross Farm	www.highcrossfarm.com
Clayton	Blackbrook Farm	www.blackbrookfarmstead.com
Elkhorn	LotFotL Community Farm	www.lotfotl.com
Ferryville	Lone Goat Farm	www.lonegoatfarm.com
Fond du Lac	Park Ridge Organics	www.parkridgeorganics.com
Fredonia	Willoway Farm	www.willowayfarm.com
Hartford	Full Harvest Farm	www.fullharvestfarm.com
Hayward	North Star Homestead Farms	www.northstarhomestead.com
Hazel Green	Sandhill Farm	www.sandhill-farm.com
High Bridge	Hermit Creek Farm	www.hermitcreekfarm.com
Jefferson	Regenerative Roots	www.regenerativeroots.com
La Valle	Hilltop Community Farm	www.hilltopcommunityfarm.org
Madison	Troy Community Farm	www.communitygroundworks.org
McFarland	Bard Family Market Garden	www.bardfamilymarketgarden.com
Menomonie	Sylvan Hills	www.sylvanhillsfarm.com
Milton	Roots Down Comm. Farm	www.rootsdowncommunityfarm.com
Milwaukee	Growing Power, Inc.	www.growingpower.org
Muskego	Godsell Farm	www.godsellfarm.com
Osceola	Foxtail Farm	www.foxtailcsa.com
Pepin	Avodah Farm	www.avodahfarm.net
Plymouth	Backyard Bounty	www.ljcomerford.wordpress.com
Potosi	Honey Hill Organic Farm	www.honeyhillorganic.com
Prescott	Borner Farm Project	www.bornerfarmproject.com

Racine	Neu Root Farm	www.neurootfarm.com
Rio	Burr Oak Gardens	www.burroakgardens.com
Turtle Lake	Keppers Pottery and Produce	www.kepperspottery.com
Watertown	Twist & Sprout Farms	www.twistandsproutfarms.com
Waunakee	Equinox Community Farm	www.equinoxcommunityfarm.com
Waupaca	Gravel Road Farm	www.gravelroadfarm.com
Wauzeka	Willow Ridge Organic Farm	www.willowridgeorganicfarm.com
West Bend	Wellspring Education Center & Organic Farm	www.wellspringinc.org
Westboro	We Grow	www.wegrowfoods.com
Westby	Knapp Creek Farm	www.knappcreekfarm.com
Wisconsin Rapids	New Season Farm	www.newseasonfarm.com

ON-FARM MARKETS

Albany	Windy Fleece Farm	www.windyfleecefarm.com
Amery	Glenna Farms	www.glennafarms.com
Amery	Pike Hole Family Farm	www.pikeholefarm.com
Bayfield	Highland Valley Farm	www.bayfieldblues.com
Bear Creek	Blueberry Haven	www.blueberryhaven.net
Belleville	Observatory Hill Farm	www.observatoryhillfarm.com
Beloit	Star & Thistle Farm	www.starandthistlefarm.com
Blanchardville	Dorothy's Grange	www.dorothysgrange.com
Bonduel	Porter's Patch	www.PortersPatch.com
Caledonia	Wick Place Candles and Farm	www.wickplacefarm.com
Campbellsport	Armstrong Apples	www.Armstrongapples.com
Cashton	Maple Ridge Orchard	www.mapleridgeorchard.com
Chilton	Heritage Orchard	www.heritageorchard.net
Chilton	Meuer Farm	www.meuerfarm.com
Clear Lake	Bull Brook Keep	www.bullbrookkeep.com
Cochrane	Cowsmo, Inc.	www.cowsmocompost.com
Colgate	Copper Kettle Farm	www.copperkfarm.com
Columbus	Sassy Cow Creamery	www.sassycowcreamery.com
Cottage Grove	Offbeat Acres	www.offbeatacres.com
Cottage Grove	West Star Organics	www.weststarfarm.com
Cross Plains	Appleberry Farm	www.theappleberryfarm.com
De Pere	Apple Valley Orchard	www.AppleValleyLLC.com
East Troy	Gardens at Michael Fields	www.michaelfields.org
Fall Creek	Out to Pasture Beef	www.outtopasturebeef.com
Fort Atkinson	Busy Barns Adventure Farm	www.busybarnsfarm.com
Gilman	Futility Farms	www.futilityfarms.com
Granton	Sternitzky/The Maple Dude	www.themapledude.com
Janesville	Skelly's Farm Market	www.skellysfarmmarket.com
Kaukauna	Star Orchard	www.starorchard.com
Kiel	Golden Bear Farm	www.goldenbearfarm.com

La Farge	Under A Rock Farm	www.underarockfarm.com
Leopolis	Eleven M Ranch	www.elevenmranch.com
Milladore	Good Earth Farms	www.goodearthfarms.com
Milton	Meyer's Farm Market	www.meyersfarmmarket.com
Neenah	Oakridge Farms	www.oakridgeberries.com
Nekoosa	Lotis Alpacas	www.lotisalpacas.com
North Prairie	Kipp Farms	www.kippfarms.com
Oconomowoc	The Garlic Underground	www.thegarlicunderground.com
Palmyra	Rushing Waters Fisheries	www.rushingwaters.net
Pittsville	Pittsview Farm Elk	www.pittsviewfarmelk.com
Prescott	Borner Farm Project	www.bornerfarmproject.com
Viroqua	Schott Farm	www.schottfarm.com
Waukesha	Field to Fork Farm	www.fieldtoforkfarms.com
Waupaca	Turners Fresh Market	www.turnersfreshmarket.com
Wausau	Sugar Hill Sugar Bush	www.sugarhillsugarbush.com
Westby	Deep Rooted	www.deeprootedorganics.com
Wisconsin Rapids	Altenburg's Country Gardens	www.altenburgsfarm.com

FOOD HUBS

Viroqua	Fifth Season Cooperative	www.fifthseasoncoop.com
Waupaca	Wisconsin Food Hub	www.wifoodhub.com

COMMUNITY SUPPORTED AGRICULTURE (CSA) PROGRAMS

Carpenter	Idle Thyme Farm	www.IdleThyeFarm.com
Cheyenne	Wind Sauna Farms	www.windsaunafarms.com
Laramie	Bright Agrotech CSA	www.brightagrotech.com
Worland	Lloyd Craft Farms CSA	www.lloydcraftfarmscsa.com

ON-FARM MARKETS

Yoder	Case Custom Meats	www.casecustommeats.com

References

1. U.S. Department of Agriculture (USDA)

2. USDA, Definition of Local Food

3. United States 2008 Farm Act, Definition of Local Food

4. Leopold Center for Sustainable Agriculture, Iowa State University, *Food, Fuel and the Future: Consumer Perceptions of Local Food, Food Safety and Climate Change in the Context of Rising Prices*

5. ATTRA National Sustainable Agricultural Information Service

6. Leopold Center for Sustainable Agriculture, Iowa State University, *Food, Fuel and Freeways*

7. USDA, Agricultural Marketing Services, *Know Your Farmer, Know Your Food* Initiative, 2008

8. Ibid.

9. Ibid.

10. USDA, *New Markets, New Opportunities: Strengthening Local Food Systems and Organic Agriculture*, 2017

11. U.S. Food and Drug Administration, *Food Safety Modernization Act*

12. USDA National Organic Program, *Organic Labeling and Seal*

13. Ibid.

14. USDA National Institute of Food and Agriculture, *Local Food Systems, Concepts, Impact and Issues*

15. Ibid.

16. Ibid.

17. Center for Sustainable Systems, University of Michigan, *U.S. Food Systems Fact Sheet*, August 2019

18. Center for Sustainable Systems, University of Michigan, *Carbon Footprint Factsheet*, August 2019

19. USDA *Know Your Farmer, Know Your Food Initiative*

20. American Farm Bureau, *America's Diverse Family Farms 2018*

21. Ibid.

22. U.S. Bureau of Labor Statistics, *Consumer Expenditures in 2017*, April 2019, Report #1080

23. National Grocers Association, *February 2018 Survey*

24. A.T. Kearney, *Firmly Rooted—the Local Food Market Expands, 2017*

25. Food Marketing Institute, *Retailer Contributions to Health and Wellness,* 2019 Report

26. Bureau of Labor Statistics, *Consumer Expenditures in 2017*, April 2019

27. National Restaurant Association, *Restaurant Industry 2030, Actionable Insights for the Future, November 2019*

28. USDA Economic Research Service

29. Food Waste Reduction Alliance

30. Urban Land Institute, *Cultivating Development: Trends and Opportunities at the Intersection of Food and Real Estate*

31. RCLCO 2018 *Housing and Community Preference Survey*
32. United Nations, *Sustainable Development Goals Report 2019, Sustainable Cities and Communities,* Page 44

33. Texas A & M University, Department of Soil and Crop Sciences

34. ATTRA National Center for Appropriate Technology, *Sustainable Agriculture, Vertical Farming*, 2016

35. Aerofarms, New Jersey

36. Gotham Greens, New York

37. Shenandoah Growers, Inc., Virginia

38. Brooklyn Grange LLC, New York

39. Edward T. McMahon, *Creating Value with Nature, Open Space and Agriculture*

40. Ibid.

41. Daron Joffe, Farmer D Consulting; author, *Citizen Farmers*

42. U.S. Green Building Council, *Leadership in Energy and Environmental Design* (LEED)

43. Building Research Establishment's Environmental Assessment Method (BREEAM)

44. U.S. Department of Energy, *Energy Star Certified Home Program*

45. U.S. Department of Energy, *Zero Energy Ready Home*

46. U.S. Department of Energy, *Solar Photovoltaic Energy*

47. U.S. Department of Energy, *Geothermal Energy*

48. U.S. Department of Energy, *Energy Star Rating*

49. Ibid.

50. U.S. Department of Energy, *Geothermal Energy*

51. Internal Revenue Service, *Federal income tax credit for energy systems*

52. Database of State Incentives for Renewables and Energy Efficiency

53. National Association of Home Builders

54. National Association of Home Builders, *Median Lot Size of Homes Sold in 2017 Preferences 2019*

55. University of Massachusetts at Amherst, Center of Agriculture, *Soil Plant Nutrient Testing Laboratory*

56. USDA Natural Resources Conservation Service

57. Ibid.

58. Debora L. Martin, *Rodale's Basic Organic Gardening*

59. Regenerative Organic Alliance, *Regenerative Organic Certification*

60. Permaculture Research Institute

61. Bee Built, Oregon

62. Apiary Inspectors of America

63. The Marijuana Break

64. Urban Ag Law, *Food Safety, State and Local Regulations*

65. USDA National Resources Conservation Service

66. USDA, *Plant Hardiness Map*

67. The Old Farmer's Almanac

68. Mel Bartholomew, *Square Foot Gardening*

69. The Old Farmer's Almanac

70. Ibid.

71. USDA, *The Role of Food Hubs in Local Food Marketing*

72. Ibid.

73. USDA, *Regional Food Hub Resource Guide*

74. Ibid.

75. Ibid.

76. USDA, Supplemental Nutritional Assistance Program (SNAP) and Special Supplemental Nutritional Program for Women, Infants and Children (WIC)

About the Author

Anna DeSimone is author of *Housing Finance 2020*, New Mortgage Programs for the New Generation of Homebuyers (*Hipoteca 2020* in Spanish). Her book received the Axiom Business Book Awards Silver Medal in Personal Finance, Retirement Planning and Investing. She is a nationally recognized expert in housing finance and author of more than 40 professional guidebooks and over 600 articles on the topic of fair and responsible lending. In 1986, she founded Bankers Advisory, a mortgage compliance audit services company, acquired by Clifton Larson Allen LLP in 2014. She has been a featured entrepreneur by *Forbes Magazine* and *Bloomberg Markets*, named one of *Housing Wire's* Women of Influence, and has received awards from *Acquisitions International* and *Wealth and Finance Magazine*.

View Anna's blog and news articles on her website:

www.annadesimone.net

Index
Page Location of Primary Description

Active Adult Community 49

Aeroponics 28

Agrihood Amenities 38

Agrihood Farms 52

Agrihood Homes 60

Apiary Inspectors of America (AIA) 77

Aquaponics, urban agriculture 28

Aquaponics, home gardening 74

Backyard Conservation (USDA) 79

Backyard Farming 69

Beekeeping 76

Bees 76

Beyond Organic 72

Beyond Sustainable 72

Biking Paths in Agrihoods 45

Biodiversity 15

Boating in Agrihoods 42

Cannabis 77

Carbon Footprint 17

Certified Organic 14

Chemical Fertilizers 71

Children's Activities in Agrihoods 48

CO_2 Emissions 18

Community Centers in Agrihoods 38

Community Gardens in Agrihoods 58

Community-Supported Agriculture (CSA) 87

Composting 79

Container Gardening 86

Cost of Food   22
Cottage Farms   78
CSA Programs   87
CSA Share Box   88
CSA Pricing and Terms   92
CSA Season   88

Early Bird Planting   81
Ecolabels   18
Energy Efficiency in Homes   61
Energy Star Rating   61
Energy Tax Credits   62

Farm Act of 2008   11
Family-owned Farms   20
Farm Activities   98
Farm Animals in Backyard Farms   78
Farm History   98
Farmers' Markets   99
Fishing in Agrihoods   42
Food and Drug Administration (FDA)   14
Food and Water Safety   79
Food Box Contents   90
Food Box Pick-up or Delivery   91
Food Hubs   101
Food Hub Role   102
Food Hub Services   104
Food Hub Structure   103
Food Safety Modernization Act   14
Food Share Add-ons   90
Food Traceback   90
Food Value Chains   103
Food Waste   25
Food Waste Reduction Alliance   25

Garden Spaces for Residents 58

Geothermal Energy 61

Genetically Modified Organisms (GMOs) 16

Golf in Agrihoods 43

Green Building 60

Greenhouse Gas Emissions, food travel 12

Greenhouse Gas Emissions, carbon footprint 17

Greenhouses 31

Grocery Shopping Trends 23

Harvest Season Chart 89

Healthy Soil 69

High Rise Farms 30

Hiking Paths in Agrihoods 45

Hobby Farms 78

Hoop Houses 13

Horseback Riding in Agrihoods 44

Housing Choices 26

How Far Food Travels 11

Hydroponics, urban agriculture 28

Hydroponics, home gardening 73

Intersection of Food and Housing 25

Know Your Farmer, Know Your Food 12

Know Your Farmer, food hubs 101

Land Conservation 36

Laws for Backyard Farming 77

LEED-Certified Construction 60

Local Food USDA Definition 11

Lot Size in Agrihoods 63

Market-style Food Box   90
Microgreens   75
Mixed-use Communities   51
Monthly Food Expenditure   22
Multi-farm CSA   93
Multi-generational Homes   50
Multi-ingredient Organic Foods   15

National Organic Program (NOP)   14
Natural Resources Conservation Service   70
Neighborhoods in Agrihoods   64
Net Zero Homes   61
Non-GMO Product Verification   16

On-farm Markets   95
Open Space in Agrihoods   64
Organic Certification   14
Organic Gardening at Home   71
Organic Materials Review Institute   71
Organic Seal (USDA   14

Permaculture   73
Pesticides, organic certification   14
Pesticides, home gardening   71
Photovoltaic Panels   62
Pick Your Own, CSA   91
Pick Your Own, On-farm   97
Plant Hardiness Zone Map   80
Plant Spacing Guide   83
Pocket Parks   64
Products Sold on the Farm   96

Raised-bed Gardening 85
Regenerative Agriculture 73
Restaurant Trends 24
Right to Farm Law 77
Rooftop Farming 31

Sale of Food by Home Gardeners 78
Schools in Agrihoods 48
Shade-tolerant Vegetables 84
Small Farmer Definition (USDA) 78
Soil Test 70
Solar Energy 61
Supplemental Nutritional Assistance 13
Sustainable Agriculture 16
Sustainable Construction 60
Sustainable Development Goals (SDG) 27
Synthetic Fertilizers 71

Urban Ag Initiatives 32
Urban Agriculture 27
Urban Agrihoods 33
U.S. Department of Agriculture (USDA) 12
USDA, food hubs 101
USDA Natural Resources Conservation 70

Vegetable Growing Season 81
Vegetable Planting Guide 82
Vertical Farming 30

Walking Paths in Agrihoods 45
Where to Buy from Local Farmers 20

Zero Energy Ready Home 70